ATLANTIS STUDIES IN COMPUTING

VOLUME 1

SERIES EDITORS: **JAN BERGSTRA, MICHAEL MISLOVE**

Atlantis Studies in Computing

Series Editors:

Jan Bergstra

Informatics Institute
University of Amsterdam
Amsterdam, The Netherlands

Michael Mislove

Department of Mathematics
Tulane University
New Orleans, USA

(ISSN: 2212-8565)

Aims and scope of the series

The series aims at publishing books in the areas of computer science, computer and network technology, IT management, information technology and informatics from the technological, managerial, theoretical/fundamental, social or historical perspective.

We welcome books in the following categories:
Technical monographs: these will be reviewed as to timeliness, usefulness, relevance, completeness and clarity of presentation.

Textbooks

Books of a more speculative nature: these will be reviewed as to relevance and clarity of presentation.

For more information on this series and our other book series, please visit our website at:

www.atlantis-press.com/publications/books

ATLANTIS PRESS

AMSTERDAM – PARIS – BEIJING

Code Generation with Templates

B.J. Arnoldus, M.G.J. van den Brand,
A. Serebrenik

Technische Universiteit Eindhoven,Den Dolech 2,5612 AZ Eindhoven
the Netherlands

J.J. Brunekreef

Fontys Hogeschool, Rachelsmolen 1, 5612 MA Eindhoven,
the Netherlands

ATLANTIS
PRESS

AMSTERDAM – PARIS – BEIJING

Atlantis Press

8, square des Bouleaux
75019 Paris, France

For information on all Atlantis Press publications, visit our website at: *www.atlantis-press.com*

Atlantis Studies in Computing

ISBNs
Print: 978-94-6239-052-2
E-Book: 978-94-91216-56-5
ISSN: 2212-8565

Preface

Templates are used to generate all kinds of text, including computer code. The last decade, the use of templates gained a lot of popularity due to the increase of dynamic web applications. Templates are a tool for programmers, and implementations of template engines are most times based on practical experience rather than based on a theoretical background. This book reveals the mathematical background of templates and shows interesting findings for improving the practical use of templates. First, a framework to determine the necessary computational power for the template metalanguage is presented. The template metalanguage does not need to be Turing-complete to be useful. A non-Turing-complete metalanguage enforces separation of concerns between the view and model. Second, syntactical correctness of all languages of the templates and generated code is ensured. This includes the syntactical correctness of the template metalanguage and the output language. Third, case studies show that the achieved goals are applicable in practice. It is even shown that syntactical correctness helps to prevent cross-site scripting attacks in web applications. We apologize in advance for any errors that may have occurred in this text, and we would be grateful to receive any comments, or suggestions about improvements for further editions.

B.J. Arnoldus
AMSTERDAM, January 2012

M.G.J. van den Brand, A. Serebrenik
EINDHOVEN, January 2012

J.J. Brunekreef
UTRECHT, January 2012

Contents

Chapter 1

Introduction

A code generator is a program being able to generate code based on an input specification, see Figure 1.1. Such programs are written to automate repetitive work, but also when a system needs to instantiate textual representations of a model, like HTML pages in web applications. Code generators are a subclass of *metaprograms*; the set of programs analyzing or manipulating other programs [Sheard (2001)]. A code generator can be written in an ad-hoc fashion or using sophisticated methodologies from compiler research.

Code generation is a projection of *input data* to output code. This input data belongs to a language with its own syntax and semantics, independently defined of the code generator. A code generator translates the input data into another representation, often a representation at a lower level of abstraction [Floridi and Sanders (2004)]. This output code can be everything, from machine code, in case of compilers, to code of a programming language, in case of computer-aided software engineering or model-driven engineering tools [Schmidt (2006); Favre (2004)]. During this translation, the code generator uses pieces of output sentences to construct the output code.

Writing code generators is not a trivial task. First, the input language has to be designed. This language should provide a complete vocabulary at the right level of abstraction for the problem domain. Defining this vocabulary requires an extensive knowledge of the problem domain. This requirement is not limited to writing code generators, but also for writing understandable and reusable domain specific libraries. Designing the input language is out

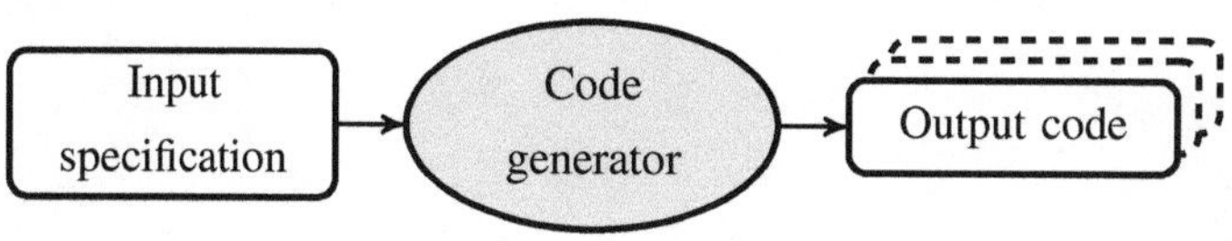

Fig. 1.1 A code generator.

of the scope of this book [Watt (2004)], but a well-defined input language definition is a crucial success factor for a code generator.
Second, writing and understanding a code generator is hard, as it contains code artifacts executed at different stages. It contains code executed at generation time, *metacode*, and code used as building blocks for the output code, the *object code*. A programmer has to be aware of the different execution stages of the different code artifacts. More confusing, artifacts belonging to different execution stages are mixed.
Finally, finding errors in code generators without tool support is difficult. Errors in the metacode are detected during compilation or during the execution of the code generator. Errors in the object code are harder to find and are detected when the output code is compiled or executed. In many code generators the object code is represented as strings without any internal structure [Sheard (2001)]. Debugging these errors is time consuming, since the code generator has to be corrected, it has to be compiled, code has to be generated and finally the generated code must be tested. Debugging tools for the metacode do not help, because the object code is handled as data, not as programs.
This chapter presents a number of approaches to implement a code generator, including templates. This book will focus on code generators using templates. Theories and concepts are presented and discussed to improve the technical quality of template based code generators, more specific, to improve the guarantees of the correctness of the output code and a formal argumentation for the necessary computational power of a template metalanguage. In the code generation parlance, the metalanguage is the language in which the code generator is written.

1.1 Safe Code Generation

This book concerns improving the reliability of template based code generators and providing better support during the development of these code generators. In order to classify the reliability of code generators, three classes of safe code generation are defined:

(1) no safety;
(2) syntax-safety;
(3) type safety.

The first safety class represents the code generators providing no guarantees of the correctness of the output at all. Code generators without a notion of the structure of the output code handle the output code as a sequence of characters. Most code generators, like Xpand[1], belong to this class. Beside the negative influence on testing and debugging code generators, this class of code generators comes with security flaws. An example of a security flaw is HTML injection in web applications. HTML injection is a vulnerability allowing an attacker to inject browser-executable content into a dynamic generated web page. The code generator cannot distinguish trusted code from malicious code since it considers the output only as a sequence of characters.

The second safety class represents the code generators guaranteeing that the output code is at least syntactical correct, i.e. the code generator is syntax-safe. A code generator is syntax-safe when for every input it is guaranteed that the generated code is a valid sentence of the desired output language. Syntax-safety eliminates parse errors in tools processing the output code and helps detecting of syntax related errors in an earlier stage of in the development process. Beside the development benefits, syntax-safety can be used to increase the protection against injection attacks.

The third safety class represents the code generators guaranteeing that the generated code is also static semantically correct. Static semantics are requirements for the code, which cannot be detected by only parsing it, such as checks for double declared variables and type errors. This class of safety guarantees that the generated code always compiles.

The next sections will show a number of approaches for implementing code generators and discuss the safety level they provide. The code generators discussed in this book are limited to *static* code generators. Static code generators write the generated code to disk, or another representation of a file, before it is processed in a next stage. The opposite case is *run-time* code generation, where the generated code is executed immediately. Also, internally generated code, such as inline function expansion or template instantiation in a compiler, is considered as run-time code generation. The code generators are divided in two categories: homogeneous systems and heterogeneous systems. Homogeneous systems are the systems where the metacode and the object code are sentences of the same language. In case of a heterogeneous system, the metacode and object code can be expressed using different languages [Sheard (2001)].

[1] http://wiki.eclipse.org/Xpand (accessed on January 23, 2012)

```
fun power n = (fn x => if n=0
              then < 1 >
              else < ~z * ~(power(n-1) x) >)

map(run < fn z => ~(power 3 < z >) >) [2,4]
```

Fig. 1.2 MetaML example.

1.2 Homogeneous Code Generators

Homogeneous is the collective term for all metaprogramming approaches where the metalanguage and object language are the same. These systems have numerous advantages over heterogeneous systems [Sheard (2001)]:

- Homogeneous systems can be multi-level, where an object-program can be a metaprogram that manipulates second-level object-programs.
- A single type system can describe the types of both the metalanguage and the object-language in a homogeneous meta-system.
- Homogeneous meta-systems can support reflection, using an operator, "run" or "eval", which translates representations of programs. This enables run-time code generation.

An example of a homogeneous metaprogramming system for *staged programming* is MetaML [Taha and Sheard (2000)]. ML is a general-purpose functional programming language. MetaML is a homogeneous metaprogramming approach using ML both as object language and metalanguage. The language is designed to enable staged programming. Staged programming, also called partial evaluation, is a technique giving control over the order of evaluation. This technique allows specializing a generic function at compile time and using the specialized version at run-time. Specifying a precise execution order allows the programmer to control time and space resources. The compiler does not choose whether a statement is executed during run-time or compile time, but this is an explicit decision of the programmer. For example a recursive function can be unfolded during compile time, so that the run-time memory usage and execution time can be predicted.

Figure 1.2 shows a staged power function defined in MetaML. The result of the `map` is `[8,64]`. In normal execution without staging, the power function is executed for each value of the list. Since the power function is only used as the cubic function, in a non-staged execution every time the same recursion is executed. By separating this calculation in two stages, the calculation of the cubic function can be done once instead of every time the power function is called. As shown in the example, first the recursion is expanded via the `run` instruction, resulting in the cubic function `map( fn z => z * z * z * 1 ) [2,4]`. In the second stage the map function is evaluated.

Another aspect of staged programming is that programs are complete compilation units and that the program is executable without staging annotations. This allows the possibility of strong typing and guarantees the syntactical correctness of the expanded code. In case of MetaML the parser of ML is used, with added grammar rules for the stage annotations and the ML type checker is reused by adding additional scope rules and bind rules for the variables in the different stages.

From here, a more liberal definition of a homogeneous system is used; a homogeneous system is a system where all the components are specifically designed to work with each other, whereas in heterogeneous systems at least one of the components is largely, or completely, ignorant of the existence of the other parts of the system [Tratt (2008)]. Using this new definition the following systems can also be considered as homogeneous systems: C++ templates [Vandevoorde and Josuttis (2003)], Template Haskell [Sheard and Peyton Jones (2002)] and Java Generics [Bracha (2004)]. As these homogeneous systems have a lot in common, we restrict ourselves to the discussion of C++ templates.

C++ templates are a C++ language feature that allows defining functions and classes based on generic types. These generic functions or classes can work on different data types without being rewritten. This is especially useful, when functionality depends on the underlying structure and not on the kind of data it operates on. Examples are operations for stacks, lists, queues and sorting algorithms. As an unintended feature, C++ templates also support staged programming [Veldhuizen (1999)].

An example of type parameterization via C++ templates is shown in Figure 1.3. This example shows the definition of a generic comparison template `GetMin`. The `main` function invokes this template in the body, where the template is parameterized with the desired type via the `<type>` syntax.

Although homogeneous code generators have certain advantages over heterogeneous code generator approaches, it is not always possible to use them. The benefits only apply when code for the same language must be generated, in that case full support for syntax checking and type checking is offered by the compiler. In a heterogeneous situation, where code for

```
#include <iostream>

template <typename T>
T GetMin(T x, T y)
{
    if(x < y) return x;
    return y;
}

int main () {
  int a=2, b=7;
  long c=20, d=4;
  std::cout << GetMin<int>(a,b) << std::endl;
  std::cout << GetMin<long>(c,d) << std::endl;
  return 0;
}
```

Fig. 1.3 C++ template example.

another language must be generated, the internal code expander of the compiler cannot be used. As a result the safety offered in the homogeneous situation is lost.

1.3 Heterogeneous Code Generators

Heterogeneous code generators are the set of code generators where the metalanguage and object language are different. These systems are not limited by a particular output language, as a result, it is possible to implement any code generator in a heterogeneous context [Tratt (2008)].

A heterogeneous code generator can be implemented in different ways [Völter (2003)]. Abstract syntax tree based, print statement based, term rewriting and text-templates are commonly used approaches. These approaches will be discussed in the coming sections.

1.3.1 *Abstract Syntax Trees*

A technique to generate code for an arbitrary target programming language is to instantiate an *abstract syntax tree* (see Section 2.5 for a formal definition) representation of the output code. The code generator instantiates a tree representation of the output code. This tree is transformed to concrete code via a so-called *unparser*.

The use of a tree ensures syntactical correctness of the output code, when the tree is based on a datatype representing the structure of the target (programming) language. It is a requirement that the programming language of the code generator is strongly typed in order to ensure that the tree is instantiated in the correct way. The syntactical correctness of the output code depends on the level of detail of the used abstract syntax tree and the correctness of the *unparser*. Unparsing is the conversion of abstract syntax tree to concrete syntax.

An abstract data type, or API, of the target language is required before one can write an abstract syntax tree based generator. This API can be defined manually, as done in Haskell/DB [Leijen and Meijer (1999)], or an API is off-the-shelf available, like Jenerator for Java [Völter and Gärtner (2001)], or an API can be generated from a grammar, like ApiGen [van den Brand *et al.* (2005)]. A Jenerator example is shown in Figure 1.4. This listing shows how the tree is constructed via instantiating types such as `CClass` and `CMethod`. These types represent nodes in the tree. The hierarchical structure of the tree is visible by the order of calls in the example. First a method node is instantiated and then a class. The result of the code generator is shown in Figure 1.5. A Hello World program is generated.

1.3.2 *Print Statements*

Print statement based generators instantiate code by printing the strings to a file or stream. It is possible, just as with abstract syntax trees, to generate code for another target language than the language of the generator. The object code specified in the generator is concrete and therefore human readable. The print statement approach can be instantly implemented in any programming language that provides print facilities. It does not depend on external libraries or tools, such as an unparser. A drawback of this approach is that no guarantees can be given with respect to the correctness of the output.
Examples of generators based on the print statements are ApiGen [van den Brand *et al.* (2005)] and NunniFSMGen[2]. Figure 1.6 shows a part of ApiGen.

1.3.3 *Term Rewriting*

Term rewriting is a branch of computer science with its foundations in equational logic [Baader and Nipkow (1998)]. It differs from equational logic, since rules are only allowed to replace the left-hand side by the right-hand side and not vice versa. Let t_1 and t_2 be a term, then a rewrite rule is defined as $t_1 \rightarrow t_2$, where a term matching t_1 is replaced by an instantiation of t_2. t_2 can again contain patterns which match on left-hand side of other rules in order to allow further rewriting.

[2]http://sourceforge.net/projects/nunnifsmgen/ (accessed on December 18, 2011)

```
package de.mathema.jenerator.paper;
// imports...
public class HelloJenerator {
  public HelloJenerator() {

    CClass createdClass = new CClass(
         "de.mathema.jenerator.paper", "HelloWorld" );

    CMethod mainMethod = new CMethod( CVisibility.PUBLIC,
                                   CType.VOID, "main" );
    mainMethod.addParameter( new CParameter(
                 CType.user( "String[]" ), "args" ) );
    mainMethod.addToBody( new ClassInstantiation(
              createdClass.getName(), "app", true ) );

    CConstructor cons = new CConstructor(
                                   CVisibility.PUBLIC );
    cons.addToBody( new CCode(
         "System.out.println(\"Hello World!\");" ) );


    createdClass.addConstructor( cons );
    createdClass.addMethod( mainMethod );

    new CodeGenerator().createCode( createdClass );
  }
  // main method following here
}
```

Fig. 1.4 Jenerator code generator example [Völter and Gärtner (2001)].

```
package de.mathema.jenerator.paper;
public class HelloWorld{
  public HelloWorld(){
    System.out.println("Hello World");
  }
  public void main(String[] args){
    new HelloWorld();
  }
}
```

Fig. 1.5 Jenerator output example [Völter and Gärtner (2001)].

Term rewriting allows to define the projection of input data to source code declaratively by a set of equations, where the left-hand side matches on the input data and the right-hand side constructs the output source code. The evaluation of rewrite rules enables generation of code in a natural way. This property makes term rewriting a suited solution

```
private void genAbstractTypeClass() {
  println("abstract public class " + getClassName()
       + " extends aterm.pure.ATermApplImpl {");
  genClassVariables();
  genConstructor();
  genToTermMethod();
  genToStringMethod();
  genSetTermMethod();
  genGetFactoryMethod();
  genDefaultTypePredicates();

  if (visitable) {
    genAccept();
  }
  println("}");
}

private void genDefaultTypePredicates() {
  Iterator<Type> types = adt.typeIterator();
  while (types.hasNext()) {
    Type type = types.next();
    genDefaultTypePredicate(type);
  }
}

private void genDefaultTypePredicate(Type type) {
  println("  public boolean isSort" +
      TypeGenerator.className(type) + "() {");
  println("    return false;");
  println("  }");
  println();
}
```

Fig. 1.6 Print statement based generator example (code snippet from ApiGen [van den Brand *et al.* (2005)]).

for generating recursive code, like nested conditionals and loops. Term rewriting offers higher level of abstraction over the implementation of a code generator in an imperative language. Despite this, rewrite rules are necessary to process the structure of the input data. Term rewrite systems come in different flavors, such as processing terms in ELAN [Borovanský *et al.* (1996)] and Stratego [Visser (2001)], or such as rewriting concrete syntax in ASF+SDF [Bergstra *et al.* (1989)].

Although term rewriting offers advantages, its learning curve is perceived as steep [Kang and Aagaard (2007)]. This experience is amplified in case the terms are based on an abstract syntax tree instead of concrete syntax. Beside that, one of the issues of term rewrite systems is the temptation to decompose the object code in almost atomic elements. Understanding

```
Entity("Person",
  [ Property("fullname", SimpleSort("String")),
    ...
    Property("homepage", SimpleSort("String"))
  ]
)
```

Fig. 1.7 Data structure containing a *Person* entity.

the resulting code is hard when all parts of the code are scattered over the rewrite rules. This is also concluded in [Sturm *et al.* (2002)], while investigating XSLT stylesheets [Clark (1999)] for code generation.

Two term rewrite approaches will be discussed. One applied to terms based on abstract syntax trees, i.e. Stratego, and one using concrete syntax, i.e. ASF+SDF.

1.3.3.1 *Stratego*

Stratego is a language based on conditional term rewriting. The form of the rewrite rules is l : t_1 `->` t_2 `where` s. The l is the name of the equation, t_1 and t_2 are terms, and s is an optional *conditional*. Normally the rewrite rules are executed via a fixed *strategy*. The Stratego system provides increased flexibility by programmable rewriting strategies, allowing control over the application of the rewrite rules.

Before starting to write the transformation one should first define the data types of the input and output. An example is borrowed from [Visser (2008)]. The input data consists of a set of *entities*. An entity can contain zero or more properties, which have a name and a type. Figure 1.7 shows a person entity definition.

This person entity can be transformed to a Java class via a rewrite rule. Since Stratego is based on terms, the right-hand side of the rule is an abstract datatype representing the hierarchical structure of the output code. This code must be unparsed to get a concrete syntax representation. An example of a Stratego rewrite rule that matches the data structure of Figure 1.7 is given in Figure 1.8.

The rewrite rule matches on the `Entity` term on the left-hand side and for each entity it instantiates a Java class. The *variable* `x` is used to parameterize the class with the name of the given entity. In case of the example person entity, `x` will get the value `Person`. The result of the equation is a tree, which is unparsed and shown in Figure 1.9. The properties of the `Entity` are ignored by this example rewrite rule and as a result not existing in the output listing. The example shows the use of Stratego for implementing a code generator.

```
entity-to-class :
  Entity(x, prop*) ->
  ClassDec(
    ClassDecHead(
      [MarkerAnno(TypeName(Id("Entity"))), Public()]
      , Id(x)
      , None(), None(), None()),
    ClassBody(
      [ConstrDec(
         ConstrDecHead([Public()],None(),Id(x),[],None()),
         ConstrBody(None(), []))
      ])
  )
```

Fig. 1.8 Stratego rewrite rule to create a class based on an entity definition.

```
@Entity
public class Person{
 public Person() {   }
}
```

Fig. 1.9 Result code of the rewrite rule.

```
entity-to-class :
  Entity(x_Class, prop*) ->
  |[
     @Entity
     public class x_Class{
       public x_Class() { }
     }
  ]|
```

Fig. 1.10 Rewrite rule using concrete syntax.

Although Stratego is based on abstract syntax trees, it does not offer syntax-safety, as every (sub) tree is casted to the generic type `Term`.

Beside the use abstract syntax trees, Stratego offers a mechanism to use *concrete* syntax in the rewrite rules [Visser (2002)]. The previous defined rule can be implemented using concrete syntax as shown in Figure 1.10. Note, the identifier `x_Class` is automatically recognized by the Stratego parser as a metavariable.

1.3.3.2 *ASF+SDF*

ASF+SDF is a concrete syntax based rewrite system [Bergstra *et al.* (1989)]. It ensures that the output code must conform to a predefined grammar and enforces syntax correctness of the generated code.

ASF+SDF consists of two formalisms. The first is SDF, an acronym for Syntax Definition Formalism, which is a formalism to specify the syntaxes of (programming) languages and to define the function signatures for ASF. Chapter 2 discusses SDF in detail. The Algebraic

Specification Formalism, ASF, is a rewriting formalism. An ASF specification is a collection of equations. The equations have a left-hand side that matches on patterns defined in SDF and a right-hand side specifying the result pattern, also defined in SDF. The form of these equations is $s = t$, where s and t are concrete syntax terms. Furthermore ASF supports conditional equations with a set of conditions, which should succeed before the equation is reduced. The form of conditional equations is $s_1 = t_1$ `, ... ,` $s_n = t_n$ `===>` $s = t$, where all variants of s and t are concrete syntax terms. During interpretation of the conditional equation, first the equations before the arrow sign are evaluated and if all succeed, the equation after the arrow sign is evaluated.

Figure 1.11 shows the Stratego example expressed in ASF. The example defines the equation for the function `generate: Term -> Java`. The equation makes use of a conditional rewrite rule. First, consider the part below the implication arrow. Its left-hand side is the `generate` function and this function includes a match pattern for the input term. The match pattern also binds variables, recognizable by the $ prefix. These variables are defined in the accompanying SDF grammar and the variables are defined for specific syntactical types. The right-hand side specifies the output Java code. The Java code contains a variable `$id`, which is not bound in the left-hand side pattern. This variable gets its value from the equation before the implication arrow. This equation assigns a value to `$id` by casting the value of the `$class` via the function `str_to_id`. ASF requires that the variables are parsed with the correct syntactical type. `$class` has the syntactical type `IdCon`, while the variable `$id` expects a Java identifier. The cast function maps the `$class` variable to the syntactical type of `$id`. This casting is specified before the implication arrow, in case the casting is not successful; the equation will not be applied.

The strict syntactical typing of the variables in ASF results in a syntactical correct mapping from the left-hand side to the right-hand side. ASF+SDF guarantees that the result is a string belonging to the language of the right-hand side type. This mechanism has inspired the template evaluator guaranteeing syntacticall correct output code, which is discussed in Chapter 6.

1.3.4 *Text-Templates*

A text-template system is the last approach to implement code generators we discuss. This approach is known from its use for instantiating HTML in web applications [Conallen (1999)]. As a result of the popularity of templates in web applications, numerous template evaluators are designed for instantiating HTML. Besides generating HTML, text-templates

```
[entity-to-class]
$id := str_to_id( $class )
====>
generate(Entity($class, $props)) =
 @Entity
 public class $id{
    public $id() { }
 }
```

Fig. 1.11 ASF example.

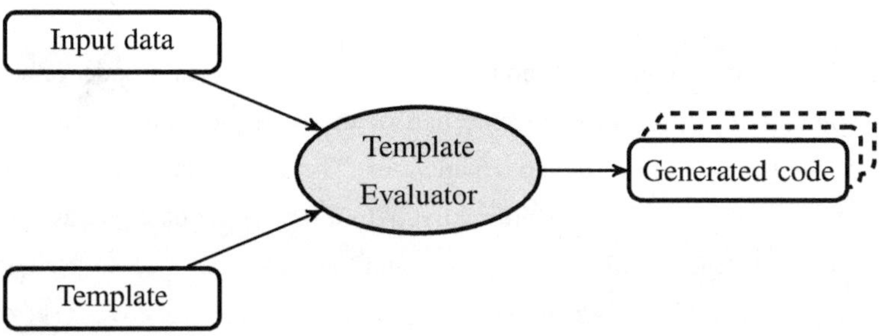

Fig. 1.12 Template based generator.

can be used for generating all kinds of unstructured text, like e-mails or code. Figure 1.12 shows the four artifacts involved in a text-template based generator. These artifacts are input data, a template, template evaluator and generated code.

Since the literature does not provide a formal definition of a template an informal operational definition provided by Parr [Parr (2004)] is given:

> "A template is an output document with embedded actions which are evaluated when rendering the template."

Following this definition a template is a text document that *can* contain *placeholders*. A placeholder is a (syntactical) entity, indicating a missing piece of text. It contains some action, or expression, declaring how to obtain a piece of text to replace it. More formally, a template is a $(\mathit{text}|\mathit{placeholder})+$ pattern, i.e. an arbitrary non-empty sequence of text fragments and placeholders. The *text* is the fixed part of the template and is one-to-one copied to the output document. The *placeholder* represents a non-complete part of the text. In case of templates, the placeholders are the metacode, which are sentences of a metalanguage. Informally, this metalanguage automatically originates at the moment placeholders are introduced in a piece of text or code. This is not only applicable for computer languages, but also happens in natural languages. For example, when one writes a generic agreement or letter where the names are replaced by a sequence of dots (...). These dots are the placeholders in the document, and can be considered as sentences of a metalanguage. Considering a template processed automatically, the metalanguage must have formal semantics and should contain explicit instructions.

Automatic processing of templates is performed by a so-called *template evaluator*. This is an application that interprets a template in order to generate text. It searches for placeholders, executes the specified action and replaces the placeholders to complete the output text.

The combination of template and template evaluator constitutes a code generator. The template contains the application specific part of the code generator, while the template evaluator is the generic part of the code generator. The generic part of the code generator is amongst others responsible for handling the output text, input data processing and other administrative tasks such as directory creation and file creation.

The understandability of the code generator improves as boilerplate code is separated from the output code patterns. Considering the abstract syntax tree approach or the print statements approach, generator code and output code fragments are mixed in the same code context. The text-template approach separates these two artifacts of a generator. Furthermore, the code patterns in a text-template are written in concrete syntax.

Text-templates can be used to generate code for every target language. It is a common pattern for writing web page generators [Conallen (1999)], but it is also used in code generator frameworks such as model-driven engineering tools like openArchitectureWare[3]. Examples of text-template evaluators are Apache Velocity[4], StringTemplate [Parr (2004)], ERb [Herrington (2003)], Java Server Pages[5], FreeMarker[6] and Smarty[7].

Figure 1.13 shows a template for the Apache Velocity template evaluator. The $ signs are used for Java object references to obtain values. Instructions for the template evaluator are prefixed by a #. The loop construction `#foreach`, is used. This construct expresses a loop over a list of objects and the body of the loop is evaluated every iteration, where the context is set to the current processed element of the list. The `#set` directive is used for setting a value. In this case it is used to upper case the first character of the identifier of the field

[3]http://www.openarchitectureware.org (accessed on December 18, 2011)
[4]http://velocity.apache.org (accessed on December 18, 2011)
[5]http://java.sun.com/products/jsp/ (accessed on December 18, 2011)
[6]http://freemarker.org (accessed on December 18, 2011)
[7]http://www.smarty.net (accessed on December 18, 2011)

```
/*
 * Created on $newDate
 * generated by a FUUT-je application using
 * Velocity templates
 */
package $package;
public class $class.Name {
  #foreach($att in $class.Attributes)
  protected $att.Type ${att.Name};
  #end

  #foreach($att in $class.Attributes)
  /**
  * @return Returns the $att.Name
  */
  #set( $uName = "${ft.capFirst($att.Name)}")
  public String get${uName}() {
    return $att.Name;
  }

  /**
  * @param $att.Name The $att.Name to set.
  */
  public void set${uName}(String ${att.Name}) {
    this.${att.Name} = $att.Name;
  }
  #end
}
```

Fig. 1.13 Example of an Apache Velocity template [van Emde Boas (2004)].

name. The upper case first character is a requirement from the Java coding standards.

1.4 Conclusions

Table 1.1 provides an overview of the advantages and disadvantages of the discussed code generator implementation approaches.

A homogeneous system is superb in terms of syntax-safety and type safety, because it is a language feature. This is also the drawback for homogeneous systems. It is only possible to generate code for the language itself. Further, the homogeneous approach can only be used when the output language can express computations, and thus can act as both metalanguage and object language. This is not always the case, for instance HTML cannot be used as metalanguage, since HTML cannot express behavior.

In case it is required to generate code for another language than the metalanguage, one can

Table 1.1 Advantages and disadvantages code generator implementation approaches.

Technique	**Advantages**	**Disadvantages**
Homogeneous	No external tools Type safety	Mono lingual
Abstract Syntax Tree	Syntax-safety	Output code not concrete Abstract Data Type required Unparser required
Print statements	Output code concrete	No safety
Term rewriting	Syntax-safety	Complex technique
Text-templates	Output code concrete Generic generator code separated	No safety

use abstract syntax trees, print statements, term rewriting systems, or text-templates. The use of abstract syntax trees enables syntax-safe code generation. However, constructing an abstract syntax tree involves additional complexity for writing and maintaining a code generator. The complexity is a result of the not concrete object code inside the generator. It is hard to read the object code, since it is encapsulated in a data structure representing the abstract syntax. A detailed knowledge of the object language grammar structure is necessary. Finally having an abstract data type is not sufficient; an unparser must also be available to transform the instantiated syntax tree into text.

The print statements approach solves the problem of not concrete object code. Print statements, or semantically equivalent, are available in all languages without the necessity of external libraries. The drawback of a print statements based generator is its simplicity. String constants contain the fragments of output code. Syntax errors are not detected by the generator or by the compiler of the metalanguage.

Term rewriting allows defining a code generator in a declarative manner by a set of equations, where the left-hand side matches on the input data and the right-hand side constructs the output source code. By nature, term rewriting supports syntactical safe code generation in case the terms are sufficient typed. However, term rewriting based code generators do not remove the entangling between the object code and the code processing the input data and file manipulation.

The text-template approach offers abstraction of most of the generic generator code. The generator related code is captured in the template evaluator. Only small chunks of metacode in the template are necessary to instruct the template evaluator. This result in a similar look of the template and the output code it instantiates. The drawback of text-templates is already in its name. The evaluator of text-templates does not consider the correctness of the object code and handles it as a sequence of characters and thus no guarantees can be given that the output code is syntactically correct.

1.5 Improving the Quality of Code Generators

The central theme of this book is to improve the technical quality of template based code generators. Templates are a widely used implementation approach for code generators, such as for generating HTML in web applications. As a result a lot of template evaluator implementations exist. However, as earlier discussed, text-templates do not offer safety and they lack of good support for all its language artifacts during development.

Theories and concepts are presented and discussed to improve the technical quality of template based code generators. This technical quality includes improving the guarantees of the correctness of the output code and includes a formal argumentation for the necessary computational power of a template metalanguage. Techniques are discussed to guarantee that the output is syntactically correct. This improves the ability to find errors as early as possible and not only when the generated code is compiled or interpreted. Finding errors in an earlier stage also reduces the chance that generated code or a code generator shipped to a client contains errors. Beside that, the presented solution also offers increased safety of applications generating code during run-time.

This book is for software professionals, researchers and students who have a basic knowledge level in software engineering. We anticipate three classes of reader:

- Software engineers designing template engines or web designers using templates, who want to understand the theoretical foundations of templates or wish to read the practical applicability of templates. They should read Chapter 4 and Chapter 7.
- Researchers who wish to understand the theoretical properties of templates. They should read Chapter 3, Chapter 5 and Chapter 6.
- Students of computer science who wants to learn about code generation and want to learn about the different roles the different languages have in the context of template-based code generation. They should read Chapter 3 to Chapter 6.

This book consists of an introduction followed by six chapters and a conclusion. Each of these chapters answers discuss a sub topic in the context of the central theme and they are arranged in order of dependency. Chapter 2 presents a literature study on the topic of formal languages. It provides the basic definitions and notations used in this book.

Chapter 3 discusses the relation between different grammar classes in order to define the requirements that a metalanguage for code generators should fulfill. These requirements for the metalanguage are based on formal languages theory. The relations between concrete syntax, abstract syntax, parser, unparser and their underlying grammars are discussed.

Using the requirements specified in Chapter 3 a metalanguage for templates is defined in Chapter 4. This metalanguage is based on existing theory of programming languages. The chapter finishes with comparing the metalanguage with a couple of different related template evaluators.

Chapter 5 discusses a method to check the syntax of the object language and metalanguage in a template simultaneously. The relation between the grammars of the object language and the metalanguage is presented. It is used to specify a template grammar containing rules for both object language as well as metalanguage. Having a grammar with rules for both languages enables checking of both languages simultaneously by a parser. The presented approach is object language parametric and every object language can be extended with a metalanguage as long the object language comes with a context-free grammar.

Checking only the syntax of the template is not sufficient to guarantee that the output of the template evaluator produces code without syntax errors. Chapter 6 shows an approach to guarantee that a template always generates code without syntax errors. The ideas of an unparser-complete metalanguage and syntax-safety are implemented in a template evaluator called *Repleo*[8].

Finally, the case studies are discussed to show the applicability of (syntax-safe) templates. Chapter 7 shows the use of Repleo used for code generation in different application domains; the generation of data structures and state machines. Furthermore protection against (HTML) injection attacks in web applications is presented.

[8]http://www.repleo.nl

Chapter 2

Preliminaries

This chapter provides basic notations, definitions and properties needed throughout this book. Whenever possible the notations and definitions are used as they appear in the literature [Comon *et al.* (2008); Engelfriet (1974); Hopcroft *et al.* (2001); Aho *et al.* (1986)]. This chapter can be skipped and referred to when necessary.

2.1 Basic Definitions and Notations

The formal language theory is used to study templates and describe their syntax. This section provides definition for common concepts of formal languages. The definitions are based on automata and language theory:

- A *symbol* is a syntactic entity without any meaning.
- An *alphabet* is a finite, non-empty set of symbols.
- The *rank* (or arity) of a symbol is the number of children.
- A *ranked alphabet* is a pair of an alphabet and ranking functions, where the rank function maps a symbol in the alphabet to a single rank.
- A *string* is a finite sequence of symbols from the given alphabet.
- A *language* is the set of all strings belonging to an alphabet, including the empty string.
- A *terminal* symbol is a symbol from which sentences are formed and it occurs literally in a sentence, i.e. terminal symbols are elements of the alphabet.
- A *nonterminal* symbol is a variable representing a sequence of symbols and it can replace a string of terminal symbols or a string existing of a combination of terminal and nonterminal symbols.

Next to strings, the concept of *tree* is used throughout the book. The trees considered here are finite (finite number of nodes and branches), directed (top-down), rooted (there is one node, the root, with no branches entering it), ordered (the children of a node are ordered left to right) and labeled (the nodes are labeled with symbols from a given alphabet) [Engelfriet (1974)]. The following terminology is be used:

- A *leaf* is a node with rank 0.
- The *top* of a tree is its root.
- A *path* through a tree is a sequence of nodes connected by branches ("leading downwards").
- A *subtree* of a tree is a tree determined by a node together with all (the subtrees of) its children.

The following list presents the naming convention and basic definitions used throughout the book.

- i, j and r are used for integer variables.
- Σ is used to denote an alphabet. For example, the binary alphabet $\Sigma = \{0,1\}$, and the set of all lower-case letters $\Sigma = \{a,b,\ldots,z\}$.
- Σ^* denotes all strings over an alphabet Σ.
- σ and c for an alphabet symbol.
- N for nonterminal alphabets.
- n for a nonterminal symbol of N.
- y for sequences of alphabet symbols combined with nonterminal symbols (i.e. strings, elements of $(N \cup \Sigma)^*$).
- z for an alphabet symbol or a nonterminal symbol ($z \in (N \cup \Sigma)$).
- ε is used for the empty string or null value.
- $\mathscr{L}$ for languages. A language contains all sentences defined by Σ^*.
- s for a sentence of a language $\mathscr{L}$ defined by Σ^*.
- r denotes the rank of a symbol and $r \in \mathbb{N}_0$. It is defined by the ranking function $r_\sigma = rank(\sigma)$ where $\sigma \in \Sigma$. Each symbol in a ranked alphabet (see Definition 2.1.1) has a unique rank.
- Σ_r for the set of symbols of rank r.
- $Tr(\Sigma)$ denotes the set of trees over a ranked alphabet Σ, i.e. Σ including a set of ranking functions over Σ.
- t for a tree (see Definition 2.1.2).
- a for an alphabet symbol with rank 0 ($a \in \Sigma_0$).
- f for an alphabet symbol with rank greater than 0 ($f \in \Sigma_r$, where $r > 0$).

- X is a set of symbols called variables, where it is assumed that the sets X and Σ_0 are disjoint.
- x is a variable $x \in X$ and is not used for integer values.
- G for grammars.

Definition 2.1.1 (Ranked alphabet). An alphabet Σ is said to be ranked if for each non-negative integer r a subset Σ_r of Σ is specified, such that Σ_r is nonempty for a finite number of r's only, and such that $\Sigma = \bigcup\limits_{r \geqslant 0} \Sigma_r$. If $\sigma \in \Sigma_r$, then σ has rank r.

Example 2.1.1 (Ranked alphabet). The alphabet $\Sigma = \{a, b, +, -, *\}$ is converted to a ranked alphabet by specifying $\Sigma_0 = \{a, b\}$, $\Sigma_1 = \{-\}$ and $\Sigma_2 = \{+, *\}$.

Definition 2.1.2 (Tree). Given a ranked alphabet Σ, the set of trees over Σ, denoted by $Tr(\Sigma)$ is the language over the alphabet $\Sigma \cup \{[\,,\,]\}$, where $\Sigma \cap \{[\,,\,]\} = \emptyset$, defined inductively as follows.

(1) If $\sigma \in \Sigma_0$, then $\sigma \in Tr(\Sigma)$.
(2) For $r \geqslant 1$, if $\sigma \in \Sigma_r$ and $t_1, \ldots, t_r \in Tr(\Sigma)$, then $\sigma[t_1 \ldots t_r] \in Tr(\Sigma)$.

Example 2.1.2 (Tree). Consider the ranked alphabet of Example 2.1.1. Then $+[*[a-[b]]a]$ is a tree of this alphabet. This tree can be visualized as:

$+[*[a-[b]]a] =$

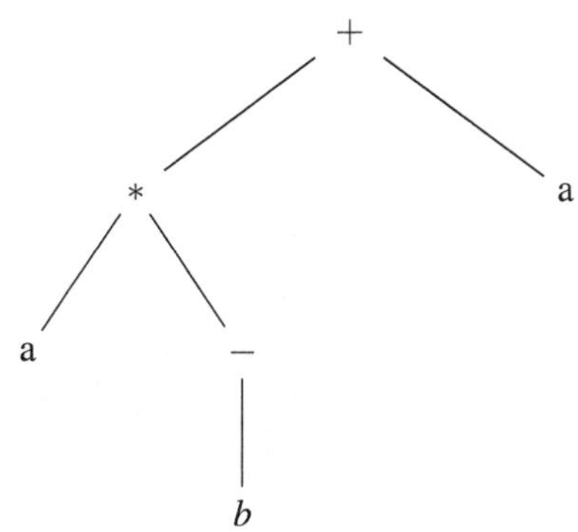

Which on its turn represents the concrete expression $(a * (-b)) + a$.

Definition 2.1.3 (Linear tree). A tree may contain variables, i.e. placeholders for subtrees. A tree $t \in Tr(\Sigma \cup X)$ is linear when each variable is at most used once in t.

Definition 2.1.4 (Substitution). A substitution (respectively a ground substitution) m is a mapping from X into $Tr(\Sigma \cup X)$ (respectively into $Tr(\Sigma)$) where there are only finitely many variables not mapped to themselves. The domain of a substitution m is the subset of

variables $x \in X$ such that $m(x) \neq x$. The substitution $\{x_1 \leftarrow t_1, \ldots, x_r \leftarrow t_r\}$ maps $x_i \in X$ on $t_i \in Tr(\Sigma \cup X)$, for every index $1 \leq i \leq r$. A substitution is ground when all terms $t_1, \ldots, t_r$ are ground terms, that is, when the terms do not contain variables.
Substitutions can be extended to $Tr(\Sigma \cup X)$ in such a way that:

$$\forall f \in \Sigma_r, \forall t_1, \ldots, t_r \in Tr(\Sigma \cup X) \;\; m(f(t_1, \ldots, t_r)) = f(m(t_1), \ldots, m(t_r)).$$

Example 2.1.3 (Substitution). Let $\Sigma = \{f(\ ,\ ,\ ), g(\ ,\ ), a, b\}$ and $X = \{x_1, x_2\}$. Consider the term $t = f(x_1, x_1, x_2)$. Consider the ground substitution $m = \{x_1 \leftarrow a, x_2 \leftarrow g(b,b)\}$ and the non-ground substitution $m' = \{x_1 \leftarrow x_2, x_2 \leftarrow b\}$. Then $m(t) = t\{x_1 \leftarrow a, x_2 \leftarrow g(b,b)\} = f(a, a, g(b,b))$ and $m'(t) = t\{x_1 \leftarrow x_2, x_2 \leftarrow b\} = f(x_2, x_2, b)$.

Definition 2.1.5 (Tree homomorphism). Let Σ and Σ' be two, not necessarily disjoint, ranked alphabets. For each $r > 0$ such that Σ contains a symbol of rank r, a set of variables $X_r = \{x_1, \ldots, x_r\}$ disjoint from Σ and Σ' is defined.
Let h_Σ be a mapping which, with $f \in \Sigma$ of rank r, associates a term $t_f \in Tr(\Sigma', X_r)$. The tree homomorphism $h : Tr(\Sigma) \rightarrow Tr(\Sigma')$ is determined by h_Σ as follows:

- $h(a) = t_a \in Tr(\Sigma')$ for each $a \in \Sigma$ of rank 0,
- $h(f(t_1, \ldots, t_n)) = t_f\{x_1 \leftarrow h(t_1), \ldots, x_r \leftarrow h(t_r)\}$
  where $t_f\{x_1 \leftarrow h(t_1), \ldots, x_r \leftarrow h(t_r)\}$ is the result of applying the substitution $\{x_1 \leftarrow h(t_1), \ldots, x_r \leftarrow h(t_r)\}$ to the term t_f.

h_Σ is called a *linear tree homomorphism* when no t_f contains two occurrences of the same x_r. Thus a linear tree homomorphism cannot copy trees.

Example 2.1.4 (Tree homomorphism). Let $\Sigma = \{g(\ ,\ ,\ ), a, b\}$ and $\Sigma' = \{f(\ ,\ ), a, b\}$. Consider the tree homomorphism h determined by h_Σ defined by: $h_\Sigma(g) = f(x_1, f(x_2, x_3)), h_\Sigma(a) = a, h_\Sigma(b) = b$. For instance: If $t = g(a, g(b,b,b), a)$, then $h(t) = f(a, f(f(b, f(b,b)), a))$.

2.2 Context-free Grammars

This book will focus on the generation of sentences of languages aimed to express programs executed or interpreted by a computer. The rules for constructing valid sentences of these languages can be specified by context-free grammars. The *syntax*[1] of a language is its valid

[1]The syntax rules do not specify the meaning of a sentence; as a result a syntactical correct sentence can be nonsense.

set of sentences. Compilers or interpreters for most programming languages are based on LL or LR parsers. LL or LR parsers can handle a subset of the context-free grammars, which implies that these programming languages are context-free languages. A context-free language $\mathscr{L}(G)$ is specified by a context-free grammar G. A sentence belonging to the set of sentences specified by a context-free grammar is called a *well-formed* sentence. The context-free grammar is defined as follows [Hartmanis (1967)]:

Definition 2.2.1 (Context-free grammar). A context-free grammar (CFG) is a four-tuple $\langle \Sigma, N, S, Prods \rangle$ where

Σ is a finite set of terminal symbols, i.e. the alphabet.

N is a finite set of nonterminal symbols and $N \cap \Sigma = \emptyset$.

S is the start symbol, or axiom, and $S \in N$.

$Prods$ is a finite set of production rules of the form $n \rightarrow y$ where $n \in N$ and $y \in (N \cup \Sigma)*$.

Each context-free grammar G_{cfg} can be transformed into a Chomsky normal form without changing the language generated by that grammar [Hotz (1980)]. A context-free grammar of the Chomsky normal form only contains rules of the forms:

(1) $n \rightarrow \varepsilon$, where $n \in N$ and A is the start symbol;

(2) $n \rightarrow s$, where $n \in N$ and $s \in \Sigma^*$;

(3) $n \rightarrow n_1 n_2$, where n, n_1, $n_2 \in N$.

Example 2.2.1 shows a context-free grammar definition for a language based on boolean algebra.

Example 2.2.1 (Context-free grammar). Let G_{bool} be a context-free grammar with, $\Sigma = \{␣, \backslash n, \tilde{}, \&, |, (,), true, false\}$, nonterminals $N = \{\text{E}, \text{T}, \text{F}, \text{L}, \text{C}\}$, start symbol $S = \text{E}$ and rules

$$Prods = \left\{ \begin{array}{lll} \text{E} \rightarrow \text{L}\,\text{T}, & \text{F} \rightarrow \text{"\textasciitilde"}\,\text{L}\,\text{F}, & \text{L} \rightarrow \text{C}\,\text{L}, \\ \text{E} \rightarrow \text{E}\,\text{"|"}\,\text{L}\,\text{T}, & \text{F} \rightarrow \text{"("}\,\text{L}\,\text{E}\,\text{")"}\,\text{L}, & \text{L} \rightarrow \varepsilon, \\ \text{T} \rightarrow \text{F}, & \text{F} \rightarrow \text{"}\textit{true}\text{"}\,\text{L}, & \text{C} \rightarrow \text{"␣"}, \\ \text{T} \rightarrow \text{T}\,\text{"\&"}\,\text{L}\,\text{F}, & \text{F} \rightarrow \text{"}\textit{false}\text{"}\,\text{L}, & \text{C} \rightarrow \text{"\textbackslash n"} \end{array} \right\}$$

The layout syntax is defined by the production rules for the nonterminal L. We assume that this layout nonterminal is inserted after every terminal symbol in the grammar and before the start nonterminal, in the case of the first production rule after nonterminal E [Johnstone *et al.* (2011)].

A context-free grammar defines a set of sentences, i.e. the language $\mathscr{L}(G)$, where for each $s \in \Sigma$ a derivation exists $S \overset{*}{\underset{G}{\Longrightarrow}} s$. If a sentence belongs to $\mathscr{L}(G)$, a parse tree can be constructed using the grammar. This tree is derived by applying the production rules of the grammar to construct the sentence and it is called the *parse tree*. Example 2.2.2 shows a parse tree derived from a sentence of $\mathscr{L}(G_{\text{bool}})$.

Example 2.2.2 (Parse tree). Let s be `~true & false | true`, the parse tree of s using the grammar G is:

$d_G(s) =$

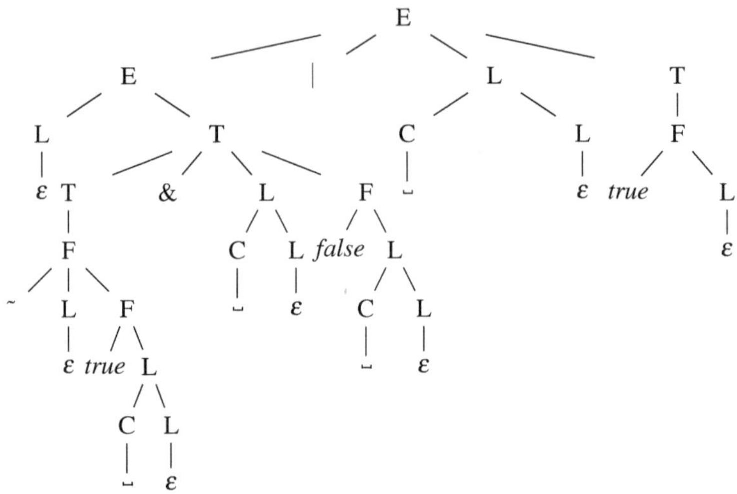

A parse tree represents the hierarchical structure of the sentence expressed by the production rules of its grammar. Normally such parse trees are automatically constructed from a given sentence when a parser is used based on the grammar. A parser can, for instance, use algorithms like LL [Aho *et al.* (1989)] and LR [Knuth (1965)].

The parse tree contains all necessary information to restore the original sentence. Consider the parse tree of Example 2.2.2, and read the leaves from left to right, the original sentence is visible. The *yield* function reconstructs the original string of a parse tree. It traverses a parse tree in order to compute the original sentence from it by concatenating the leaves (taking the leaf symbols as letters) from left to right.

Definition 2.2.2 (Yield). The *yield* function is defined by the following two rules:

- $yield(a) = a$ if $a \in \Sigma_0$;
- $yield(f(t_1,\ldots,t_r)) = yield(t_1)\cdot\ldots\cdot yield(t_r)$ if $f \in \Sigma_r$ and $t_i \in Tr(\Sigma \cup N)$, where $\cdot$ denotes the string concatenation.

2.3 Regular Tree Grammars

A *regular tree language* is a set of trees generated by a *regular tree grammar*. The definition of regular tree grammars is:

Definition 2.3.1 (Regular tree grammar). A regular tree grammar (RTG) is a four-tuple $\langle \Sigma, N, S, Prods \rangle$, where:

Σ is a finite set of terminal symbols with rank $r \geq 0$.

N is a finite set of nonterminal symbols with rank $r = 0$ and $N \cap \Sigma = \emptyset$.

S is a start symbol and $S \in N$.

Prods is a finite set of production rules of the form $n \to t$, where $n \in N$ and $t \in Tr(\Sigma \cup N)$.

Example 2.3.1 shows a regular tree grammar (taken from [Cleophas (2008)]).

Example 2.3.1 (Regular tree grammar). Let G be the regular tree grammar with $\Sigma = \{a(\, , \,), b(\,), c\}$, nonterminals $N = \{E, W\}$, start symbol E, and rules

$$
\begin{aligned}
Prods = \{ & \\
& \mathrm{E} \to \mathrm{W}, \\
& \mathrm{W} \to \mathrm{b(W)}, \\
& \mathrm{W} \to \mathrm{b(a(c,c))} \\
\} &
\end{aligned}
$$

The language of this grammar is

$$\mathscr{L}(G_{rtg}) = \{b(a(c,c)), b(b(a(c,c))), b(b(b(a(c,c)))), \ldots\}.$$

The parse steps of the term $b(b(a(c,c)))$ are $E \Rightarrow W \Rightarrow b(W) \Rightarrow b(b(a(c,c)))$, where $\Rightarrow$ is a derivation step.

Regular tree languages have a number of properties [Cleophas (2008)], the one being important for this book is *recognizability* of regular tree languages. Recognizable tree languages are the languages recognized by a finite tree automaton. Regular tree languages are recognizable by (non)-deterministic bottom up finite tree automata and non-deterministic top-down tree automata [Comon *et al.* (2008)]. The set of languages recognizable by deterministic top-down tree automata is limited to the class of path-closed tree languages [Virágh (1981)], a subset of regular tree languages (see Section 3.3).

2.4 Relations between CFL and RTL

A number of relations can be defined between context-free languages and regular tree languages [Cleophas (2008)]. Amongst others, a tree can be represented as a term. These terms can be parsed using a context-free grammar, since printing a (sub)tree to text does not depend on the sibling nodes of that (sub)tree. This context-free grammar of the used term representation is given in Figure 2.4. For example the tree of Example 2.2.1 can be represented by the term

$$
\begin{array}{l}
E(\\
\;E(L(\varepsilon), \\
\;T(T(F(\tilde{}\,,L(\varepsilon),F(\mathit{true},L(C(\textvisiblespace),L(\varepsilon))))), \\
\;\&,L(C(\textvisiblespace),L(\varepsilon)),F(\mathit{false},L(C(\textvisiblespace),L(\varepsilon))))), \\
\;|,L(C(\textvisiblespace),L(\varepsilon)),T(F(\mathit{true},L(\varepsilon))) \\
)
\end{array}
$$

The goal of this book is the formal definition of code generators based on templates. For this purpose, the relation between regular tree languages and the parse trees of context-free languages is relevant. The *parse* function takes a string and a grammar and returns the parse tree of that string when the string can be produced by that grammar. The way parse algorithms create a parse tree shows regularity, which suggests that the parse trees are indeed regular. A proof that the set of parse trees of a context-free grammar is a regular tree language can be found in [Comon *et al.* (2008)]. The following definition shows the derivation of the regular tree grammar $\mathscr{L}(G_{\mathrm{pt}})$ defining the set of parse trees of a context-free grammar $\mathscr{L}(G_{cfg})$.

Definition 2.4.1 (Regular tree grammar for parse trees). Let $G_{cfg} = \langle \Sigma, N, S, \mathit{Prods} \rangle$ be a context-free grammar. The regular tree grammar $G_{\mathrm{pt}} = \langle \Sigma', N', S', \mathit{Prods}' \rangle$ defining the parse trees of G_{cfg} is derived by the following rules:

- The start symbol of both grammars is equal: $S = S'$,
- The set of nonterminals of both grammars is equal: $N = N'$,
- The alphabet of G_{pt} is derived by the following rule: $\Sigma' = \Sigma \cup \{\varepsilon\} \cup \{(n,r) \mid n \in N,\ \exists n \to y \in \mathit{Prods}$ with r equal to the number of symbols of $y\}$. In parse trees, a symbol can normally have a different number of children, when alternative production rules have a different pattern length. In tree languages a symbol must have a fixed rank, so

the symbol (n,r) is introduced for each $n \in N$ such that there is a rule $n \to y$ where y has r symbols.

- The set of productions $Prods'$ of G_{pt} is derived by the following rules:

  if $n \to \varepsilon \in Prods$ then $n \to (n,0)(\varepsilon) \in Prods'$.

  if $(n \to n_1 \ldots n_r) \in Prods$ then $n \to (n,r)(n_1,\ldots,n_r) \in Prods'$.

Example 2.4.1 (Regular tree grammar for parse trees). Since normally in parse trees a symbol can have different number of children, an updated version of the parse tree displayed in Example 2.2.2 is given: $d_G(s) =$

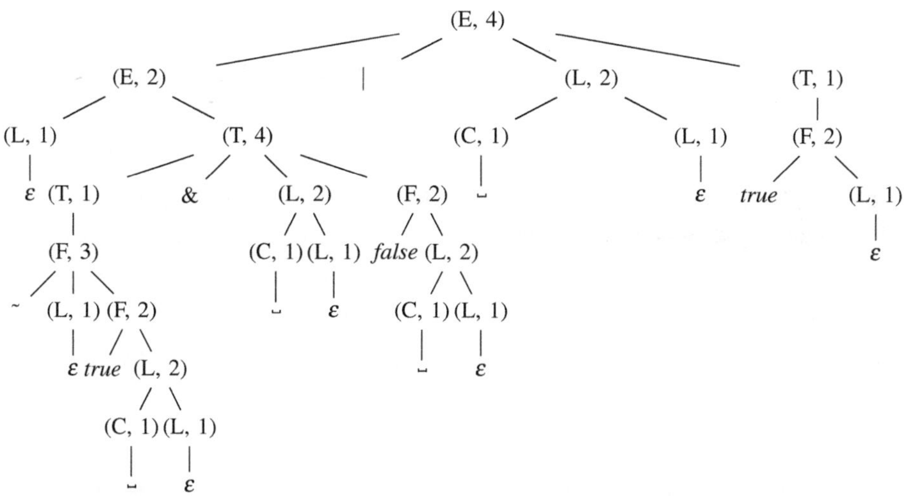

Using the definition given above, the G_{pt} defining the language of parse trees of G_{bool} can be derived. The result of the derivation is a regular tree grammar G_{pt} with, $\Sigma = \{␣, \backslash n, \tilde{}, \&, |, (,), true, false\}$, nonterminals $N = \{(\mathrm{E},4), (\mathrm{E},2), (\mathrm{T},4), (\mathrm{T},1), (\mathrm{F},5), (\mathrm{F},3), (\mathrm{F},2), (\mathrm{L},2), (\mathrm{L},1), (\mathrm{C},1)\}$, start symbol $S = \mathrm{E}$ and rules

$$Prods = \left\{ \begin{array}{lll} (\mathrm{E},2) \to \mathrm{L\,T}, & (\mathrm{F},3) \to \text{“~”}\,\mathrm{L\,F}, & (\mathrm{L},2) \to \mathrm{C\,L}, \\ (\mathrm{E},4) \to \mathrm{E}\,\text{“|”}\,\mathrm{L\,T}, & (\mathrm{F},5) \to \text{“(”}\,\mathrm{L\,E}\,\text{“)”}\,\mathrm{L}, & (\mathrm{L},1) \to \varepsilon, \\ (\mathrm{T},1) \to \mathrm{F}, & (\mathrm{F},2) \to \text{“}\textit{true}\text{”}\,\mathrm{L}, & (\mathrm{C},1) \to \text{“␣”}, \\ (\mathrm{T},4) \to \mathrm{T}\,\text{“\&”}\,\mathrm{L\,F}, & (\mathrm{F},2) \to \text{“}\textit{false}\text{”}\,\mathrm{L}, & (\mathrm{C},1) \to \text{“\textbackslash n”} \end{array} \right\}$$

The following statements hold for context-free grammars and regular tree grammars:

- $\mathscr{L}(G_{\text{pt}}) = parse(\mathscr{L}(G_{cfg}))$
- $\mathscr{L}(G_{cfg}) = yield(\mathscr{L}(G_{\text{pt}}))$

Hence, also

- $\mathscr{L}(G_{cfg}) = yield(parse(\mathscr{L}(G_{cfg})))$
- $\mathscr{L}(G_{\text{pt}}) = parse(yield(\mathscr{L}(G_{\text{pt}})))$

Sentences can be mapped to a parse tree and back to the original sentence. This is a result of the fact that the *parse* function does not throw away information, but it builds a tree with the original sentence distributed over its leaves.

2.5 Abstract Syntax Trees

The set of abstract syntax trees of a language is called the abstract syntax and this abstract syntax is defined by a regular tree grammar. These abstract syntax trees are considered as the abstract representation of well-formed sentences [Donzeau-Gouge *et al.* (1984)]. The abstract syntax representation of a sentence is unique, while the textual representation is usually cluttered with optional and semantically irrelevant details such as blanks and line feeds. These optional and semantically irrelevant details are called *syntactic sugar*.
The *abstract syntax tree* is a representation of a sentence without superfluous nodes, such as nodes corresponding to keywords and *Chain rules* [Koorn (1994)]. A chain rule is a grammar rule of the form $n_1 \rightarrow n_2$, where both n_1 and n_2 are nonterminals.

Example 2.5.1 (Abstract syntax tree). An example of an abstract syntax tree of the sentence s given in Example 2.2.2 is:

$AST(s) =$

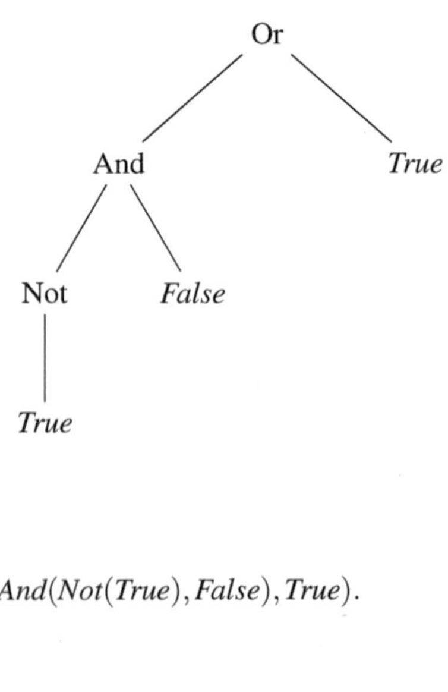

It can also be represented as a term

$$AST(s) = Or(And(Not(True), False), True).$$

```
begin declare input : natural,
              output : natural,
              repnr : natural,
              rep : natural;
      input := 14;
      output := 1;
      while input - 1 do
          rep := output;
          repnr := input;
          while repnr - 1 do
             output := output + rep;
             repnr := repnr - 1
          od;
          input := input - 1
      od
end
```

Fig. 2.1 A PICO program.

2.6 Used Languages and Formalisms

This section discusses the syntax of the formalisms used throughout the book. The language PICO is also presented here. PICO is used for illustrating purposes.

2.6.1 *The PICO Language*

The goal of PICO [Bergstra *et al.* (1989)] is to have a simple language, large enough to illustrate the concepts of parsing, type checking and evaluation. Informal, the PICO language is the language of while-programs. The main features of PICO are:

- Two types: natural numbers and strings.
- Variables must be declared in a separate section.
- Expressions can be made of constants, variables, addition, subtraction and concatenation.
- Statements: assignment, if-then-else and while-do.

A PICO program consists of declarations followed by statements. Variables must be declared before they can be used in the program. Statements and expressions can be used in the body of the program. An example PICO program that computes the factorial function is given in Figure 2.1[2].

[2]Example borrowed from http://www.meta-environment.org/doc/books/extraction-transformation/language-definitions/language-definitions.html (accessed on December 18, 2011)

2.6.2 *Syntax Definition Formalism*

Template grammars, as presented in Chapter 5, can easily become ambiguous and dealing with ambiguities is a primary requirement for parsing templates. The Scannerless Generalized LR (SGLR) algorithm, and its implementation the SGLR parser [Visser (1997)], can deal with these ambiguities. Grammars for the SGLR parser are defined using the Syntax Definition Formalism (SDF) [Heering *et al.* (1989)], which is the main reason for using SDF in this book.

In contrast with other parser algorithms, such as LL or LALR, and their used BNF-like [Backus *et al.* (1960)] grammar formalisms, SDF supports the complete class of context-free grammars. This enables the support for modular grammar definitions. Pieces of grammar can be embedded in modules and imported by other modules. Modules may have formal symbol parameters, which can be bound by actual symbols using imports. The syntax of module parameters is: module <ModuleName> [<Symbol>+]. When the module is imported, all occurences of the formal parameters will be substituted by the actual parameters The modularity enables combining and reusing of grammars.

The core of an SDF module consists of the elements of the mathematically four-tuple definition of a context-free grammar as defined in Section 2.2. In SDF nonterminals are called *sorts* and declared after the similar keyword sorts. *Symbols* is the global name for literals, sorts and character classes and form the elementary building blocks of SDF syntax rules. Start symbols are declared after the keyword context-free start-symbols. Production rules are declared in sections context-free syntax and lexical syntax. The *productions rules* contain a *syntactical pattern* at the left-hand side and a resulting sort at the right-hand side. This left-hand side pattern is based on a combination of symbols, i.e. terminals in combination with nonterminals. Symbols can be declared as optional via a postfix question mark. In the context-free syntax section a LAYOUT sort is automatically injected between every symbol in the left-hand side of a production rule. The LAYOUT sort is an SDF/SGLR embedded sort for white spaces and line feeds. This mechanism differs from the earlier presented approach, where the layout nonterminal should be present explicitly in the production rules. To illustrate SDF, the SDF module shown in Figure 2.2 defines the PICO language.

SDF also supports concise declaration of associative lists. A list is declared by its elements and a postfix operator * or +, with the respectively meaning of at least zero times or at least one time. Lists may contain a separator, which are declared via the pattern {Symbol Literal}*, where Symbol defines the syntax of the elements and Literal de-

```
module languages/pico/syntax/Pico

imports basic/NatCon
imports basic/StrCon
imports basic/Whitespace

hiddens
  context-free start-symbols
    PROGRAM

exports
  sorts PROGRAM DECLS ID-TYPE STATEMENT EXP TYPE PICO-ID

  context-free syntax
    "begin" DECLS {STATEMENT";" }* "end"
                              -> PROGRAM {cons("program")}
    "declare" {ID-TYPE "," }* ";"
                              -> DECLS {cons("decls")}
    PICO-ID ":" TYPE  -> ID-TYPE {cons("decl")}

    PICO-ID ":=" EXP  -> STATEMENT {cons("assignment")}
    "if" EXP "then" {STATEMENT ";" }*
              "else" {STATEMENT ";" }* "fi"
                              -> STATEMENT {cons("if")}
    "while" EXP "do" {STATEMENT ";" }* "od"
                              -> STATEMENT {cons("while")}

    PICO-ID                   -> EXP {cons("id")}
    NatCon                    -> EXP {cons("natcon")}
    StrCon                    -> EXP {cons("strcon")}
    EXP "+" EXP               -> EXP {cons("add")}
    EXP "-" EXP               -> EXP {cons("sub")}
    EXP "||" EXP              -> EXP {cons("concat")}
    "(" EXP ")"               -> EXP {cons("bracket")}

    "natural"                 -> TYPE {cons("natural")}
    "string"                  -> TYPE {cons("string")}

  lexical syntax
    [a-z] [a-z0-9]*   -> PICO-ID   {cons("picoid")}

  lexical restrictions
    PICO-ID -/- [a-z0-9]
```

Fig. 2.2 The PICO grammar in SDF.

fines the separator syntax, for example: `{STATEMENT ";" }*`. This kind of lists are called *separated lists*.

The production rules can be annotated with a list of properties between curling brackets at the right-hand side of the rule. The parser includes these annotations in the parse tree at the node produced by the production rule. Tools processing the parse tree can use these annotations.

For example, an abstract syntax for an SDF grammar can be specified using annotations. The label of the abstract syntax representation of a production rule is assigned by a so-called constructor value. This constructor value is used during desugaring to instantiate the nodes of the abstract syntax tree. The constructor is declared via a `cons` value. SDF requires that a constructor is unique for a given sort, and in that way suffices the first uniqueness requirement of the *desugar* function of Definition 3.1.1. It does not require that a constructor is only used for a fixed rank and thus SDF does not satisfy the requirements to generate a legal regular tree language. Production rules can also annotated with the keyword `reject`. The `reject` annotation specifies that strings specified by the rule is rejected for that nonterminal. Rejects should only used for nonterminals defining lexical syntax. The rejects are used to specify the lexical disambiguation rule "prefer keywords".

Besides these core features of SDF, it supports modularization of grammar definitions. Every grammar definition file is declared as a module with a name, which can be imported by other modules. Modules are imported via the `imports` keyword followed by the name(s) of imported modules. Sections of a grammar module can be declared hidden or visible via the keywords `hiddens` and `exports` to prevent unexpected collisions between grammar modules result in undesired ambiguities. Exported sections are visible in the entire grammar, while hidden sections are only visible in the local grammar module. Although the namespace of a nonterminal is global, adding a new alternative to a nonterminal, which is defined in an imported module, does not change the recognized language of imported module. This is because per module an LR parse table is generated, based on the module dependency graph. SDF also provides syntax to define priorities and associativity to express disambiguation rules in a grammar.

Considering again the SDF module shown in Figure 2.2. The nonterminals and production rules are declared in the exported section. The start symbol is `PROGRAM`, which is the root sort for a PICO program. In the PICO module the start symbol is declared hidden to prevent automatic propagation to modules importing this grammar. The annotation feature of SDF is also used in the PICO module to specify the abstract syntax tree. The definition for the sorts `NatCon` and `StrCon`, and a module defining white space (spaces, tabs, and new lines) are imported.

The grammar of Figure 2.2 is used to parse PICO programs, like Figure 2.1. The abstract syntax tree, result of parsing the program and desugaring the parse tree is shown in Fig-

```
program(
  decls([
    decl( "input", natural ),
    decl( "output", natural ),
    decl( "repnr", natural ),
    decl( "rep", natural )
  ]),
  [
    assignment( "input", natcon( 14 ) ),
    assignment( "output", natcon( 1 ) ),
    while( sub( id( "input" ), natcon( 1 ) ),[
      assignment( "rep", id( "output" ) ),
      assignment( "repnr", id( "input" ) ),
      while( sub( id( "repnr" ), natcon ( 1 ) ),[
        assignment( "output", add( id( "output" ),
                                   id( "rep" ) ) ),
        assignment( "repnr", sub( id( "repnr" ),
                                  natcon( 1 ) ) )
        ]),
      assignment( "input", sub( id( "input" ),
                                natcon( 1 ) ) )
    ])
  ]
)
```

Fig. 2.3 Abstract syntax tree of PICO program of Figure 2.1.

ure 2.3. The tree is displayed in the ATerm format, to be discussed in Section 2.6.3.

2.6.3 *ATerms*

The syntax for terms used in this book is based on a subset of the ATerms syntax [van den Brand *et al.* (2000)]. ATerms have support for lists, which are not directly supported by the presented regular tree grammars. Lists must be binary trees to stay fully compatible with the regular tree grammars. The serialized term notation of the list is only a shorthand notation for these binary trees, i.e. the list

```
[ "a", "b", "c" ]
```

has the internal representation

```
[ "a", [ "b", [ "c" , []]]].
```

Since the lists of ATerms are internally stored as binary trees, where the left branch is the element and right branch the list or empty list, the use of ATerms meets this requirement. The subset of the ATerm language is defined by the SDF definition of Figure 2.4.

```
module ATerms

imports StrCon
        IdCon

exports
  sorts AFun ATerm

  context-free syntax
        StrCon  -> AFun
        IdCon   -> AFun
        AFun                              -> ATerm
        AFun "(" {ATerm ","}+ ")"         -> ATerm
        "[" {ATerm ","}* "]"              -> ATerm
```

Fig. 2.4 Subset of ATerm syntax used in this book.

The `IdCon` and `StrCon` are respectively defined as the following character classes `[A-Za-z] [A-Za-z\-]*`[3] and `["]~[\0-\31\n\t\"\\]*["]`.

[3]The original character class for IdCon allows numeric symbols in the tail. These characters are not allowed to prevent ambiguities in the tree path queries presented later on.

Chapter 3

The Unparser

Code generators are metaprograms translating a regular tree to a sentence of a context-free language. The metalanguage used to implement the code generator should be, on the one side, expressive enough to be of practical value, and, on the other side, restricted enough to enforce the separation between the view and the model, according to the model-view-controller architecture (MVC, see Section 7.1.3) [Krasner and Pope (1988)]. In the MVC architecture, templates are commonly used to implement the *view* of the internal data of an application (*model*).

The MVC architecture decouples the models and its transformations from the view components, hereby reducing the complexity and increasing the flexibility of the system. This separation of concerns also allows different views for the same underlying model.

While in the original paper on MVC [Krasner and Pope (1988)] the *view* was expected to send editing messages to the model, already in [Burbeck (1992)] this functionality was restricted to the *controller*, and the *view* was only allowed to receive the messages from the model to update the way the model is shown. This intuition was formalized in [Parr (2004)], where it was argued that the view should neither alter the model nor perform calculations depending on the semantics of the model. Unfortunately, the separation of view and logic is not enforced in most existing template engines, such as JSP, i.e., it is possible to write JSP templates with all logic in a single file. Typically, such a file will contain fragments in HTML, JSP-tags, Java, and SQL. Not only does this file violate the MVC architecture principle, because logic (model) and presentation (view) are not separated, but it is also hard to understand the file due to different escaping characters required to support multiple programming languages, executed at different stages.

In this chapter the unparser code generation pattern is presented and is shown that unparser-complete metalanguages provide the right level of expressivity, i.e. not too weak and not too powerful [Arnoldus *et al.* (2011)]. An unparser-complete metalanguage is capable of expressing an unparser: a code generator that translates any legal abstract syntax tree into a semantically equivalent sentence of the corresponding context-free language. A metalanguage not able to express an unparser will fail to produce all sentences belonging to the corresponding context-free language.

The unparser translates an abstract syntax tree into a sentence of a context-free language. It is semantically neutral, that means that parsing and desugaring the output sentence produced by an unparser can reproduce the abstract syntax tree. The unparser is capable to instantiate all sentences of the output language, modulo layout and other semantically irrelevant syntax. This chapter discusses the properties and requirements of the unparser and shows that a linear deterministic tree-to-string transducer is powerful enough to express the unparser.

An unparser can be seen as a part of the "circle of code" shown in Figure 3.1, i.e. the circle from concrete syntax to parse tree to abstract syntax and back to concrete syntax. The textual representation of a program obeying a context-free grammar ($\mathscr{L}(G_{cfg})$ in Figure 3.1) can be *parse*d to obtain the corresponding parse tree ($\mathscr{L}(G_{pt})$). The set of parse trees of a context-free grammar is a regular tree language [Comon *et al.* (2008)]. Since the parse tree contains exactly the same information as the textual representation, the textual representation can be restored using the parse tree. The corresponding mapping from $\mathscr{L}(G_{pt})$ to $\mathscr{L}(G_{cfg})$ is the *yield* function (see Definition 2.2.2). Alternatively, one can *desugar* the parse tree, i.e., simplify it by removing the semantically irrelevant layout information. In this way, an abstract syntax tree ($\mathscr{L}(G_{ast})$) is obtained. Finally, the *unparse* function closes the circle and maps elements of $\mathscr{L}(G_{ast})$ to $\mathscr{L}(G_{cfg})$. Section 3.1 discusses the *desugar* function followed by the discussion of the *unparse* in Section 3.2. After that, unparser-completeness is discussed in Section 3.3.

3.1 Deriving Abstract Syntax Trees

A parse tree can be transformed in an abstract syntax tree. This transformation requires that the *meaning* of the original sentence is not altered during the translation from a parse tree to an abstract syntax tree. This requirement is expressed in Figure 3.1 by the cycle of the application of $unparse \circ desugar \circ parse$. Equal meaning of a program is defined by the following property: Given a parse tree t_{pt} and an abstract syntax tree t_{ast} representing the same piece of object code and given a function f_1 operating on t_{pt}, resulting in a term t, and f_2 operating on t_{ast} resulting in the same t, it is required that $f_1(t_{pt}) = f_2(t_{ast})$, where $t_{ast} = desugar(t_{pt})$. For example, the parse tree of a C program and the abstract syntax tree

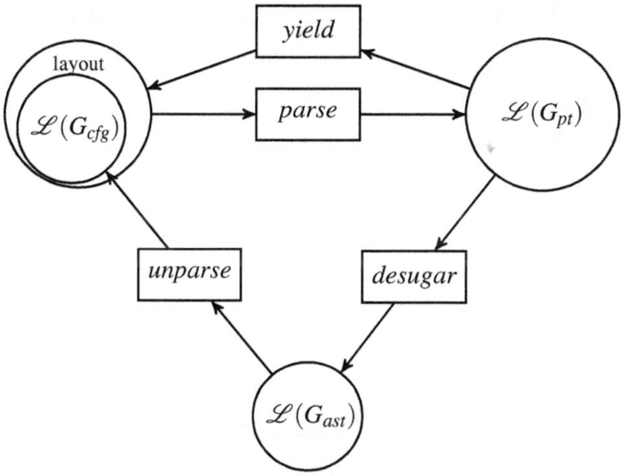

Fig. 3.1 Relations between languages and their grammars.

of the same program should result in the same assembler code after compilation. By means of that definition, the required detail of the abstract syntax is dependent on the information used by the function f_2 processing it. In other words, a function, only interested in a subset of the semantics of a programming language, can use a less detailed abstract syntax than a function using every detail of the programming language. Therefor, the *desugar* function is defined in the context of the required detail of the input tree for function f_2 and not generic. In this chapter, we present a generic *desugar* function, where the level of detail of the resulting t_{ast} is defined by labels in the parse tree t_{pt}.

The topic of this chapter is to derive the *unparse* function from the context-free grammar of the output language. However, in order to generate a textual representation from an abstract syntax tree the unparser should be aware of the mapping between concrete syntax constructs and abstract syntax constructs. It is not a goal to design the most compact abstract syntax for a given f_2, but a formal notion of abstract syntax is necessary to discuss the properties of metaprograms instantiating code. In practice, an abstract syntax tree representation is based on the parse tree modulo layout information and keywords. In the next paragraphs an approach for transforming a parse tree to an abstract syntax tree is presented. The *desugar* function can be manually defined in the parser definition, like in parser implementations such as YACC [Johnson (1975)], ANTLR [Parr and Quong (1995)] and Beaver[1]. These parsers allow associating a production rule with a *semantic action* in the

[1]http://beaver.sourceforge.net/ (accessed on December 18, 2011)

grammar. These semantic actions, for example specified in a third generation programming language, can directly instantiate an abstract syntax tree. Another way to construct the mapping is by means of heuristics [Wile (1997)]. This approach will introduce machine-generated names for the abstract syntax tree nodes.

A *desugar* function can also be defined in a semi-automatic manner. In order to retain the full control of the abstract syntax constructs, the abstract syntax constructs (signature labels) are integrated with the production rules of a context-free grammar. Formally, a production rule in the augmented context-free grammar has the form $n \rightarrow z\{c\}$ where $n \in N$, $z \in (N \cup \Sigma)^*$ and c is an element of an alphabet Σ'. The set Σ' is the alphabet of the regular tree grammar belonging to the abstract syntax and is not necessarily disjoint from $N \cup \Sigma$. It is not allowed to use a signature label c multiple times. In order to remove the layout and other superfluous syntax, it is allowed, under strict conditions, to have production rules without signature labels. These conditions are in the case of:

- **Layout syntax** - The nonterminals belonging to the layout syntax, such as whitespaces and comment, should not be defined with a signature label. The desugar function, as defined in Section 3.1, excludes these syntax from the tree. It is mandatory, that the layout syntax include the empty string ε, as the layout is not restored by the automatic derived unparser.
- **Chain rules** - It is allowed that production rules of the form $n_1 \rightarrow n_2$, are not accompanied with a signature label. The abstract syntax belonging to n_2 is propagated to n_1, which is allowed, since all signature labels are unique. Furthermore, it is allowed that n_2 is surrounded by layout nonterminals, as these layout syntaxes contain the empty string.

Example 3.1.1 (Augmented context-free grammar). The following set of production rules show the extension of the context-free grammar of Example 2.2.1 with signature labels:

$$
Prods = \left\{ \begin{array}{lll}
\mathrm{E} \rightarrow \mathrm{L\,T} & \mathrm{F} \rightarrow \text{“\textasciitilde”}\,\mathrm{L\,F}\,\{Not\} & \mathrm{L} \rightarrow \mathrm{C\,L} \\
\mathrm{E} \rightarrow \mathrm{E}\,\text{“|”}\,\mathrm{L\,T}\,\{Or\} & \mathrm{F} \rightarrow \text{“(”}\,\mathrm{L\,E}\,\text{“)”}\,\mathrm{L}\,\{Br\} & \mathrm{L} \rightarrow \varepsilon \\
\mathrm{T} \rightarrow \mathrm{F} & \mathrm{F} \rightarrow \text{“}\textit{true}\text{”}\,\mathrm{L}\,\{True\} & \mathrm{C} \rightarrow \text{“␣”} \\
\mathrm{T} \rightarrow \mathrm{T}\,\text{“\&”}\,\mathrm{L\,F}\,\{And\} & \mathrm{F} \rightarrow \text{“}\textit{false}\text{”}\,\mathrm{L}\,\{False\} & \mathrm{C} \rightarrow \text{“\textbackslash n”}
\end{array} \right\}
$$

In presence of signature labels the term notation for the parse trees is adapted and written as $parse(s_1 \cdot s'_1 \cdot s_2 \cdot \ldots \cdot s_r \cdot s'_r \cdot s_{r+1}) = < n, c > (s_1, t'_1, s_2, \ldots, s_r, t'_r, s_{r+1})$, where n is the top nonterminal, $t'_1 \ldots t'_r$ are sub parse trees with top nonterminals $n_1 \ldots n_r$, strings $s_1 \ldots s_{r+1}$ are the terminals and c is the label associated with $n \rightarrow s_1, n_1, s_2, \ldots, s_r, n_r, s_{r+1}$. If there is no such label, $parse(s_1 \cdot s'_1 \cdot s_2 \cdot \ldots \cdot s_r \cdot s'_r \cdot s_{r+1})$ is defined as $n(s_1, t'_1, s_2, \ldots, s_r, t'_r, s_{r+1})$. Furthermore, the function *parse* used in this article is complete.

The parse tree of $s =$`~true & false | true`, which results from parsing with the grammar with signature information, will have the following form: $d_G(s) =$

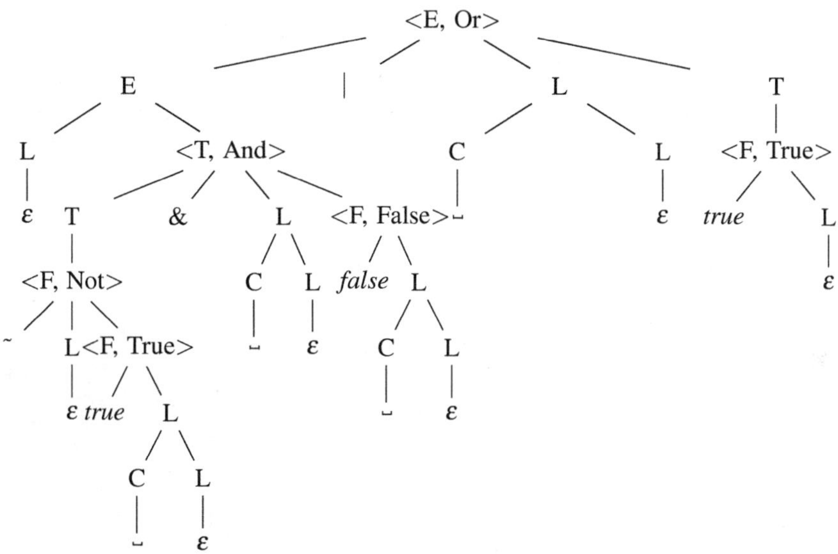

and the term representation is:

$d_G(s) =$

```
< E , Or >(
  E( L (),
    < T, And >(
      T( <F, Not>( ~, L (),
          <F, True>( true, L( C( ), L() ))
      )),
      &,
      L( C( ), L() ),
      <F, False>(false, L( C( ), L() ))
    )
  ),
  |,
  L( C( ), L() ),
  T( <F, True>( true, L() ))
)
```

Having a context-free grammar with signature labels, the abstract syntax tree can be automatically instantiated from a parse tree. This is executed by the *desugar* function, which replaces the nodes in the parse tree with new nodes labeled by signature labels. The rank of signature label c is equal to the number of augmented nonterminals in the corresponding production rule of the context-free grammar. Nodes in the parse tree without a signature label are removed from the tree. This mechanism facilitates the removal of nodes that do not contain semantically significant information, such as layout syntax.

Definition 3.1.1 (Desugar). The *desugar* function is defined by the following equations:

$$
\begin{aligned}
&desugar(x) = \varepsilon \qquad \text{if } x \in \Sigma\\
&desugar(f(x_1,\ldots,x_r)) = dc(x_1,\ldots,x_r)\\
&desugar(<f,c>(x_1,\ldots,x_r)) =\\
&\quad\begin{cases} c & \text{if } dc(x_1,\ldots,x_r) = \varepsilon\\ c(dc(x_1,\ldots,x_r)) & \text{if } dc(x_1,x_2,\ldots,x_r) \neq \varepsilon \end{cases}
\end{aligned}
$$

and

$$
\begin{aligned}
&dc() = \varepsilon\\
&dc(x_1,x_2,\ldots,x_r) =\\
&\quad\begin{cases} dc(x_2,\ldots,x_r) & \text{if } x_1 \in \Sigma\\ desugar(x_1), dc(x_2,\ldots,x_r) & \text{if } x_1 \notin \Sigma \text{ and}\\ & dc(x_2,\ldots,x_r) \neq \varepsilon\\ desugar(x_1) & \text{otherwise} \end{cases}
\end{aligned}
$$

Example 3.1.2 (Desugar). Applying the *desugar* function to the parse tree t of `~true & false | true` using the grammar of Example 3.1.1 will result in the abstract syntax tree: $desugar(t) = Or(And(Not(True), False), True)$. ■

Observe that Definition 3.1.1 ensures termination of *desugar* as long as its argument is a finite tree. Indeed, each subsequent call to *desugar* or *dc* reduces the size of the input argument either by removing the function symbol, e.g., $desugar(f(x_1,\ldots,x_r)) = dc(x_1,\ldots,x_r)$ or by reducing the number of arguments in the call, e.g., $dc(x_1,x_2,\ldots,x_r) = dc(x_2,\ldots,x_r)$.

Theorem 3.1.1. *The abstract syntax tree obtained by applying the desugar function to a parse tree belongs to a regular tree language* [Cleophas (2009)].

Proof. Recognizability of trees by finite tree automata is closed under linear tree homomorphism [Engelfriet (1974)]. The *desugar* function is a linear tree homomorphism; subtrees are only removed and not duplicated. Since the abstract syntax tree is a linear tree homomorphism of the parse tree and the set of parse trees of a context-free language is a regular tree language [Comon *et al.* (2008)], the abstract syntax tree belongs to a regular tree language. ∎

The mapping of a parse tree to an abstract syntax tree is regular, which suggests there exists a mapping between the regular tree grammar of the parse tree G_{pt} and the regular tree grammar of the abstract syntax tree G_{ast}. There is indeed a mapping:

Definition 3.1.2 (Mapping parse tree grammar to abstract syntax tree grammar). Let $G_{pt} = \langle \Sigma, N, S, Prods \rangle$ be the regular tree grammar of the parse tree (see Definition 2.4.1), the regular tree grammar $G_{ast} = \langle \Sigma', N', S', Prods' \rangle$ is derived via the following rules:
The start symbol of both grammars is equal: $S = S'$. The set of nonterminals of the regular tree grammar is a subset of N, i.e. $N' \subset N$. N' contains all nonterminals n, which at least appears one time in the left-hand side of a production rule augmented with a signature label c. The alphabet of G_{ast} is $\Sigma' = \Sigma_c$. Σ_c is the alphabet containing the symbols $c_1, \ldots, c_j$ used for augmenting the production rules of a context-free grammar with signature labels. The set of productions $Prods'$ of G_{ast} is the result set obtained by matching every production rule in $Prods$ on the following patterns:

- $n \rightarrow <n,c> (z_1 \ldots z_r)$, then $n \rightarrow c(makeRhs(z_1, \ldots, z_r))) \in Prods'$ when $makeRhs(z_1, \ldots, z_r) \neq \varepsilon$
- $n \rightarrow n(z_1 \ldots z_r)$, then $n \rightarrow makeRhs(z_1, \ldots, z_r) \in Prods'$ when $|makeRhs(z_1, \ldots, z_r)| = 1$
- Otherwise, no production rule is added to $Prods'$

where

$$
\begin{aligned}
&makeRhs() = \varepsilon \\
&makeRhs(z_1, z_2, \ldots, z_r) = \\
&\begin{cases}
makeRhs(z_2, \ldots, z_r) & \text{if } z_1 \notin N' \\
z_1, makeRhs(z_2, \ldots, z_r) & \text{if } z_1 \in N' \text{ and } makeRhs(z_2, \ldots, z_r) \neq \varepsilon \\
z_1 & \text{otherwise}
\end{cases}
\end{aligned}
$$

Example 3.1.3 (Mapping G_{pt} to G_{ast}). The result of the mapping of G_{pt} to G_{ast} for the language of Example 2.2.1 is a regular tree grammar with $\Sigma = \{$ And(,), Or(,), Not( ), Br( ), True, False $\}$, nonterminals $N = \{$E, T, F$\}$, start symbol $S =$ E and rules

$$
Prods = \left\{
\begin{array}{lll}
\mathrm{E} \rightarrow \mathrm{T} & \mathrm{F} \rightarrow \mathrm{Not(F)} & \mathrm{T} \rightarrow \mathrm{F} \\
\mathrm{T} \rightarrow \mathrm{And(T,F)} & \mathrm{E} \rightarrow \mathrm{Or(E,T)} & \mathrm{F} \rightarrow \mathrm{Br(E)} \\
\mathrm{F} \rightarrow \mathrm{True} & \mathrm{F} \rightarrow \mathrm{False} &
\end{array}
\right\}
$$

3.2 The Unparser Generation Pattern

In contrast with the *parse* ∘ *yield* couple, where the *yield* always restores the original code including layout from a parse tree, this is not the case for abstract syntax trees. The abstract syntax trees lack information to reconstruct the original sentences, since the original keywords are implicitly stored in the nodes and not explicitly in leaves. As a result, it is necessary to define a function per G_{ast} to reconstruct a concrete syntax representation of its abstract syntax trees. This function is called the *unparse* function: It translates an abstract syntax tree into a textual representation of the sentence.
In contrast with the *yield* function, it is not possible to guarantee that unparsed code is syntactically equivalent to the parsed code. Superfluous information, like layout, is not present in the abstract syntax tree and has to be induced by default rules in the unparser definition. The *unparse* function can indeed be used as a code formatter [van den Brand and Visser (1996)]. The unparser cannot restore the original code for an arbitrary case, except the one, where the layout of the original code matches the layout syntax defined in the unparser. The following relation reflects this property:

$$\mathscr{L}(G_{cfg}) \supseteq unparse(desugar(parse(\mathscr{L}(G_{cfg}))))$$

However, the *unparse* function should produce a text which is syntactically correct and represents the original abstract syntax tree. The unparser is correct if and only if re-parsing its output sentences reproduce the same abstract syntax trees as the original inputs [Ramsey (1998)]. That is, as the couple of *unparse* and *desugar* only executes a syntactical mapping and does not alter the meaning of the code represented by the concrete syntax or the abstract syntax. The abstract syntax contains all semantic information, and this information should be present in the unparsed sentence without altering it. Parsing and desugaring this unparsed code must result in the same abstract syntax tree, otherwise information is lost or altered somewhere in the process. The following relation reflects this property:

$$\mathscr{L}(G_{ast}) = desugar(parse(unparse(\mathscr{L}(G_{ast}))))$$

The signature of the *unparse* function is:

$$unparse : Tree \rightarrow String$$

The *unparse* function traverses a tree, just as the *yield* function does. The unparser differs from the *yield* function (see Definition 2.2.2) as it is not a generic tree traversal function, but is tailored for the abstract syntax grammar of the input. The *yield* function is a traversal function accepting every parse tree, while an *unparse* function has an action for every production rule in the regular tree grammar of the abstract syntax. The *unparse* function restores the mapping defined by the *desugar* function. Where the *desugar* function removes terminals from the parse tree, the unparser actions must restore the removed terminals. Terminals are removed from nodes at different levels in the parse tree and to restore them actions must be defined in the *unparse* function to restore these terminals. As a result the *unparse* function follows the structure of the abstract syntax grammar and can only be applied to trees produced by that grammar.

The *unparse* function can be derived from a context-free grammar extended with signatures. For each production rule in the context-free grammar there is a case in the definition of *unparse*, called an *action*, allowing *unparse* to traverse the abstract syntax tree and to restore terminals whenever needed. For instance, in Example 3.1.1, given the production rule T → T "&" L F $\{And\}$, the definition of the unparser should have an action for $unparse(And(x',x''))$. Each action in *unparse* has a left-hand side and a right-hand side, see Example 3.2.2. First, the definition to derive an unparser from a given context-free grammar is provided.

Definition 3.2.1 (Unparse). Let $G_{cfg} = \langle \Sigma, N, S, Prods \rangle$ be a context-free grammar augmented with signature labels, where N' is the set of non-terminals defined by the production rules with a signature label. Then, the corresponding function *unparse* is defined by a set of actions *Actions* such that for any $n \rightarrow z_1 \ldots z_r\{c\} \in Prods$

- either $makeLhs(z_1, \ldots, z_r, 1) \neq \varepsilon$ and
  $unparse(c(makeLhs(z_1, \ldots, z_r, 1))) = makeRhs(z_1, \ldots, z_r, 1) \in Actions,$
- or $makeLhs(z_1, \ldots, z_r, 1) = \varepsilon$ and
  $unparse(c) = makeRhs(z_1, \ldots, z_r, 1) \in Actions,$

where

$$
\begin{aligned}
&makeLhs(i) = \varepsilon \\
&makeLhs(z_1, z_2, \ldots, z_j, i) = \\
&\quad \begin{cases}
makeLhs(z_2, \ldots, z_j, i+1) & \text{if } z_1 \notin N' \\
x_i, makeLhs(z_2, \ldots, z_j, i+1) & \text{if } z_1 \in N' \text{and} \\
 & \quad makeLhs(z_2, \ldots, z_j, i+1) \neq \varepsilon \\
x_i & \text{otherwise}
\end{cases}
\end{aligned}
$$

and

$$
\begin{aligned}
&\mathit{makeRhs}(i) = \varepsilon\\
&\mathit{makeRhs}(z_1, z_2 \ldots, z_j, i) =\\
&\begin{cases}
z_1 \cdot \mathit{makeRhs}(z_2, \ldots, z_j, i+1) & \text{if } z_1 \in \Sigma\\
\mathit{unparse}(x_i) \cdot \mathit{makeRhs}(z_2, \ldots, z_j, i+1) & \text{if } z_1 \in N'\\
\mathit{makeRhs}(z_2, \ldots, z_j, i+1) & \text{if } z_1 \notin (N' \cup \Sigma)
\end{cases}
\end{aligned}
$$

and $\cdot$ denotes the string concatenation operation.

Example 3.2.1. Definition 3.2.1 is illustrated using the production rule T $\rightarrow$ T "&" L F $\{And\}$ from Example 3.1.1. Then, the set N' of non-terminals corresponding to production rules with signature labels is $\{$E, F, T$\}$. Hence, "&" and L should be omitted from the left-hand side of the unparser action:

$$
\begin{aligned}
\mathit{makeLhs}(\text{T}, \text{“\&”}, \text{L}, \text{F}, 1) &= x_1, \mathit{makeLhs}(\text{“\&”}, \text{L}, \text{F}, 2)\\
&= x_1, \mathit{makeLhs}(\text{L}, \text{F}, 3) =\\
&= x_1, \mathit{makeLhs}(\text{F}, 4) =\\
&= x_1, x_4
\end{aligned}
$$

since $\mathit{makeLhs}(5) = \varepsilon$. Similarly, for the right-hand side of the action, L is ignored :

$$
\begin{aligned}
\mathit{makeRhs}(\text{T}, \text{“\&”}, \text{L}, \text{F}, 1) &= \mathit{unparse}(x_1) \cdot \mathit{makeRhs}(\text{“\&”}, \text{L}, \text{F}, 2) =\\
&\mathit{unparse}(x_1) \cdot \text{“\&”} \cdot \mathit{makeRhs}(\text{L}, \text{F}, 3) =\\
&\mathit{unparse}(x_1) \cdot \text{“\&”} \cdot \mathit{makeRhs}(\text{F}, 4) =\\
&\mathit{unparse}(x_1) \cdot \text{“\&”} \cdot \mathit{unparse}(x_4) \cdot \mathit{makeRhs}(5) =\\
&\mathit{unparse}(x_1) \cdot \text{“\&”} \cdot \mathit{unparse}(x_4) \cdot \varepsilon =\\
&\mathit{unparse}(x_1) \cdot \text{“\&”} \cdot \mathit{unparse}(x_4)
\end{aligned}
$$

Since $\mathit{makeLhs}(\text{T}, \text{“\&”}, \text{L}, \text{F}, 1) \neq \varepsilon$, the action corresponding to T $\rightarrow$ T "&" L F $\{And\}$ is $\mathit{unparse}(\mathit{And}(x_1, x_4)) = \mathit{unparse}(x_1) \cdot \text{“\&”} \cdot \mathit{unparse}(x_4)$. ■

The left-hand side matches on a node in the abstract syntax tree with the signature label c and the variables $x_1, \ldots, x_r$ are assigned to the subtrees belonging to the label c. Following the previous definition, the rank of c, i.e., the number of arguments of c created by *makeLhs*, is not necessarily equal to r: the rank of c is equal to the number of nonterminals in the pattern of the production rule labeled c in the augmented context-free grammar. Therefore, the variable x_i only exists in the action $\mathit{unparse}(c(\ldots)) = \ldots$ if a symbol at index i in the right-hand side of the corresponding production rule is a nonterminal $n \in N'$. The *right-hand side* constructs a string $s_1 \cdot \ldots \cdot s_r$. The number of strings r is equal to the number of symbols in the pattern of the corresponding production rule. Each s_i is either a string or a recursive unparser invocation. Specifically, s_i is a string, if a terminal is defined at index i in the production rule; an unparser invocation, if a nonterminal $n \in N'$ is defined at position i, and ε for the remaining case if $n_i \notin (N' \cup \Sigma)$.

Example 3.2.2. Example 3.2.1, continued. Given the aforementioned production rules, the following unparser is derived:

$$\begin{aligned}
unparse(Not(x_3)) &= \text{``$\sim$''} \cdot unparse(x_3) \\
unparse(And(x_1,x_4)) &= unparse(x_1) \cdot \text{``\&''} \cdot unparse(x_4) \\
unparse(Or(x_1,x_4)) &= unparse(x_1) \cdot \text{``|''} \cdot unparse(x_4) \\
unparse(Br(x_3)) &= \text{``(''} \cdot unparse(x_3) \cdot \text{``)''} \\
unparse(True) &= \text{``true''} \\
unparse(False) &= \text{``false''}
\end{aligned}$$

■

In the presented boolean example removing the spaces has not changed the meaning, nor the recognizability by the parser, of the boolean expression. However, for some languages it is not allowed to yield a string without a whitespace character between the unparsed sub strings, since two unparsed sub strings can become one string without a natural separation. In that case the right-hand patterns of the unparser must be $s_1 \cdot \sqcup \cdot \ldots \cdot \sqcup \cdot s_r$, where $\sqcup$ is a whitespace character. An example of this problem is a sequence of two identifiers, which are separated by a space in the original code. They will be parsed as a single identifier when they are concatenated by an unparser without using a whitespace character separating them. This can happen with a language such as Java where method declarations have a type followed by a method name, where both can be an identifier.

The unparser derived according to Definition 3.2.1 is linear and deterministic. An unparser is *linear* if for each action in the unparser and every x_i in the action, x_i occurs not more than once in the action's right-hand side. The unparser is called *deterministic* if actions have incompatible left-hand sides, i.e., for every tree there exists only one applicable unparser action.

Theorem 3.2.1. *The unparser derived according to Definition* 3.2.1 *is linear and deterministic.*

Proof. Linearity follows from Definition 3.2.1: every variable appearing on the right hand side appears only once. Recall that a signature label c is used once in the augmented context-free tree grammar. A signature label c directly corresponds to one action in $unparse(c(x_1,\ldots,x_k))$. Since a signature label c is used for only one production rule, the left-hand sides of the unparser are unique and thus the unparser is deterministic. ∎

Definition 3.2.1 also ensures that *unparse* always terminates if its argument is a finite tree. Recall that $unparse(\ldots)$ for $n \to z_1 \ldots z_r\{c\}$ distinguishes between $makeLhs(z_1,\ldots,z_r,1) = \varepsilon$ and $makeLhs(z_1,\ldots,z_r,1) \neq \varepsilon$. However, $makeLhs(z_1,\ldots,z_r,1) = \varepsilon$ holds only if $z_i \in \Sigma$ for all i, $1 \leq i \leq r$. Therefore, the right-hand side expression $makeRhs(z_1,z_2\ldots,z_r,1) = z_1 \cdot \ldots \cdot z_r$ and *unparse* is defined as $unparse(c) = z_1 \cdot \ldots \cdot z_r$. Since the right-hand side of the latter equation does not contain calls to *unparse*, it cannot introduce non-termination. The remaining case is $makeLhs(z_1,\ldots,z_r,1) \neq \varepsilon$. In this case *unparse* is defined as $unparse(c(makeLhs(z_1,\ldots,z_r,1))) = makeRhs(z_1,\ldots,z_r,1)$. Termination stems from the fact that every variable appearing on the right hand-side appears in the left-hand side, and from the reduction in the term size between the left-hand side and the right-hand side terms.

3.3 Unparser Completeness

In the past sections the *desugar* function and *unparse* function are defined. A metalanguage capable to express an unparser function is called *unparser-complete*. In this section it is shown that unparser-completeness is a *more* restricted notion than Turing-completeness. To establish this result it is shown that the unparser as defined in Definition 3.2.1 can be expressed by a linear deterministic top-down tree-to-string transducer, and recall that the top-down tree-to-string transducer is strictly less powerful than a Turing machine, i.e., the languages top-down-tree-to-string transducers accept are a subset of the languages Turing machines can accept [Virágh (1981)].

Definition 3.3.1 (Top-down tree-to-string transducer). [Engelfriet *et al.* (1980)]. A top-down tree-to-string transducer is a 5-tuple $M = \langle Q, \Sigma, \Sigma', q_0, R\rangle$, where Q is a finite set of states, Σ is the ranked input alphabet, Σ' is the output alphabet, $q_0 \in Q$ is the initial state, and R is a finite set of rules of the form:

$$q(\sigma(x_1,\ldots,x_k)) \to s_1 q_1(x_{i_1}) s_2 q_2(x_{i_2}) \ldots s_p q_p(x_{i_p}) s_{p+1}$$

with $k,p \geq 0$; $q,q_1,\ldots,q_p \in Q$; $\sigma \in \Sigma_k$; $s_1,\ldots,s_{p+1} \in \Sigma'^*$, and $1 \leq i_j \leq k$ for $1 \leq j \leq p$ (if $k = 0$ then the left-hand side is $q(c)$). M is called *deterministic* if different rules in R have different left-hand sides. M is called *linear* if, for each rule in R, no x_i occurs more than once in its right-hand side.

Example 3.3.1. Unparser in Example 3.2.2 can be seen as a top-down tree-to-string transducer $\langle Q, \Sigma, \Sigma', q_0, R\rangle$ such that the set of states $Q = \{unparse\}$, the input alphabet $\Sigma = \{Not, And, Or, Br, True, False\}$, the output alphabet $\Sigma' = \{$"~","&","|","(",")", "true","false"$\}$ and the finite set of rules R is given by actions defining the unparser in Example 3.2.2.

Next, for each context-free grammar an unparser can be defined using a linear and deterministic top-down tree-to-string transducer. Furthermore, any unparser corresponding to Definition 3.2.1 can be mapped on a top-down tree-to-string transducer.

Theorem 3.3.1. *An unparser based on a linear deterministic top-down tree-to-string transducer can be defined for every context-free grammar augmented with signature labels.*

Proof. Every production rule in a context-free grammar can be projected on the form $n \rightarrow s_1 n_1 s_2 \ldots s_r n_r s_{r+1}\{c\}$, where $s_1, \ldots, s_{r+1}$ are strings and may be the empty string ε, and $n, n_1, \ldots, n_r$ are the nonterminals. In case the pattern $s_1 s_2$ occurs, the strings can be concatenated into a new string s'_1. It is assumed that the augmented grammar meets the requirements for augmenting a grammar with signature labels as sketched in Section 3.1. The abstract syntax tree belonging to this production rule is: $t_{ast} = c(t_1, \ldots, t_r)$, where $t_1, \ldots, t_r$ are the abstract syntax trees belonging to $n_1 \ldots n_r$. The corresponding tree-to-string transducer rule is: $q(c(x_1, \ldots, x_r)) \rightarrow s_1 q_1(x_1) s_2 \ldots s_r q_r(x_r) s_{r+1}$, where $q, q_1, \ldots, q_r$ are transducer states. Application of the transducer to the abstract syntax tree consists in *matching* the tree against the pattern $c(x_1, \ldots, x_r)$ and *replacing* it with a string originating from $s_1 q_1(x_1) s_2 \ldots s_r q_r(x_r) s_{r+1}$, where $q_1(x_1), \ldots, q_r(x_r)$ have been recursively applied to $t_1, \ldots, t_r$, i.e., $q(c(t_1, \ldots, t_r)) = s_1 \cdot s'_1 \cdot s_2 \cdot \ldots \cdot s_r \cdot s'_r \cdot s_{r+1}$, where $s'_1 = q_1(t_1) \ldots s'_r = q_r(t_r)$. In Chapter 4 this match-replace intuition will be used to define an eponymous construct in the unparser-complete metalanguage.
Parsing $s_1 \cdot s'_1 \cdot s_2 \cdot \ldots \cdot s_r \cdot s'_r \cdot s_{r+1}$ produces a parse tree $parse(s_1 \cdot s'_1 \cdot s_2 \cdot \ldots \cdot s_r \cdot s'_r \cdot s_{r+1}) = < n, c > (s_1, t'_1, s_2, \ldots, s_r, t'_r, s_{r+1})$, where $t'_1 \ldots t'_r$ are sub parse trees with top nonterminals $n_1 \ldots n_r$ and strings $s_1 \ldots s_{r+1}$ are the terminals. The abstract syntax tree is $desugar(< n, c > (s_1, t'_1, s_2, \ldots, s_r, t'_r, s_{r+1})) = c(t_1 \ldots t_r)$, where $t_1 = desugar(t'_1)$, $\ldots$, $t_r = desugar(t'_r)$, which is equal to the original abstract syntax tree. Since this relation holds for every production rule in a context-free language, the unparser can be defined using a top-down tree-to-string transducer for every context-free language. ∎

The proof that $\mathscr{L}(G_{cfg}) \supseteq unparse(desugar(parse(\mathscr{L}(G_{cfg}))))$ also holds is almost similar to the proof of Theorem 3.3.1. One should take the string s as starting point instead of the abstract syntax tree. The superset relation is a result of the fact that layout is not available in the abstract syntax tree and as a result it cannot be literally restored during unparsing. The language produced by the unparser is thus always a sentence of $\mathscr{L}(G_{cfg})$, but the set of sentences of $\mathscr{L}(G_{cfg})$ is greater than the set of sentences the unparser can produce.

Theorem 3.3.2. *The relation $\mathscr{L}(G_{cfg}) \supseteq unparse(desugar(parse(\mathscr{L}(G_{cfg}))))$ holds for the unparser.*

Proof. First, similarly to the proof of Theorem 3.3.1, the relation

$$\mathscr{L}(G_{ast}) = desugar(parse(unparse(\mathscr{L}(G_{ast}))))$$

holds when using a context-free grammar without production rules for layout syntax. Next $\mathscr{L}(G_{cfg})$ is extended with layout syntax resulting in $\mathscr{L}(G_{cfg})'$, then $\mathscr{L}(G_{cfg})' \supset \mathscr{L}(G_{cfg})$, since every sentence without layout must be in $\mathscr{L}(G_{cfg})'$, otherwise the languages are not semantically equal. Thus every sentence the unparser produce must be at least in $\mathscr{L}(G_{cfg})$, otherwise the *unparse* function does not meet the requirement of the unparser to be semantically transparent. ∎

The last step is that the unparser is linear and deterministic.

Theorem 3.3.3. *The unparser of Definition* 3.2.1 *is a linear and deterministic top-down tree-to-string transducer.*

Proof. The derivation of an unparser using Definition 3.2.1 can be mapped on a top-down tree-to-string transducer. Considering Definition 3.2.1 the unparser contains actions of the form:

$$\begin{aligned} unparse(c) &= s \\ unparse(c(x_1,\ldots,x_r)) &= s_1 \cdot unparse(x_1) \cdot \ldots \cdot s_r \\ &\quad \cdot unparse(x_r) \cdot s_{r+1} \end{aligned}$$

The similarity with the top-down tree-to-string transducer is obvious. Substitute the occurrences of *unparse* by states named q and the unparser becomes a tree-to-string transducer. The unparser is linear, since each x_i occurs once on the left-hand side and once on the right-hand side.
The unparser is also deterministic, since it is derived from a context-free grammar augmented with signature labels, where each signature label is only used for one production rule. ∎

These theorems show that an unparser can be specified using a linear deterministic top-down tree-to-string transducer.
Recall that the top-down tree-to-string transducer is strictly less powerful than the Turing machine, i.e., top-down-tree-to-string transducers accept a subset of the languages Turing machines can accept [Virágh (1981)]. Indeed, the class of tree languages a top-down tree-to-string transducer can recognize is equal to its corresponding finite tree automaton [Engelfriet *et al.* (1980)]. Unlike a Turing machine, a top-down tree-to-string transducer cannot change the input tree on which it operates but only emit a string while processing the input tree. The class of languages the top-down tree-to-string transducer accepts is the class of *path-closed tree languages* [Virágh (1981)]. This class of tree languages is a subset of regular tree languages [Comon *et al.* (2008)]. The languages of abstract syntax trees of the augmented grammar are path-closed, since a signature label is only used for one production rule.

3.4 Conclusions

The relations between concrete syntax, abstract syntax trees and their grammars are discussed. The unparser translates an abstract syntax to a concrete syntax and is a metaprogram instantiating code with two specific properties: parsing and desugaring its output results in the original abstract syntax tree of the used input, and the unparser can instantiate all meaningful sentences of the output language.
The formal notion and properties of unparser-completeness are defined. Unparser-completeness of a metalanguage provides the balance between expressivity and restrictiveness. On one hand, the metalanguage is expressive enough to implement an unparser, and, hence, can instantiate any semantically correct program in the object language. On the other hand, the metalanguage is restricted enough to enforce the model-view separation in terms of [Parr (2004)]. In the next chapter this notion of unparser-completeness is used to define a metalanguage for templates.
A linear deterministic top-down tree-to-string transducer is powerful enough to implement an unparser. Using the notion of the top-down tree-to-string transducer it has been shown that unparser-completeness is a weaker notion than Turing-completeness, i.e., unparser-complete metalanguages are not necessarily Turing-complete. The enforcement of separation of concerns is also met, as this transducer does not allow expressing calculations or modifying the model.

Chapter 4

The Metalanguage

This chapter introduces an unparser-complete metalanguage for templates. The syntax and operational semantics of the constructs are given. The constructs of this metalanguage are based on the concepts of the theoretical framework of Chapter 3. As a result, the metalanguage is strong enough to specify unparsers, and still enforces a separation of model and view.

The requirements for the metalanguage are:

- Powerful enough to express an unparser.
- Minimize the possibilities for expressing calculations in the template.

The first requirement guarantees that the metalanguage enforces no unnecessary limitations on the sentences that templates can instantiate, since an unparser is capable to instantiate all meaningful sentences of its output language.

The second requirement is to enforce separation of model and view. Inspired by [Parr (2004)], the unparser-complete metalanguage should be strong enough to express the view, i.e. unparsers, but it should limit the possibility that model specific code and calculations are specified in the metaprogram instantiating the code. This is essential to prevent the use of templates for computations that are not part of rendering the view. The availability of a general-purpose metalanguage does not prevent to write complete programs in the template, which breaks the model-view-controller (MVC) architecture. The MVC architecture is discussed in Section 7.1.3.

In Section 4.1, a formal definition of code generators is provided. Section 4.2 discusses the metalanguage and provides a formal specification of its operational semantics. The unparser-complete metalanguage is compared with related template systems in Section 4.4. The comparison uses a case study based on the implementation of an unparser for the PICO language.

4.1 Code Generators

Two metaprograms for instantiating code are already presented in Chapters 2 and 3. The first is the *yield* function, see Definition 2.2.2. The second is the *unparse* function, see Definition 3.2.1. The *yield* function reconstructs a sentence from an arbitrary parse tree of an arbitrary context-free language. It is the most generic metaprogram as it generates a sentence from every arbitrary parse tree. The *yield* function does not depend on the structure of the tree and only considers the leaves of the tree. The only requirement for the *yield* function to get a well-formed output sentence is a well-formed input parse tree.
The *unparse* function is not limited to parse trees and allows abstract syntax trees as input. The abstract syntax tree lacks syntactic information, like layout information, to restore the original code it represents. The *unparse* function contains the missing syntax in its rules to restore the syntactic sugar missing in the abstract syntax tree. For both the *yield* function and *unparse* function it should be noticed that no semantic information is added to or removed from the generated sentence. Only the representation of the sentence is changed.
The *unparse* function can be considered as a set of small templates, where each unparse equation contains a subtemplate based on the corresponding production rule. For instance, consider the right-hand side of the unparser for the `or` case in Example 3.2.2:

$$unparse(Or(x_1,x_4)) = unparse(x_1)\cdot\text{``}|\text{''}\cdot unparse(x_4).$$

It consists of two recursive calls to the *unparse* function in order to convert subtrees x_1 and x_4 to strings and it contains the lexical representation of the *Or* operator, i.e. `|`. This metaprogram transforms an input tree with the *Or* signature to a concrete syntax representation without altering its meaning.
Just as the *unparse* function, the code generator function *CG* converts a tree into a string and has the signature:

$$CG : Tree \rightarrow String$$

The properties of a code generator are defined by the following definition:

Definition 4.1.1 (Code generator). A code generator *CG*, instantiating sentences of a given $\mathscr{L}(G_{cfg})$ modulo layout, is a function producing at least two sentences of $\mathscr{L}(G_{cfg})$ and at most the set of sentences defined by $\mathscr{L}(G_{cfg})$.

This definition excludes metaprograms producing exactly one sentence of $\mathscr{L}(G_{cfg})$:

$$CG(x) = s, \text{ where } s \in \mathscr{L}(G_{cfg}) \text{ and } x \text{ matches every tree.}$$

No external information is necessary to complete the sentence; it is already complete. All semantic information is *a priori* available in the result sentence of the code generator and the input data has no influence on it. Given that input data is not necessary, the language of the output code is independent of the input data language. When the input data is empty, i.e. no semantic information is specified, this metaprogram will always generate a sentence s. Since only one sentence s is generated, its functionality domain is limited to the semantics of s.

The unparser is a kind of code generator, however the domain of code generators is broader. The relation

$$\mathscr{L}(G_{rtg}) = desugar(parse(cg(\mathscr{L}(G'_{rtg}))))$$

does not have to hold for a code generator , and it is not required that G_{rtg} and G'_{rtg} are equal, since the input data may contain less details than the output code. A code generator is not necessarily linear and data may be copied, i.e. it may contain rules of the form $CG(f(x)) = CG(x) \cdot CG(x)$. The code generator must be deterministic; otherwise it can generate different output sentences for a given input tree.

Example 4.1.1 (Code generator). Considering the *unparse* function of Example 3.2.2, once one or more recursive calls in the right-hand side of the equations is substituted by a fixed sentence of terminals or a variable is used more than once in the right-hand side, the unparser becomes a code generator. To illustrate it, the unparse rule for the *Or* is changed. First by substituting one call by a fixed sentence of terminals:

$$unparse(Or(x_1, x_4)) = unparse(x_1) \cdot \text{``}|\text{''} \cdot unparse(x_4)$$

is changed to:

$$CG(f(x)) = \text{``}true\text{''} \cdot \text{``}|\text{''} \cdot CG(x)$$

It is no longer possible to use it as *unparse* function, since the set of sentences the code generator can produce is a subset of the sentences belonging to the output language $\mathscr{L}(G_{bool})$. The $unparse(x_1)$ call can return all sentences belonging to the output language $\mathscr{L}(G_{bool})$, while in *CG* it is replaced by "*true*". "*true*" $\subset \mathscr{L}(G_{bool})$, so the sentences *CG* can produce is a subset of $\mathscr{L}(G_{bool})$.

An example of the second case is the nonlinear code generator:

$$CG(f(x)) = CG(x) \cdot \text{``}|\text{''} \cdot CG(x)$$

This code generator always produces sentences of the form $s_1 \mid s_2$, where s_1 and s_2 are equal and s_1 and s_2 are sentences of $\mathscr{L}(G_{bool})$, while the unparser allows to generate sentences where s_1 and s_2 are not necessarily equal. This code generator only produces a subset of sentences of $\mathscr{L}(G_{bool})$, as the set of sentences produced by the template $s_1 \mid s_2$, where s_1 and s_2 are equal, is a subset of the sentences where s_1 and s_2 are not necessarily equal. Finally, it is not necessary that *CG* accept the abstract syntax language of the output language G_{bool}.

The way an unparser is changed into a code generator is related to partial evaluation [Futamura (1999)]. Informally, some code generators can be obtained by evaluating the unparser using a non-complete abstract syntax tree. The result is a not complete evaluated template. Considering the semantics, a code generator has the following properties. First, without input data the code generator cannot produce a valid well-formed output sentence, since information is missing. Second, the code generator is not semantic neutral. Contrary to the unparser, the code generator is allowed to add semantic information to the input data or remove semantic information from the input data. As a result the input data tree will only generate a subset of sentences belonging to the output language, or the input data tree can contain more meaningful information than the sentences of the output language can reflect.

4.2 The Unparser Complete Metalanguage

The *unparse* function, see Definition 3.2.1, is the starting point for the design of the unparser-complete metalanguage. This section discusses the provided metalanguage constructs, which are based on the requirements for implementing an unparser. Beside the syntax of the constructs, their formalized operational semantics are presented.
In this chapter a template is considered as a string of characters[1], where it is allowed to have placeholders containing instructions. A placeholder is written between the character sequences `<:` and `:>`; the so-called *hedges*. These hedges act as markers to indicate the transition between the object code and the metacode. Since a template is a string with placeholders these hedges are obligatory; otherwise it is not possible to make a distinction between object code and metacode. The syntax of the hedges is free, as long as they are disjoint of character sequences used in the object language.
The template evaluator executes the evaluation of the placeholders. It searches for placeholders in the string and replaces them using information from the input data tree. The instructions of the placeholders are evaluated to obtain a string to replace the placeholders. When all placeholders are replaced the evaluator is finished.

[1] A template is a sentence of a template grammar in Chapter 5.

Considering the *unparse* function of Section 3.2 two kinds of instructions can be identified. The first selects an unparse action based on matching a pattern on a piece of the input data and binds metavariables to subtrees of it. Second, equations have names of the form *unparse*, which are called in the right-hand side of the equations having a variable as argument. Two constructs implement this functionality:

- Match-replace (Section 4.2.4);
- Subtemplates (Section 4.2.3).

Match-replace is a mechanism to *match* on input data (sub)trees and depending on a match, returning another (sub) sentence. Subtemplates enable generation of recursive structures, like lists and trees. Next to these kernel constructs derived placeholders are available, which are abbreviations for constructions using subtemplates and match-replace placeholders:

- Substitution (Section 4.2.5);
- Conditional (Section 4.2.6);
- Iteration (Section 4.2.7).

These placeholder constructs are discussed in the coming sections. The metalanguage is discussed by means of a (informal) syntax definition and operational semantics. The operational semantics of the different metalanguage constructs depends on the way templates are evaluated. First, the general function evaluating a template is discussed. After the general function is introduced, the syntax and operation semantics of the different placeholder constructs are described.

4.2.1 *Template Evaluation*

This section discusses the *eval* function, which defines the interpretation of the unparser-complete metalanguage. This *eval* function evaluates a template using some input data resulting in an output sentence and has the following signature:

$$eval : Template \times Templates \times MVars \rightarrow String.$$

The *eval* function has three arguments, the first argument *Template* contains the current template (a string containing placeholders) under evaluation, the other two arguments are context information. The *String* is the result of the template evaluation. For now, assume that the *eval* function can detect metalanguage code in the template string and call itself recursively to replace these placeholders with strings. This detection of placeholders is not

discussed in detail, since an approach based on a combination of object language grammar and metalanguage grammar will be presented in Chapter 5 .
The context arguments, *Templates* and *MVars*, are both symbol tables, where *Templates* contains (sub)templates and *MVars* contains metavariables. The symbol table *Templates* is initialized with all (sub)templates defined at the start of the evaluation. The symbol table *MVars* contains all assigned metavariables. During evaluation *MVars* is continuously updated.

The *eval* function is not directly invoked to start a template evaluation, but a helper function *start* is used. This function initializes the context of the *eval* function and has the following signature:

$$start : Templates \times InputData \rightarrow String$$

where *Templates* is a set of (sub)templates stored in a symbol table and *InputData* is a tree representing the input data. Before presenting the equations of the *eval* function, it must be noted that the equations used in this book should be interpreted as a conditional term rewriting system [Alpuente *et al.* (1994)]. The equations have the form:

$$\frac{\begin{array}{c} t_1 \mapsto t_1' \\ \dots \\ t_i \mapsto t_i' \end{array}}{t \mapsto t'}$$

where t, t', t_1, $t_1', \dots, t_i$, t_i' are terms. The $\mapsto$ must be read as *results in* or *maps to*. The equation should be then read as "If the rewriting of t_1 results in t_1', …, of t_i results in t_i' then rewriting of t results in t'". Terms after the $\mapsto$ sign may contain an updated value, used in the remaining (sub) equations. For example, consider the equation:

$$add(bst_{vars}, \$\text{root}, t) \mapsto bst_{vars}$$

If before the equation bst_{vars} equals to $\{\ \}$, then after evaluation bst_{vars} will hold the value $\{root \mapsto t\}$. Next to $\mapsto$, the equations support the operators $=$ and $\in$. The "=" should be read as "If t_1 is equal to t_2 then continue with …". The "$\in$" should be read as "If t_1 is an element of the set t_2 then continue with …". These are conditional operations and the equation is only completed when all statements are true.

The *start* function is defined as follows:

$$\frac{\begin{array}{c} startblk([]) \mapsto bst_{vars1} \\ add(bst_{vars1}, \$\mathrm{root}, t) \mapsto bst_{vars2} \\ add(bst_{vars2}, \$\$, t) \mapsto bst_{vars3} \\ startblk(bst_{vars3}) \mapsto bst_{vars4} \end{array}}{start(st_{tmps}, t) \mapsto eval(<: \mathrm{template}() :>, st_{tmps}, bst_{vars4})}$$

where st_{tmps} is a symbol table containing the subtemplates, t is the input data tree and bst_{vars} contains the block-structured symbol table for the metavariables. The functions *startblk*, *add* and *eval* used in the equation of the *start* function are defined in the following subsections. The *start* function has some operational consequences: First it assigns the input data tree to the metavariables $\$root$ and \$\$, where $\$root$ is intended as a global metavariable containing the original input data tree. The \$\$ metavariable is an internal metavariable which is updated to hold a current context of the input data tree. It has the same behavior as the "normal" metavariables, but is only implicitly accessible, since the concrete syntax of metavariables does not allow to write \$\$ as identifier for a metavariable. Furthermore the *start* function shows that a template with the name *template* is the starting point of evaluation, since the fixed template in the right-hand side of the *start* function contains a call to that template.

The different equations for the recursive *eval* function are defined by the semantics of the placeholders in the coming subsections. For completeness, the cases for the string without placeholders and the empty string are given by the following equations:

$$eval(\varepsilon, st_{tmps}, bst_{vars}) \mapsto \varepsilon;$$

$$eval(s, st_{tmps}, bst_{vars}) \mapsto s, \text{ when } s \text{ does not contain a placeholder.}$$

4.2.2 *Block-Structured Symbol Table*

The (sub)templates and metavariables are stored in symbol tables. A simple symbol table is used to store the (sub)templates and a block-structured symbol table for metavariables. The block-structured symbol table is a simple symbol table extended with the operations for starting and finishing a block. Both kinds of symbol tables are defined in [Hayes (1987)]. The operations supported by these symbol tables are:

- *add* - Adds a metavariable to a block.
- *lookup* - Searches for a metavariable and returns its value.
- *startblk* - Starts a new block to add metavariables.

- *stopblk* - Removes the latest added block of metavariables.

The standard operations of a symbol table *delete* and *update* are not necessary for this metalanguage, since reassignment of metavariables with a new value is not possible in a scope and deletion of metavariables is also not possible.
The operations and behavior of a simple symbol table are discussed. A *symbol table* is modeled by a partial function from symbol, *SYM*, to values, *VAL*:

$$st : SYM \nrightarrow VAL$$

The arrow "$\nrightarrow$" indicates that a function from *SYM* to *VAL* is not necessarily defined for all elements of *SYM* (hence 'partial'). The subset of *SYM* for which the symbol table provides a value is defined as: $dom(st)$. The set of symbols defined by $dom(st)$ is the alphabet Σ_{st} of the symbol table. If a symbol $a \in \Sigma_{st}$, that is $a \in dom(st)$, then $st(a)$ is the unique value associated with a and hence $st(a) \in VAL$. The notation $\{a \mapsto t\}$ describes a function that is only defined for a

$$dom(\{a \mapsto t\}) \mapsto \{a\}$$

which maps a to t

$$\{a \mapsto t\}(a) \mapsto t$$

More generally, the notation

$$\{a_1 \mapsto t_1, a_2 \mapsto t_2, \ldots, a_j \mapsto t_j\}$$

where all the a_i's are distinct is used to define a function whose domain is

$$\{a_1, a_2, \ldots, a_j\}$$

and whose value for each a_i is the corresponding t_i. For example, if a number of metavariables are assigned to a subtree of the input data

$$st = \{\$lhs \mapsto \text{sub(id("repnr"), natcon(1))}, \$natcon \mapsto 1, \$id \mapsto \text{"repnr"}\}$$

The domain of *st* is $dom(st) = \{\$lhs, \$natcon, \$id\}$ and

$$\begin{aligned} st(\$lhs) &\mapsto \text{sub(id("repnr"), natcon(1))} \\ st(\$natcon) &\mapsto 1 \\ st(\$id) &\mapsto \text{"repnr"} \end{aligned}$$

The notation { } is used to denote the empty symbol table, where $dom(\{\}) = \varnothing$. Initially the symbol table is empty, i.e. $st = \{\}$.

The next step is to introduce block-structured symbol tables. The requirement for a block-structured symbol table is that metavariables assigned in a parent block can be looked up in a child block and that a metavariable assigned in a child block can override an earlier assigned metavariable of its parent block(s). A block-structured symbol table is a sequence of simple symbol tables, one for each nested block, where functions in the last defined simple symbol table override the functions of earlier instantiated symbol tables. First a definition of function overriding is provided.

Definition 4.2.1 (Function overriding [Hayes (1987)]). The operator $\oplus$ combines two functions of the same type to a give a new function. The new function $f \oplus g$ is defined for an argument a if either

- $dom(f \oplus g) = dom(f) \cup dom(g)$;
- $(f \oplus g)(a) = g(a)$, when $a \in dom(g)$;
- $(f \oplus g)(a) = f(a)$, when $a \notin dom(g)$ and $a \in dom(f)$.

Example 4.2.1 (Function overriding). An example of function overriding is shown by the following equations:

$$
\begin{aligned}
&\{\$id \mapsto \text{“repnr”}, \$lhs \mapsto \text{sub(id(“repnr”), natcon(1))}\}\\
&\qquad \oplus \{\$lhs \mapsto \text{id(“repnr”)}, \$rhs \mapsto \text{natcon(1)}\}\\
&= \{\$id \mapsto \text{“repnr”}, \$lhs \mapsto \text{id(“repnr”)}, \$rhs \mapsto \text{natcon(1)}\}
\end{aligned}
$$

A block-structured symbol table *bst* is modeled as a sequence of symbol tables *st*, where the first symbol table *st* is the outermost block and the last st' is the innermost block. The empty block-structured symbol table is $bst = [\ ]$. For example at a given point in the template the *bst* contains the blocks $bst = [st, st']$, where $st = \{\$id \mapsto \text{“repnr”}, \$lhs \mapsto \text{sub(id(“repnr”) natcon(1))}\}$ and $st' = \{\$lhs \mapsto \text{id(“repnr”)}, \$rhs \mapsto \text{natcon(1)}\}$. The environment for that point is a single st_{env} obtained by combining all the symbol tables of *bst* using the equation: $st_{env} = st_1 \oplus \ldots \oplus st_i$, where st_i refers to the innermost block.

The function *env*, with the signature $env : bst \rightarrow st$, obtains an st_{env} from a given *bst* and is defined by the following equations:

$$env([]) \mapsto \{\}$$

$$env([st]) \mapsto st$$

$$env([st_1, st_2, \ldots, st_i]) \mapsto st_1 \oplus env(st_2, \ldots, st_i)$$

The function *startblk*, with the signature $startblk : bst \rightarrow bst$, appends an empty symbol table *st* to *bst* and is defined by the following equations:

$$startblk([]) \mapsto [\{\}]$$

$$startblk([st_1, \ldots, st_i]) \mapsto [st_1, \ldots, st_i, \{\}]$$

The function *stopblk*, with the signature $stopblk : bst \rightarrow bst$, removes the last symbol table *st* to *bst* and is defined by the following equations:

$$stopblk([]) \mapsto []$$

$$stopblk([st_1]) \mapsto []$$

$$stopblk([st_1, \ldots, st_{i-1}, st_i]) \mapsto [st_1, \ldots, st_{i-1}]$$

The function *add*, with the signature $add : bst \times a \times t \rightarrow bst$, adds a new metavariable to the last added symbol table and is defined by the following equations:

$$\frac{a \notin dom(st)}{add([st], a, x) \mapsto [st \cup \{a \mapsto x\}]}$$

$$\frac{a \notin dom(st_i)}{add([st_1, \ldots, st_i], a, x) \mapsto [st_1, \ldots, st_i \cup \{a \mapsto x\}]}$$

The function *lookup*, with the signature $lookup : bst \times a \rightarrow t$, uses the given block-structured symbol table to lookup the latest defined value *t* of a given *a* and is defined by the following equation:

$$\frac{\begin{array}{c} env(bst) \mapsto st \\ a \in dom(st) \end{array}}{lookup(bst, a) \mapsto st(a)}$$

The use of the symbol table has two requirements. First, the operation *add* has the requirement that the symbol *a* should not be present in the innermost symbol table. Second, the operation *lookup* has the requirement that the symbol *a* is present in the symbol table *env*(*bst*). In case these requirements are not met an error must be generated such as `metavariable "a" already defined` or `metavariable "a" not found`.

4.2.3 *Subtemplates*

Subtemplates are a mechanism to compose a template of multiple smaller fragments. The first reason for having subtemplates is to enable recursion, i.e. that it is possible that a (sub)template can instantiate itself. Recursion is essential to generate tree or list structures. The second reason for a subtemplate mechanism is to reduce the number of code clones in a template definition.

Two constructs are necessary to implement subtemplates, i.e. the declaration and invocation. The concrete syntax of the declaration of a (sub)template is:

```
IdCon[ String ]
```

where `IdCon` is the name of the subtemplate and `String` contains the (sub)template which contains output document characters with placeholders. A set of (sub)templates is a list of these declarations, which is mapped to the symbol table st_{tmps} used for the evaluation of the templates. The symbol table st_{tmps} is initialized by mapping subtemplates of the form `IdCon[ String ]` to symbol table functions of the form $a \mapsto t$, where a is equal to the `Identifier` and t is equal to the `String`. The symbol table requires that each a is unique, thus each template must have a unique identifier. The lexical character class for `IdCon` is equal to the character class as defined in Section 2.6.3. The *start* function requires that at least one template is defined with the name `template`.

The second construct is the subtemplate call statement. This placeholder is used in a template and replaced by the result of an evaluated subtemplate. The syntax of a subtemplate call placeholder is:

```
<: IdCon( Expr ) :>
```

where `IdCon` is the identifier of the called subtemplate and `Expr` contains an expression to set a new value for the context metavariable \$\$. The evaluator replaces this placeholder by the result of the evaluated subtemplate with the identifier `IdCon`. Before the subtemplate is evaluated, the expression is evaluated to obtain a new context metavariable \$\$. The operational semantics of the subtemplate call placeholder is defined by the following equation:

$$\frac{\begin{array}{c} st_{tmps}(idcon) \mapsto s \\ eval(s_1, st_{tmps}, bst_{vars1}) \mapsto s'_1 \\ eval(s_3, st_{tmps}, bst_{vars1}) \mapsto s'_3 \\ startblk(bst_{vars1}) \mapsto bst_{vars2} \\ add(bst_{vars2}, \$\$, evalexpr(expr, bst_{vars2})) \mapsto bst_{vars3} \\ eval(s, st_{tmps}, bst_{vars3}) \mapsto s'_2 \end{array}}{eval(s_1 <: idcon(expr) :> s_3, st_{tmps}, bst_{vars1}) \mapsto s'_1 \cdot s'_2 \cdot s'_3}$$

The expression `Expr` is used to obtain a new value for the internal context metavariable $$.
`Expr` supports the following operations:

- Metavariable lookup (`$IdCon`);
- String constants (`"Lorem ipsum"`);
- Tree path queries (`a1b2`), see Definition 4.2.2;
- String concatenation (`Expr + Expr`);
- No operation.

The syntax of the expressions is defined by the following set of context-free production rules:

$$\begin{array}{l} \text{Expr} \rightarrow \text{Expr} + \text{Expr} \\ \text{Expr} \rightarrow \$\text{IdCon} \\ \text{Expr} \rightarrow \text{String} \\ \text{Expr} \rightarrow \text{Treequery} \\ \text{Expr} \rightarrow \$\text{IdCon Treequery} \\ \text{Expr} \rightarrow \varepsilon \end{array}$$

The string concatenation is only allowed when both expressions reduces to strings, i.e. a leaf symbol. The evaluation of the expressions is defined by the following equations:

$$\frac{\begin{array}{c} evalexpr(e_1, bst_{vars}) \mapsto e'_1 \\ evalexpr(e_2, bst_{vars}) \mapsto e'_2 \\ rank(e'_1) = 0 \\ rank(e'_2) = 0 \end{array}}{evalexpr(e_1 + e_2, bst_{vars}) \mapsto e'_1 \cdot e'_2}$$

$$\frac{c \in \Sigma_{vars} \qquad lookup(bst_{vars}, c) \mapsto t}{evalexpr(c, bst_{vars}) \mapsto t}$$

$$\frac{lookup(bst_{vars}, \$\$) \mapsto t \qquad evaltreequery(t, tq) \mapsto t'}{evalexpr(tq, bst_{vars}) \mapsto t'}$$

$$\frac{c \in \Sigma_{vars} \qquad lookup(bst_{vars}, c) \mapsto t \qquad evaltreequery(t, tq) \mapsto t'}{evalexpr(ctq, bst_{vars}) \mapsto t'}$$

$$evalexpr(c, bst_{vars}) \mapsto c$$

$$evalexpr(\varepsilon, bst_{vars}) \mapsto lookup(bst_{vars}, \$\$)$$

The tree path queries are (sub) sentences of the path language belonging to the regular tree grammar of the input data. Path languages for regular tree languages are defined by the following definition:

Definition 4.2.2 (Path language [Comon *et al.* (2008)]). Let t be a ground term, the path language $\pi(t)$ is defined inductively by:

- if $t \in \Sigma_0$, then $\pi(t) = t$;
- if $t = f(t_1, \ldots, t_r)$ then $\pi(t) = \bigcup_{i=1}^{i=r} \{f \cdot i \cdot s | s \in \pi(t_i)\}$.

Example 4.2.2 (Path language [Cleophas (2008)]). For $t = a(b(c), a(c, c))$ the path language $\pi(t)$ is $\pi(t) = \{a1b1c, a2a1c, a2a2c\}$.

A tree path query is a (sub) sentence of $\pi(t)$, where t is the tree of the current context metavariable $$ or the tree obtained from the metavariable symbol table. The evaluation of a tree path query starts at the root of the tree t and selects a subtree or leaf symbol by sequential stepping down through the tree using the nodes specified in the query. The subtree or leaf symbol where the tree path query points to is returned by the tree path query evaluator for further processing by the expression evaluator.
The input is represented as an ATerm [van den Brand *et al.* (2000)], see Section 2.6.3. The ATerm format supports lists, but it is not supported to select an element in these lists; a tree path query may only point to a list node.

The evaluation equations for a tree path query are given below:

$$\frac{f = c \qquad r \geq i}{evaltreequery(f(x_1,\ldots,x_r),\langle c,i,t\rangle) \mapsto evaltreequery(x_i,t)}$$

$$\frac{f = c \qquad r \geq i}{evaltreequery(f(x_1,\ldots,x_r),\langle c,i\rangle) \mapsto x_i}$$

$$\frac{f = c \qquad r < i}{evaltreequery(f(x_1,\ldots,x_r),\langle c,i,t\rangle) \mapsto \varepsilon}$$

$$\frac{f = c \qquad r < i}{evaltreequery(f(x_1,\ldots,x_r),\langle c,i\rangle) \mapsto \varepsilon}.$$

$$\frac{f \neq c}{evaltreequery(f(x_1,\ldots,x_r),\langle c,i,t\rangle) \mapsto \varepsilon}$$

$$\frac{f \neq c}{evaltreequery(f(x_1,\ldots,x_r),\langle c,i\rangle) \mapsto \varepsilon}$$

$$evaltreequery([x_1,\ldots,x_r],\langle c,i,t\rangle) \mapsto \varepsilon$$

$$evaltreequery([x_1,\ldots,x_r],\langle c,i\rangle) \mapsto \varepsilon$$

$$evaltreequery([x_1,\ldots,x_r],\langle c\rangle) \mapsto \varepsilon$$

$$evaltreequery(f(x_1,\ldots,x_r),\langle c\rangle) \mapsto \varepsilon$$

$$\frac{c' = c}{evaltreequery(c,\langle c'\rangle) \mapsto c}$$

$$\frac{c' \neq c}{evaltreequery(c,\langle c'\rangle) \mapsto \varepsilon}$$

Note for expressing tree path queries in the *evaltreequery*, a tree path query string is mapped to a nested set of tuples of the form $\langle c,i,t\rangle$, $\langle c,i\rangle$ or $\langle c\rangle$, where c is the current node label, i the index and t the tail of the tree path query. For example $a1b1c$ is mapped to $\langle a,1,\langle b,2,\langle c\rangle\rangle\rangle$.

Example 4.2.3 (Expressions). Table 4.1 shows the evaluation result of a number of different kinds of expressions. The tree provided as context for the tree path query evaluation is: $t = a(b(\text{“}s_1\text{”}), a([c(\text{“}s_2\text{”}), c(\text{“}s_3\text{”})]))$.

Table 4.1 Expression examples.

Expression	**Result**
“a”	“a”
“a” + “b”	“ab”
$a1b1$	“s_1”
$a1$	$b(\text{“}s_1\text{”})$
$a2a1$	$[c(\text{“}s_2\text{”}), c(\text{“}s_3\text{”})]$
$a2a1c1$	ε
$b1$	ε
$a1b1 +$ “a”	“s_1a”
$a1b1 + a1b1$	“s_1s_1”

Example 4.2.4 (Subtemplate placeholder). An example of the declarations of subtemplates is shown in Figure 4.1. The result of this template is after evaluation:

```
Lorem ipsum dolor sit amet, consectetur adipiscing elit.
Integer elementum porta facilisis.
```

The `<: sub( ) :>` calls the subtemplate `sub` and inserts the result in the calling template. The call has no expression, since no input data context has to be selected.

```
template[
  Lorem ipsum dolor sit amet, <: sub( ) :>.
  Integer elementum porta facilisis.
]

sub[
  consectetur adipiscing elit
]
```

Fig. 4.1 Subtemplate example.

4.2.4 *Match-Replace*

The match-replace placeholder is a construct to specify a finite set of match-rules containing a result string. This result string may contain placeholders, which are evaluated before it is used to replace the match-replace placeholder. The behavior of the construct is comparable to a switch-case statement, i.e. a match-rule is selected based on the first match. The syntax of the match-replace is:

```
<: match :>
   <: Matchpattern =:> String
   ...
   <: Matchpattern =:> String
<: end :>
```

As the syntax shows, the match-replace contains a set of match-rules *mr*, which return a string. The match-rules contain a match-pattern and a result string, in the equations the abstract notation $\langle mp, s\rangle$ for match-rules is used, where *mp* is the `Matchpattern` and *s* the `String`. A simple match-rule selection algorithm is used, where the first rule with a successful match is selected. It is possible that no match-rule matches the current (sub)tree of the input data. In that case an error is generated.
Match-rules are matched against the current tree assigned to the internal metavariable $$. The match-pattern may define metavariables, which are bound to subtrees of the matched tree. These assigned metavariables are stored in a new scope of the symbol table. The string of the selected match-rule is evaluated using the symbol table containing the metavariables assigned during the matching process. The scope of a metavariable is the evaluated string, including recursively applied placeholders. Metavariables assigned in inner blocks hide metavariables assigned in parent blocks, as the semantics of the block-structured symbol table already defines.
First the evaluation of the match-replace placeholder itself is discussed. After that, the match-patterns and tree matching algorithm are formalized. In case of an error the match-

replace returns an object *ERROR*. The *ERROR* is used to inform the user about the failure.

$$\frac{\begin{array}{c} eval(s_1, st_{tmps}, bst_{vars1}) \mapsto s'_1 \\ eval(s_3, st_{tmps}, bst_{vars1}) \mapsto s'_3 \\ lookup(bst_{vars1}, \$\$) \mapsto t \\ startblk(bst_{vars1}) \mapsto bst_{vars2} \\ findmatch(t, [mr_1, \ldots, mr_i], bst_{vars2}) \mapsto \langle s, bst_{vars3} \rangle \\ eval(s, st_{tmps}, bst_{vars3}) \mapsto s'_2 \end{array}}{eval(s_1 \text{<: match :>} [mr_1, \ldots, mr_i] \text{ <: end :>} s_3, st_{tmps}, bst_{vars1}) \mapsto s'_1 \cdot s'_2 \cdot s'_3}$$

$$\frac{\begin{array}{c} eval(s_1, st_{tmps}, bst_{vars1}) \mapsto s'_1 \\ eval(s_3, st_{tmps}, bst_{vars1}) \mapsto s'_3 \\ lookup(bst_{vars1}, \$\$) \mapsto t \\ startblk(bst_{vars1}) \mapsto bst_{vars2} \\ findmatch(t, [mr_1, \ldots, mr_i], bst_{vars2}) = \varepsilon \end{array}}{eval(s_1 \text{<: match :>} [mr_1, \ldots, mr_i] \text{ <: end :>} s_3, st_{tmps}, bst_{vars1}) \mapsto ERROR}$$

$$\frac{match(t, mr_1, bst_{vars}) = \varepsilon}{findmatch(t, [mr_1, mr_2 \ldots, mr_i], bst_{vars}) \mapsto findmatch(t, [mr_2 \ldots, mr_i], bst_{vars})}$$

$$\frac{match(t, mr, bst_{vars}) = \varepsilon}{findmatch(t, [mr], bst_{vars}) \mapsto \varepsilon}$$

$$\frac{match(t, mr_1, bst_{vars}) \mapsto \langle s, bst_{vars} \rangle}{findmatch(t, [mr_1, mr_2 \ldots, mr_i], bst_{vars}) \mapsto \langle s, bst_{vars} \rangle}$$

$$\frac{match(t, mr, bst_{vars}) \mapsto \langle s, bst_{vars} \rangle}{findmatch(t, [mr], bst_{vars}) \mapsto \langle s, bst_{vars} \rangle}$$

The syntax of the match-pattern is similar to the ATerm tree syntax, defined in Section 2.6.3, augmented with syntax for metavariables. `IdCon` syntactically limits the alphabet of the labels of these trees Σ. The syntax of the metavariables is defined as an `IdCon` prefixed with a dollar sign. The alphabet of metavariables Σ_{vars} is thus always disjoint from Σ, since the dollar-sign is not allowed for `IdCon`. Note that the internal used metavariable $\$\$$ is always disjoint of $\Sigma \cup \Sigma_{vars}$, since its syntax is not a sentence of `IdCon` neither of `IdCon` prefixed with a dollar-sign. The rank of a metavariable is $c \in \Sigma_{vars}$ is $rank(c) = 0$, as it is always a leaf node. It is allowed to have lists in the ATerm tree syntax. These lists are a shorthand notation for binary trees, and are matched via the pattern $[mp_1, \ldots, mp_k]$, where $mp_1, \ldots, mp_k$ are match-patterns. The underlying binary tree structure of lists has as effect that the last match-pattern mp_k in the pattern $[mp_1, \ldots, mp_k]$ is matched against the tail of the list. The tail contains the remaining list or empty list.

The tree pattern matcher is implemented as a root-to-frontier pattern matcher [Cleophas (2008)]. The matching mechanism is minimalistic and does for example not support associative-commutative matching such as provided by TOM [Moreau *et al.* (2003)]. It tries to match the tree, and during matching it adds the assigned metavariables to the symbol table bst_{vars}. The *match* function has the signature: $Tree \times Matchpattern \times MVars \rightarrow MVars$. Its operations are defined by the following equations:

$$\frac{\begin{array}{c} f = f' \\ match(x_1, mp_1, bst_{vars1}) \mapsto bst_{vars2} \\ \ldots \\ match(x_r, mp_r, bst_{vars(r)}) \mapsto bst_{vars(r+1)} \end{array}}{match(f(x_1, \ldots, x_r), f'(mp_1, \ldots, mp_r), bst_{vars1}) \mapsto bst_{vars(r+1)}}$$

$$\frac{f \neq f'}{match(f(x_1, \ldots, x_r), f'(mp_1, \ldots, mp_r), bst_{vars}) \mapsto \varepsilon}$$

$$\frac{\begin{array}{c} match(x_1, mp_1, bst_{vars1}) \mapsto bst_{vars2} \\ match([x_2, \ldots, x_r], [mp_2, \ldots, mp_k], bst_{vars2}) \mapsto bst_{vars3} \end{array}}{match([x_1, x_2, \ldots, x_r], [mp_1, mp_2, \ldots, mp_k], bst_{vars1}) \mapsto bst_{vars3}}$$

$$\frac{match(x, mp, bst_{vars1}) \mapsto bst_{vars2}}{match([x], [mp], bst_{vars1}) \mapsto bst_{vars2}}$$

$$\frac{match([x_1, \ldots, x_r], mp, bst_{vars1}) \mapsto bst_{vars2}}{match([x_1, \ldots, x_r], [mp], bst_{vars1}) \mapsto bst_{vars2}}$$

$$match([], [], bst_{vars}) \mapsto bst_{vars}$$

$$\frac{\begin{array}{c} c' \notin \Sigma_{mvar} \\ c = c' \end{array}}{match(c, c', bst_{vars}) \mapsto bst_{vars}}$$

$$\frac{\begin{array}{c} c' \notin \Sigma_{mvar} \\ c \neq c' \end{array}}{match(c, c', bst_{vars}) \mapsto \varepsilon}$$

$$\frac{\begin{array}{c} c \in \Sigma_{mvar} \\ bst_{vars} \neq \varepsilon \end{array}}{match(t, c, bst_{vars}) \mapsto add(bst_{vars}, c, t)}$$

$$\frac{c \in \Sigma_{mvar} \quad bst_{vars} = \varepsilon}{match(t, c, bst_{vars}) \mapsto \varepsilon}$$

Table 4.2 Match pattern examples.

Input Data	**MatchPattern**	bst_{vars}
"a"	"b"	ε
"b"	"b"	$\langle\{\}\rangle$
a("b")	$a(\$x)$	$\langle\{\$x \mapsto$ "b"$\}\rangle$
$a(b($"c"$), d($"e"$))$	$a(\$x, d(\$y))$	$\langle\{\$x \mapsto b($"$c$"$), \$y \mapsto$ "e"$\}\rangle$
[]	[]	$\langle\{\}\rangle$
["a"]	[$x, $y]	$\langle\{\$x \mapsto$ "a"$, \$y \mapsto [\,]\}\rangle$
["a", "b", "c"]	[$x, $y]	$\langle\{\$x \mapsto$ "a"$, \$y \mapsto [$"$b$", "$c$"$]\}\rangle$
["a", "b"]	[$x, $y, []]	$\langle\{\$x \mapsto$ "a"$, \$y \mapsto$ "b"$\}\rangle$

The Table 4.2 shows some examples of trees, match patterns and the resulting symbol table. When a match fails the result is ε.

The match-replace placeholder can also be accompanied with an expression:

```
<: match Expr :>
   <: Matchpattern =:> String
   ...
   <: Matchpattern =:> String
<: end :>
```

This construction is an abbreviation for a combination of the match-replace placeholder and subtemplates and can be rewritten to the following subtemplate call placeholder:

```
<: id( Expr ) :>
```

and subtemplate:

```
id[
 <: match :>
   <: Matchpattern =:> String
   ...
   <: Matchpattern =:> String
```

```
 <: end :>
]
```

where the value of id should be unique to prevent collisions with other subtemplates, i.e. the value of id should be hygienic [Kohlbecker *et al.* (1986)].
The match-replace is a verbose construction for some common operations like substitution, iteration and conditional. The next presented placeholders are abbreviations for the match-replace and are more intuitive for programmers with an imperative background.

4.2.5 *Substitution*

The substitution placeholder provides a one-to-one insertion of a leaf symbol of the input data tree into the template. The syntax of the substitution placeholder is:

```
<: Expr :>
```

The evaluator replaces the substitution placeholder by a string. The value of this string is obtained by evaluating the Expr.
The informal operational semantics of this placeholder are straightforward. The expression is evaluated, which must yield a string, otherwise an error is generated. This result of the expression substitutes the placeholder in the template.
Formally, the evaluation of the substitution placeholder can be written as a combination of subtemplates and match-replace placeholders. Consider Figure 4.2, the substitution placeholder on the left side of the arrow can be replaced by a subtemplate call placeholder, i.e. `<: id(Expr) :>` accompanied by two subtemplates. This subtemplate call placeholder sets a new value for the context metavariable $$. It calls the subtemplate *id*, which iterates over the list of characters in the string, and a string can indeed be mapped to a list of characters. The subtemplate *idc* is called per character, which maps every character in the input data to a character in the object code. The number of match-rules in this mapping is equal to the number of characters supported by the string type of the input data. Note that the names of the subtemplates *id* and *idc* must be unique to ensure they do not conflict with other declared subtemplates.

```
                          <: id(Expr) :>

                          id[
                            <: match :>
                              < [$mchar;$chars] =:>
                                <: idc($mchar) :><: id($chars) :>
                              <: [] =:>
                            <: end :>
                          ]
<: Expr :>          ⇒
                          idc[
                            <: match :>
                              <: a =:>a
                              .
                              .
                              .
                              <: Z =:>Z
                            <: end :>
                          ]
```

Fig. 4.2 Translation of substitution placeholder to match-replace and subtemplates.

4.2.6 *Conditional*

The conditional placeholder selects a result string based on the result of a condition. The syntax of the conditional placeholder is inspired by the if-then(-else) construct that can be found in most imperative languages:

```
<: if Expr == Matchpattern then :>
  String ( <: else :> String )?
<: fi :>
```

The if-then(-else) construct consists of an condition to select the result strings. The condition contains an `Expr` and a `Matchpattern`. The `Expr` is used to calculate a value from the input data. This result of the expression is matched against the `Matchpattern`; when the match is successful the string of the then-part is inserted. In case of an unsuccessful match the else-part is inserted, or when this part is unspecified, nothing is inserted. The chosen string may contain placeholders and is evaluated before inserting it in the template. The conditional placeholder can be rewritten to a match-replace placeholder. The translation is defined by the mappings of Figure 4.3 and Figure 4.4. The first mapping is the if-then-else, the second mapping is the if-then. At the translation of the if-then, the missing else-part must be defined in the match-replace placeholder. Without this second rule for the empty result, the evaluation of the match-replace placeholder will produce an error when the first match pattern does not match. Since the if-then(-else) is rewritten to a match-replace placeholder, it is possible to have metavariables in the match pattern of the conditional. During translation the match pattern is only used for the then-part, as a result the metavariables of that match pattern are only available in that part. The else part uses the default match pattern $\$x$, so $\$x$ is assigned to the result of the expression in case the then part is selected.

```
<:if Expr == Matchpattern then:>
  s1
<:else:>
  s2
<:fi:>
```

⇒

```
<: match Expr :>
  <: Matchpattern =:> s1
  <: $x =:> s2
<: end :>
```

Fig. 4.3 Translation of if-the-else to match-replace.

```
<:if Expr == Matchpattern then:>
  s
<:fi:>
```

⇒

```
<: match Expr :>
  <: Matchpattern =:> s
  <: $x =:>
<: end :>
```

Fig. 4.4 Translation of if-then to match-replace.

4.2.7 *Iteration*

The iteration placeholder is an abbreviation for the match-replace placeholder for handling lists. It contains an expression to select a list from the input data and it contains a result string, which is instantiated for every element in the list. During iteration the current element is assigned to a user definable metavariable $\$IdCon$ in order to use it in the placeholders of the string. The syntax of the iteration placeholder is:

```
<: foreach $IdCon in Expr do :>
  String  ( <: sep :> String )?
<: od :>
```

A separator can be defined in case of a separated list. The mapping of an iteration placeholder to a match-replace placeholder is defined in Figure 4.5 and Figure 4.6. The metavariable *$IdCon* contains the element of the iteration. The metavariable *$tail* is bound to the tail of the list and recursively invokes the subtemplate *id* with this new context via a subtemplate call. The identifier of the subtemplate *id* must be unique to remove possible conflicts. The first translation, of Figure 4.5, is for non-separated lists and the second translation, of Figure 4.6, is for separated lists. In the second case, three match-rules are necessary to handle the separator in a correct way. A separator must only be inserted between two elements and is not allowed to terminate a list, which is prevented by the second rule. Section 6.7 discusses why this extra rule becomes superfluous in a syntax-safe template evaluator.

```
                                   id[<: match Expr :>
<: foreach $IdCon in Expr do :>      <: [] =:> e
  s                          ⇒       <: [$IdCon;$tail] =:>
<: od :>                               s <: id($tail) :>
                                   <: end :>]
```

Fig. 4.5 Translation of iteration placeholder to match-replace placeholder (non-separated lists).

```
                                    id[<: match Expr :>
                                      <: [] =:> e
<:foreach $IdCon in Expr do:>         <: [$IdCon] =:> s
 s <: sep :> s(sep)            ⇒      <: [$IdCon;$tail] =:>
<:od:>                                   s s(sep) <: id($tail) :>
                                    <: end :>]
```

Fig. 4.6 Translation of iteration placeholder with separator to match-replace placeholder (separated lists).

4.2.8 *Unparser Completeness*

The presented metalanguage is intentionally minimalistic to prevent it for using for computations other than rendering the view. The next theorem shows that the presented minimalistic metalanguage is unparser-complete:

Theorem 4.2.1. *A metalanguage containing constructions for subtemplates and match-replace placeholders is unparser-complete.*

Proof. Every production rule in a context-free grammar can be projected on the form $n \rightarrow s_1 n_1 s_2 \ldots s_r n_r s_{r+1}\{c\}$, where $s_1, \ldots, s_{r+1}$ are strings and may be the empty string ε, and $n, n_1, \ldots, n_r$ are the nonterminals. In case the pattern $s_1 s_2$ occurs, the strings can be concatenated into a new string s'_1. It is assumed that the augmented grammar meets the requirements for augmenting a grammar with signature labels as sketched in Section 3.1. The abstract syntax tree belonging to this production rule $t_{ast} = c(t_1, \ldots, t_r)$, where $t_1, \ldots, t_r$ are the abstract syntax trees belonging to $n_1 \ldots n_r$. The template belonging to this production rule is: $tmp =$

```
unparse[
<: match :>
 <: c( $x1, ... ,$xr ) =:>
   s1 <: unparse( $x1 ) :> s2 ...
   sr <: unparse( $xr ) :> sr+1
<: end :>
]
```

Normally, a grammar contains multiple production rules. Each production rule must be implemented as a match rule in the *unparse* template.
Evaluating the template using the abstract syntax tree t_{ast} results in

$$start(tmp, t_{ast}) \Rightarrow s_1 \cdot s'_1 \cdot s_2 \cdot \ldots \cdot s_r \cdot s'_r \cdot s_{r+1},$$

where s_1 is the result of evaluating the template *unparse* with the input data tree bound to $\$x_1$, and s_r is the result of evaluating the template *unparse* with the input data tree bound to $\$x_r$. Parsing the string $s_1 \cdot s'_1 \cdot s_2 \cdot \ldots \cdot s_r \cdot s'_r \cdot s_{r+1}$ produces a parse tree $parse(s_1 \cdot s'_1 \cdot s_2 \cdot \ldots \cdot s_r \cdot s'_r \cdot s_{r+1}) = <n, c> (s_1, t'_1, s_2, \ldots, s_r, t'_r, s_{r+1})$, where $t'_1 \ldots t'_r$ are sub parse trees with top nonterminals $n_1 \ldots n_r$ and strings $s_1 \ldots s_{r+1}$ are the terminals. The abstract syntax tree is $desugar(<n, c> (s_1, t'_1, s_2, \ldots, s_r, t'_r, s_{r+1})) = c(t_1 \ldots t_r)$, where $t_1 = desugar(t'_1), \ldots,$ $t_r = desugar(t'_r)$. This abstract syntax tree is equal to the original abstract syntax tree. Since this relation holds for every production rule in a context-free language, the unparser can be defined using a metalanguage providing subtemplates and match-replace placeholders. ■

Theorem 4.2.1 shows that not every feature of the presented metalanguage is necessary to meet the requirements for an unparser-complete metalanguage. First only metavariable lookups are necessary, the other operations are for convenience during implementing code generators. Second the stack of metavariables supporting blocks is superfluous when implementing an unparser, since metavariables are only used in the scope of a match-replace placeholder. However, referring to earlier assigned metavariables is sometimes necessary (see case studies of Chapter 7), if only just for identifiers based on multiple labels in the input data tree. An example is generating a get function with the name of the class and field: `getNaturalValue`, where `Natural` is the class name and `Value` the field name.

4.3 Example: The PICO Unparser

The template of Figure 4.7 is an implementation of an PICO unparser and reconstructs the concrete syntax for an abstract syntax tree of PICO. An example of such an abstract syntax tree of a PICO program is shown in Figure 2.3. It is obtained by parsing and desugaring the PICO program of Figure 2.1. This abstract syntax tree can be used as input data for the template to obtain a concrete syntax representation of the PICO program. The layout is not literally restored, since layout information is missing in the abstract syntax tree. The template evaluator uses the layout as it is defined in the template.

This unparser implementation shows the application of the subtemplates, match-replace placeholders and substitution placeholders. The unparser consists of the start template *template* and a subtemplate for each nonterminal appearing in the right-hand side of a context-free production rule. The subtemplates are necessary to handle the list structures of the declarations and statements, and to handle the recursive structure of the statements and expressions. They contain a match-replace placeholder to match on the subtree of the abstract syntax belonging to the nonterminal of the sentences the match-replace placeholder instantiates. The number of match-rules of the match-replace placeholders is equal to the number of alternatives belonging to these nonterminals.

```
template[
<: match :>
<: program( decls($decls), $stms ) =:>
begin declare
<: decls( $decls ) :>;
<: stms( $stms ):>
end
<: end :>]
decls[
<: match :>
<: [] =:>
<: [ $head ] =:>  <: idtype($head) :>
<: [ $head, $tail] =:> <: idtype($head) :>, <: decls($tail) :>
<: end :>]
stms[
<: match :>
<: [] =:>
<: [ $head ] =:> <: stm($head) :>
<: [ $head, $tail] =:> <: stm($head) :>; <: stms($tail) :>
<: end :>]
stm[
<: match :>
 <: assignment( $id, $expr ) =:>
                                  <: $id :> := <: expr( $expr ) :>
 <: while( $expr, $stms ) =:> while <: expr($expr) :> do
                                  <: stms($stms):> od
 <: if( $expr, $thenstms, $elsestms ) =:> if <: expr($expr) :>
      then <: stms($thenstms) :> else <: stms($elsestms) :> fi
<: end :>]
expr[
<: match :>
 <: natcon( $natcon ) =:> <: $natcon :>
 <: strcon( $strcon ) =:> "<: $strcon :>"
 <: id( $id ) =:> <: $id :>
 <: sub( $lhs, $rhs ) =:> <: expr($lhs) :> - <: expr($rhs) :>
 <: concat( $lhs, $rhs ) =:> <: expr($lhs) :> || <: expr($rhs) :>
 <: add( $lhs, $rhs ) =:> <: expr($lhs) :> + <: expr($rhs) :>
<: end :>]
idtype[
<: match :>
<: decl( $id, $type ) =:> <: $id :> : <: type($type) :>
<: end :>]
type[
<: match :>
 <: natural =:> natural
 <: string  =:> string
<: end :>]
```

Fig. 4.7 PICO unparser based on templates.

4.4 Related Template Systems

This section discusses the metalanguage of some related template systems. Three industrially used template evaluators (ERb [Herrington (2003)], JSP [Bergsten (2002); Roth and Pelegrí-Llopart (2003)], and Velocity[2]) and an evaluator presented in the academic literature (StringTemplate [Parr (2004)]) are discussed. This selection is based on availability of a working template evaluator and to show different metalanguages.

A metalanguage can be minimalistic, for example only using placeholders containing reference labels. The template evaluator replaces a placeholder with the referred label with a piece of data instead that the placeholder describes an expression. Next to a minimalistic programming language, a language, like Ruby or Java, can be used as metalanguage. Template systems using a rich metalanguage are ERb, JSP, and Velocity. A system like StringTemplate provides a metalanguage that is less powerful than a Turing-complete metalanguage.

The next sections present the industrial template evaluators ERb, JSP, and Velocity. They are designed to generate HTML in web applications, although Herrington [Herrington (2003)] uses ERb to generate code in a model driven engineering approach. The last discussed template evaluator, StringTemplate, finds also its origin in the application as a template evaluator for a dynamic website[3]. StringTemplate is used to investigate template evaluators and metalanguage features in an academic setting. For each of these template evaluators an implementation of the PICO unparser is provided. In Section 4.4.5 a brief evaluation is given about the differences and similarities between the different metalanguages.

4.4.1 *ERb*

ERb is a text-template interpreter for the programming language Ruby[4]. ERb introduces special syntax constructs to embed Ruby code in a text file. There is no restriction on the language ERb can generate as the metalanguage Ruby is Turing-complete.

The first main construct is `<%= Ruby expression %>`. Its behavior is similar to the earlier defined substitution placeholder. The Ruby expression is evaluated and the result is emitted to the output. An example of this construct is: `Hello <%= "Jack" %>` which yields `Hello Jack` after evaluation.

[2]http://velocity.apache.org (accessed on December 18, 2011)
[3]http://www.jguru.com (accessed on December 18, 2011)
[4]http://www.ruby-lang.org (accessed on December 18, 2011)

The second main construct is `<% Ruby code %>`, which embeds Ruby code in a template. The code is executed, but output text is only emitted in the generated text when print statements are used inside the Ruby code. Ruby statements can span multiple placeholders, so it is possible to use the conditional and iteration statement provided by the Ruby language. This approach to embed Ruby in a template is flexible. When a new language construct is added to Ruby, it can immediately be used in an ERb template, because ERb does not have any assumptions about the metalanguage, except that it must be Ruby.

```
<%
names = []
names.push({'first' => "Jack", 'last' => "Herrington"})
names.push({'first' => "Lori", 'last' => "Herrington"})
names.push({'first' => "Megan", 'last' => "Herrington"})
%>
<% names.each { |name| %>
Hello <%= name[ 'first' ] %> <%= name[ 'last' ] %>
<% } %>
```

Fig. 4.8 ERb example [Herrington (2003)].

An example of an ERb template is presented in Figure 4.8. The first placeholder initializes the array `names`. The second placeholder and the last placeholder are an iteration formed by the Ruby iterator `.each`. The template text between those placeholders is emitted for each element in the array `names`. The same construction of placeholders can also be used for `if` statements and other Ruby constructs.

Figure 4.9 shows an implementation of the PICO unparser using ERb. The abstract syntax trees of PICO represented as ATerms are mapped one-to-one to an XML representation, such that it can be queried using XPath. The unparser is grouped in three subtemplates: `root`, `statements` and `expr`. The `root` is the starting point of the unparser. At lines 4–9 it generates the variable declarations. Typical for the ERb implementation is the deletion of the quote-sign (`"`) in the query result, see the use of the `gsub` construct in line 6. This is necessary as strings returned by the XML queries are surrounded by quotes. Also typical for the ERb implementation is the separator handling using an `if` statement to check for the last element, see line 8.

The way Ruby is embedded in ERb results in a limitation of the use of Ruby. Variables in ERb are global accessible and writable in all (sub)templates, which makes out of the box recursive evaluation impossible since earlier assigned variables with the same name in a calling template are overwritten. This is an important limitation, resulting in additional boilerplate code to implement a stack mechanism in the template.

```
root.erb:
begin
  declare
   <% decls = input_data.xpath('//program/decls/list/decl');
              decls.each { |decl| %>
     <%= decl.xpath('value').text.gsub(/\"/, '') %>:
       <%= decl.xpath('*[2]').last.name %>
     <% if decl != decls.last %>,<% end %>
  <% } %>;
  <% last_stm = nil %>
  <% statements = input_data.xpath('//program/list/*') %>
  <%= subtemplate("statements.erb", binding)%>
end

statements.erb:
<% statements.each { |stm| %>
   <% stack.push stm != statements.last %>
   <% case stm.node_name when "assignment" then %>
         <%= stm.xpath('value').text.gsub(/\"/, '') %> :=
            <% expr = stm.xpath('*[2]');
            print subtemplate("expr.erb", binding) %>
     <% when "while" then %> while
            <% expr = stm.xpath('*[1]');
               print subtemplate("expr.erb", binding) %> do
            <% stack.push statements %>
               <% statements = stm.xpath('*[2]/*'); %>
               <%= subtemplate("statements.erb", binding) %>
               <% statements = stack.pop %> od
     <% when "if" then %> if <% expr = stm.xpath('*[1]');
            print subtemplate("expr.erb", binding) %> then
            <% stack.push statements %>
            <% statements = stm.xpath('*[2]/*'); %>
            <% statements2 = stm.xpath('*[3]/*'); %>
            <% stack.push statements2 %>
            <%= subtemplate("statements.erb", binding) %>
            else
            <% statements = stack.pop %>
            <%= subtemplate("statements.erb", binding) %>
            <% statements = stack.pop %> fi
   <% end %>
   <% if stack.pop then %>;<% end %>
<% } %>
```

Fig. 4.9 PICO unparser implemented using ERb.(to be continued)

```
   expr.erb:
44 <% case expr.first.name
        when "natcon" then %> <%= expr.xpath('value').text %>
46 <%   when "strcon" then %> <%= expr.xpath('value').text %>
   <%
   when "id" then %> <%= expr.xpath('value').text.gsub(/\"/, '') %>
48 <%   when "sub" then %> <% exprl = expr.xpath('*[1]');
        stack.push expr.xpath('*[2]'); expr = exprl;
50      print subtemplate("expr.erb", binding) %> -
       <% expr = stack.pop; print subtemplate("expr.erb", binding) %>
52 <%   when "concat" then %> <% exprl = expr.xpath('*[1]');
        stack.push expr.xpath('*[2]'); expr = exprl;
54      print subtemplate("expr.erb", binding) %> ||
       <% expr = stack.pop; print subtemplate("expr.erb", binding) %>
56 <%   when "add" then %> <% exprl = expr.xpath('*[1]');
        stack.push expr.xpath('*[2]'); expr = exprl;
58      print subtemplate("expr.erb", binding) %> +
       <% expr = stack.pop; print subtemplate("expr.erb", binding) %>
60 <% end %>
```

Fig. 4.10 PICO unparser implemented using ERb.(continued)

It is obligatory to support recursive template evaluation with scoped variables to have an unparser-complete template evaluator. Since Ruby is offered as metalanguage, the problem of global variables in ERb could be solved using an explicit stack mechanism in the templates. Consider the `statements` subtemplate, it iterates (line 16) over a list of statements provided by the caller. At line 17 the current state of the iteration, i.e. whether the iteration is not finished, is pushed on the stack. For correct separator handling, this value is popped and used to generate a separator at line 41.

Lines 18–40 contain a case-switch, similar to the match-replace placeholder. It checks the kind of the statement node in the input data to select the corresponding concrete syntax. The `if` statement and `while` statement recursively contain statements and need to call the `statements` subtemplate. When the `statements` subtemplate is recursively called, the variable `statements` is pushed on the stack and a new value is assigned to the variable. For example the `while` at lines 22–28, the content of the variable `statements` is pushed at line 25, a new value is assigned to the variable at line 26 and the subtemplate is called at line 27, finally the original value of the `statements` variable is reassigned to it at line 28. The subtemplate `expr` for generating expressions works in a similar way.

4.4.2 *Java Server Pages*

Java Server Pages (JSP) is a template based system developed by Sun Microsystems. It is designed for generating dynamic web pages and XML messages in Java-based enterprise systems. The aim of JSP is to provide separation between the object code and the content generation. The complete Java language is available as metalanguage in JSP pages.

The evaluation of JSP pages is tuned for performance. This is achieved by having two phases: a translation phase and a request phase. In a web environment a page is requested via a client. The translation phase is done once per page at the first request. The *JSP compiler* translates the JSP page to a Java servlet class where all object code is embedded in `println(...)` statements, i.e. the translation phase converts the JSP page to a print statement based code generator (Section 1.3.2). This servlet class is instantiated to answer requests to generate the output code, i.e. HTML.

JSP provides two levels of instructions: JSP directives and JSP scripting elements. JSP directives provide information for the translation phase that is independent of any specific request. The scripting elements are the instructions that are executed at every request of the servlet. These scripting elements are the placeholders of JSP.

JSP directives provide global information for instructing the JSP Compiler for creating the servlet class. They have the following syntax:

```
<%@ directive { attr="value" }* %>.
```

Table 4.3 shows the standard directives. Lines 2–5 of Figure 4.11 contain directives to define the basic page settings for the JSP implementation of the PICO unparser. JSP supports tag libraries, Java classes containing functionality, which can be called from a JSP page. In Figure 4.11, the tag libraries for XML querying, string manipulation functions and core functions are imported[5].

Table 4.3 JSP Directives.

Element	**Description**
`<%@ page ... %>`	Defines page-dependent attributes, such as session tracking, error page, and buffering requirements.
`<%@ include ... %>`	Includes a file during the translation phase.
`<%@ taglib ... %>`	Declares a tag library, containing custom actions, that is used in the page.

[5]http://java.sun.com/products/jsp/jstl/1.1/docs/tlddocs/c/tld-summary.html (accessed on December 18, 2011)

JSP provides three types of scripting elements, see Table 4.4. The first two are equivalent to the ERb placeholders; one for embedding Java code in a JSP page and one to define expressions, where the output is directly emitted in the result. The third type of placeholder is used to declare variables and methods that get inserted into the main body of the servlet class. It can be used to declare methods, to be called from the template and to specify fields for storing global information independent of single request.

Table 4.4 JSP Scripting Elements.

Element	Description
`<% ... %>`	Scriptlet, used to embed Java scripting code.
`<%= ... %>`	Expression, used to embed scripting code expressions when the result shall be added to the output code.
`<%! ... %>`	Declaration, used to declare variables and methods in the servlet body of the JSP page implementation class.

The JSP PICO unparser is shown in Figure 4.11. Comparing to the implementation of Section 4.3, the following differences can be noticed. First, iteration is supported by a `foreach` statement, as shown at lines 10–16. It generates a list of declarations, separated by a comma. The list separator handling is implemented by a check at line 15. The `if` prevents the generation of a comma at the last cycle of the iteration. The other difference is the variable scoping supported by JSP. In contrast with the unparser-complete metalanguage, JSP does not support a stack where variables are pushed and popped. The requirement for the stack is that variables must be passed to a called (sub)template and variables in the scope of the calling (sub)template should not be overwritten in the called (sub)template. In case of recursion this easily happens, when the (sub)template calls itself and the same variable names are used. For example in the `Expr.jsp` subtemplate defined at lines 65–100 of Figure 4.11. JSP offers a scoping mechanism for variables, where the *page* scope and *request* scope are used. The variables in the page scope are only available in the page itself and not in a called (sub)template, while variables in the request scope are also available in the called (sub)templates. An example is shown at lines 77–82. Values extracted from the input data are stored in variables in the page scope, lines 77–78, otherwise they are overwritten by the recursively called (sub)template. Since page scoped variables are not passed to a called (sub)template, they are assigned to a request scoped variable before calling the (sub)template, see lines 79–82.

```
pico.jsp:
<%@ page language="java" contentType="text/plain"%>
<%@ taglib prefix="c" uri="http://java.sun.com/jsp/jstl/core" %>
<%@ taglib prefix="x" uri="http://java.sun.com/jsp/jstl/xml" %>
<%@ taglib prefix="fn" uri="http://java.sun.com/jsp/jstl/functions" %>
<c:import url="input.xml" var="url" />
<x:parse xml="${url}" var="input" />
begin
  declare
   <x:forEach var="decl" varStatus="status"
                      select="$input/program/decls/list/decl">
     <x:set var="identifier" select="string($decl/value)"
          scope="page"/>${fn:replace( identifier, "\"", "")}:
         <x:out select="name($decl/*[2])" />
     <c:if test="${status.last=='false'}" >,</c:if>
   </x:forEach>;
   <x:set var="statements" select="$input/program/list"
                                              scope="request"/>
   <jsp:include page="statements.jsp"/>

end

statements.jsp:
<%@ taglib prefix="c" uri="http://java.sun.com/jsp/jstl/core" %>
<%@ taglib prefix="x" uri="http://java.sun.com/jsp/jstl/xml" %>
<%@ taglib prefix="fn" uri="http://java.sun.com/jsp/jstl/functions" %>

<x:forEach var="stm" varStatus="status" select="$statements/*">
   <x:choose>
     <x:when select="name($stm)=\"assignment\"" >
      <x:set var="identifier" select="string($stm/value)"
              scope="page"/>${fn:replace( identifier, "\"", "")}
              := <x:set var="expr" select="$stm/*[2]"
              scope="request"/><jsp:include page="expr.jsp"/>
     </x:when>

     <x:when select="name($stm)=\"while\"">
            while <x:set var="expr" select="$stm/*[1]"
            scope="request"/><jsp:include page="expr.jsp"/> do
           <x:set var="statements" select="$stm/*[2]"
            scope="request"/>
           <jsp:include page="statements.jsp"/>
          od
     </x:when>
     <x:when select="name($stm)=\"if\"">
      if <x:set var="expr" select="$stm/*[1]" scope="request"/>
                <jsp:include page="expr.jsp"/>then
                <x:set var="statements1" select="$stm/*[2]"
                scope="page"/><x:set var="statements2"
                select="$stm/*[3]" scope="page"/>
```

Fig. 4.11 PICO abstract syntax tree unparser in JSP.(to be continued)

```
                    <c:set var="statements" value="${statements1}"
                    scope="request" />
                    <jsp:include page="statements.jsp"/>
         else       <c:set var="statements" value="${statements2}"
                    scope="request" />
                    <jsp:include page="statements.jsp"/> fi
         </x:when>
    </x:choose> <c:if test="${status.last=='false'}" >;</c:if>
  </x:forEach>

  expr.jsp:
<%@ taglib prefix="c" uri="http://java.sun.com/jsp/jstl/core" %>
<%@ taglib prefix="x" uri="http://java.sun.com/jsp/jstl/xml" %>
<%@ taglib prefix="fn" uri="http://java.sun.com/jsp/jstl/functions" %>
<x:choose>
 <x:when select="name($expr)=\"natcon\"" >
  <x:out select="$expr/*[1]"/>
 </x:when>
 <x:when select="name($expr)=\"strcon\"" >
  <x:out select="$expr/*[1]"/>
 </x:when>
 <x:when select="name($expr)=\"id\"" >
  <x:set var="identifier" select="string($expr/*[1])"
  scope="page"/> ${fn:replace( identifier , "\"", "")}
 </x:when>
 <x:when select="name($expr)=\"sub\"" >
  <x:set var="exprl" select="$expr/*[1]" scope="page"/>
  <x:set var="exprr" select="$expr/*[2]" scope="page"/>
  <c:set var="expr" value="${exprl}" scope="request" />
  <jsp:include page="expr.jsp"/> - <c:set var="expr"
  value="${exprr}" scope="request" />
  <jsp:include page="expr.jsp"/>
 </x:when>
 <x:when select="name($expr)=\"concat\"" >
  <x:set var="exprl" select="$expr/*[1]" scope="page"/>
  <x:set var="exprr" select="$expr/*[2]" scope="page"/>
  <c:set var="expr" value="${exprl}" scope="request" />
  <jsp:include page="expr.jsp"/> || <c:set var="expr"
  value="${exprr}" scope="request" />
  <jsp:include page="expr.jsp"/>
 </x:when>
 <x:when select="name($expr)=\"add\"" >
  <x:set var="exprl" select="$expr/*[1]" scope="page"/>
  <x:set var="exprr" select="$expr/*[2]" scope="page"/>
  <c:set var="expr" value="${exprl}" scope="request" />
  <jsp:include page="expr.jsp"/> + <c:set var="expr"
  value="${exprr}" scope="request" />
  <jsp:include page="expr.jsp"/>
 </x:when>
</x:choose>
```

Fig. 4.12 PICO abstract syntax tree unparser in JSP.(continued)

4.4.3 *Velocity*

Velocity[6] is a template evaluator for Java. It provides a basic template metalanguage to reference Java objects, called Velocity Template Language. Velocity is text-based and has no assumptions on the language it generates. The aim of Velocity is to separate the presentation tier and the business tier, according to the model-view-controller (MVC) architecture in web applications. The metalanguage of Velocity supports complex computations, since it is possible to assign variables and write expressions. An example of a Velocity template is already discussed in Section 1.3.4.

The Velocity Template Language (VTL) has two core notations: object references written as a $ followed by its variable name, and statements starting with a # followed by the instruction. The object references can be directly used in the object code, similar to the substitution placeholder, or as variables in the statements. The VTL statements are shown in Table 4.5.

[6]http://velocity.apache.org (accessed on December 18, 2011)

Table 4.5 VTL Statements.

Statement	Description
`#set`	Assigns a value to a variable.
`#if( Expression )...`	Selects a text based on the result of the expression.
`#elseif( Expression ) ...#else...#end`	
`#foreach( Expression )...#end`	Iterates over a list returned by the expression and instantiates the text for each element in the list.
`#literal()...#end`	Disables the evaluator for a section.
`#include( filename )`	Includes the file named `filename` without interpretation of metacode.
`#parse( filename)`	Includes the file named `filename` with interpretation of metacode.
`#stop`	Stops the evaluator.
`#evaluate`	Evaluates a string containing metacode.
`#define`	Assigns a block of VTL to a reference.
`#macro`	Defines a repeated segment of a VTL template.

The Velocity PICO unparser is shown in Figure 4.13. Velocity provides internal handling of XML data, which enables a compact definition of the unparser. The difference between the Velocity PICO unparser and the implementation based on the unparser-complete metalanguage is the use of the `foreach` statement and `if`.

Velocity has the same problem with the variable scopes as JSP. As a consequence temporary variables are necessary when a subtemplate is recursively called multiple times, for example at lines 45–46.

```
begin
 declare
  #foreach ($decl in
   $root.getRootElement().getChild("decls")
                                   .getChild("list").getChildren() )
   $decl.getChild("value").getText().replace('"', ''):
   $decl.getChildren().get(1).getName()
   #if( $velocityHasNext ),#end
   #end;
   #set( $statements = $root.getRootElement().getChild("list") )
   #statements( $statements )
end

#macro (statements $statements)
#foreach ( $stm in $statements.getChildren() )
#if( $stm.getName() == "assignment" )
    $stm.getChild("value").getText().replace('"', '') :=
    #set($expr = $stm.getChildren().get(1) )#expr($expr)
#elseif( $stm.getName() == "while" )
    while #set($expr = $stm.getChildren().get(0) )
          #expr($expr) do #set($statements =
          $stm.getChildren().get(1))#statements( $statements )
    od
#elseif( $stm.getName() == "if" )
  #set($stms1 = $stm.getChildren().get(1) )
     #set($stms2 = $stm.getChildren().get(2) )
    if #set($expr = $stm.getChildren().get(0) )
        #expr($expr) then
        #set($statements = $stms1)#statements( $statements )
    else
        #set($statements = $stms2)#statements( $statements )
    fi
#end
#if( $velocityHasNext );#end
#end
#end
```

Fig. 4.13 PICO abstract syntax tree unparser in Velocity.(to be continued)

```
#macro (expr $expr )
#if( $expr.getName() == "natcon" )
  $expr.getValue()
#elseif( $expr.getName() == "strcon" )
  $expr.getValue()
#elseif( $expr.getName() == "id" )
  $expr.getValue().replace('"', '')
#elseif( $expr.getName() == "sub" )
  #set($exprl = $expr.getChildren().get(0) )
  #set($exprr = $expr.getChildren().get(1) )
  #expr($exprl)-#expr($exprr)
#elseif( $expr.getName() == "concat" )
  #set($exprl = $expr.getChildren().get(0) )
  #set($exprr = $expr.getChildren().get(1) )
  #expr($exprl)||#expr($exprr)
#elseif( $expr.getName() == "add" )
  #set($exprl = $expr.getChildren().get(0) )
  #set($exprr = $expr.getChildren().get(1) )
  #expr($exprl)+#expr($exprr)
#end
#end
```

Fig. 4.14 PICO abstract syntax tree unparser in Velocity.(continued)

4.4.4 *StringTemplate*

StringTemplate is a text-template system designed to enforce strict separation of model and view in a model-view-controller architecture. The developers of StringTemplate have designed the metalanguage using an evolution process starting from a simple "document with holes" to a sophisticated template evaluator. This separation of model and view is achieved by enforcing that the view cannot modify the model or perform calculations based on data from the model. Therefore, in comparison to JSP or ERb, the design of StringTemplate is optimized for enforcement of separation, not for Turing-completeness, nor amazingly-expressive "one-liners" [Parr (2004)].

This limited metalanguage enforces a template developer to exclude any calculations in the template and enforces to only consider the output code. It supports attribute references, subtemplates, implicit `for`-loops and `if` constructs. The authors of StringTemplate distilled four important metalanguage constructs, shown in Table 4.6.

Table 4.6 StringTemplate statements.

Statement	Description
$attribute$	Attribute references. For example: $user.name$.
$if(attribute)$subtemplate $else$subtemplate2$endif$	Conditional template inclusion. For example: $if(attr)$<title>$attr$</title>$endif$.
$template(argument-list)$	(Recursive) template references. For example: $item()$.
attribute:{anonymous-template}	Template application to a multi-valued attributes, i.e. iteration. For example: $users:{<tr><td>$it.name$</td><td> $it.age$</td></tr>}.

This set of constructs is, in their experience, powerful enough to specify templates for complex dynamic websites. They discovered a similarity between templates and grammars. The analogy with grammars is that (sub)templates are production rules and the attribute references are the terminals. The result of this observation is that the explicit for-loop construction is not necessary to generate lists. Instead of a for-loop, a kind of regular expression notation can be used, like $names:item()$, where the subtemplate item() is invoked for every element of the list names. Although the notation is shorter, the behavior is equal to an iteration placeholder.

Figure 4.15 shows the PICO unparser specified in StringTemplate. The compact notation for the iterator results in a compact definition of the unparser. The PICO unparser based on StringTemplate has the fewest lines of code compared to the other unparser specifications. The handling of the input data in StringTemplate is not as flexible as the other systems. StringTemplate uses a Java Map structure as input data, which is instantiated via a JavaScript Object Notation tree (JSON) [Crockford (2008)][7] of the input abstract syntax tree. JSON trees differ from the trees used in this book. JSON nodes are a representation of JavaScript objects with fields, such fields do not have an index and are only accessible via their labels. Fortunately, JSON supports ordered lists and as a workaround the ordered trees are emulated by pushing the children of a node into a list. Consider an ATerm of the form $f(t_1,\ldots,t_r)$, which is translated to a JSON node of the form $\{\text{“}f\text{”} : [t_1,\ldots,t_r]\}$, where the branches are stored in an ordered list, which can be queried using the location of an element. When t_i is a list, the translation will result in a nesting of listings, which cannot be queried by the mechanism of StringTemplate. Therefore, an ATerm t_i is translated to $\{\text{“}list\text{”} : t_i\}$, when t_i is a list. Alternatively index labels could be used for the branches, for

[7] http://www.json.org (accessed on December 18, 2011)

example $f(t_1,\ldots,t_r)$ to $\{``f": \{``one": t_1\},\ldots,\{``r": t_r\}\}$. The last translation is mapping the keyword `if` in the abstract syntax tree to `when`, since `if` is a keyword in StringTemplate and thus not allowed as label reference.

StringTemplate is not able to select an element in a list based on its position, but only provides standard list functions `first`, `last` and `rest`, where `first` returns the first element, `last` the last element of the list and `rest` the original list without the first element. The `first` and `last` functions are used to directly request an element of the list when possible, for the other arguments the `rest` function is used to obtain them. If the element at index k, where $k > 1$, is needed, the `rest` function is applied $k-1$ times and the first element of the last `rest` call is fetched: `first(rest( ... rest( list ) ... ))`. Line 23 of Figure 4.15 shows this approach.

4.4.5 *Evaluation*

The PICO unparser is implemented in ERb, JSP, Velocity and StringTemplate. The notable differences and similarities are summarized in this section.

StringTemplate and the unparser-complete metalanguage do not allow manipulation of data, and as a result calculations cannot be expressed. The metalanguages of the industrial approaches, ERb, JSP and Velocity, are Turing-complete. A Turing-complete metalanguage allows manipulating of data and storing of data. This is unnecessary to implement an unparser and can only lead to undesired programming in templates. Programming in templates can result in undesired tangling of concerns [Hunter (2000)].

Although the metalanguages of the three industrial approaches are Turing-complete, these systems share the same problem. They support recursion, but the assigned metavariables are by default globally available instead of scoped for the block where they are defined. Some workarounds are used to enable block scoping of metavariables, but it introduced undesired boilerplate code. In case of JSP and ERb an explicit stack mechanism for the metavariables must be defined. In case of Velocity helper metavariables is used to prevent updates of metavariables from an inner scope.

The PICO unparser based on StringTemplate has the fewest lines of code. StringTemplate provides a block scoping mechanism making explicit definition of a stack unnecessary. However, in comparison to the unparser-complete metalanguage, StringTemplate has the limitation that it can only handle unordered trees. An extra transformation is necessary to convert the input data from an ordered tree to an unordered tree.

```
picounparser.st:
begin
  declare
  $first(program).decls:decl(); separator=","$;
  $last(program).list:statements(); separator=";"$
end

decl.st:
$first(it.decl).value$:$last(it.decl).keys$

statements.st:
$if(it.assignment)$

$first(it.assignment).value$ :=
  $expr(expr=last(it.assignment))$
$elseif(it.while)$

while $expr(expr=first(it.while))$ do
  $last(it.while).list:statements(); separator=";"$
od
$else$
if $expr(expr=first(it.when))$ then
  $first(rest(it.when)).list:statements(); separator=";"$
else
  $last(it.when).list:statements(); separator=";"$
fi
$endif$

expr.st:
$if(expr.natcon)$
$expr.natcon$
$elseif(expr.strcon)$
"$expr.strcon$"
$elseif(expr.id)$
$expr.id$
$elseif(expr.sub)$
$expr(expr=first(expr.sub))$-$expr(expr=last(expr.sub))$
$elseif(expr.concat)$
$expr(expr=first(expr.concat))$||$expr(expr=last(expr.concat))$
$elseif(expr.add)$
$expr(expr=first(expr.add))$+$expr(expr=last(expr.add))$
$endif$
```

Fig. 4.15 PICO abstract syntax tree unparser in StringTemplate.

Besides the metalanguage, the (implicit) behavior of the template evaluator is important. Some versions of ERb print text to the output at spurious moments instead of building a string and returning it at the end of the evaluation. This is not a problem when having a single template, but with the recursively called subtemplates, the output characters are printed in the wrong order. Subtemplates must be first evaluated and the resulting string must be inserted in the calling template and not directly be sent to the output stream.

4.5 Conclusions

In this chapter an unparser-complete metalanguage is defined. This metalanguage is based on the linear deterministic top-down tree-to-string transducer. Five constructs are provided: subtemplates, match-replace placeholder, substitution placeholder, iteration placeholder and conditional placeholder. This metalanguage is unparser-complete as it supports match-replace placeholders and subtemplates, including recursive template evaluation. The substitution placeholder, iteration placeholder and conditional placeholder are abbreviations for combinations of subtemplates and match-replace placeholders. This metalanguage cannot change the input data to enforce separation of model and view.

Implementations of unparsers for the PICO language are discussed to compare the unparser-complete metalanguage with the metalanguages of ERb, Velocity, JSP and StringTemplate. The unparser implemented using StringTemplate has the fewest lines of code, but in contrast with the unparser-complete metalanguage, StringTemplate cannot directly accept all regular trees without a translation function. The metalanguages of ERb, Velocity, JSP are Turing-complete. Increased expression power of a metalanguage increases the chance of undesired programming in templates. Programming in templates may result in tangling of concerns. Although these industrial approaches provide a Turing-complete metalanguage they do not have a block scoping mechanism for the metavariables. A workaround for proper handling of metavariable scopes was necessary to implement the PICO unparser.

Chapter 5

Syntax-Safe Templates

Writing templates, and code generators in general, is a complex and error prone task. This complexity[1] mainly results from mixing multiple languages in a template, executed at different stages, and the incompleteness of the object code. Manual verification of incomplete object code is hard to do and computers cannot execute incomplete code.

Text-based template evaluators do not improve the situation, as they are not able to check the object code. They are only aware of the syntax of the metalanguage, while the object language is considered as a string without any required structure. These evaluators only process and check the metacode and do not deal with the correctness of the rest of the template. Ignorance of the correctness of the object code can lead to undetected syntax errors [Sheard (2001)]. Misspellings in the object code, such as missing semicolons, are easily made and in such case text-based template evaluators generate syntactically incorrect code without giving a warning.

A test approach based on generating all possible outputs followed by verifying the result using a compiler or interpreter seems a valid route. However, to guarantee that a template generates syntactically correct sentences during production use, a possibly exploding amount of input data test cases must be defined for every template. Furthermore, an error must be manually traced back to its origin, which is not always obvious, such as sometimes experienced when using the C preprocessor [Ernst *et al.* (2002)], where the compiler error messages point to the post-processed code instead of the original source code. Checking the template directly offers accurate error messages, pointing to the origin of the error.

Beside the problems during development, dynamic text-based code generation as used in web applications can result in serious security issues, like malicious code injection. An example of malicious code injection is discussed in Chapter 7.

[1] The complexity here considered is complexity in the broadest sense of the word and not for example computational complexity.

In order to remove the possibility of syntax errors in the generated code, the notion of *syntax-safety* for templates is introduced in this chapter [Arnoldus *et al.* (2007)]. Syntax-safety is a property of a code generator, where for every possible input the output of a syntax-safe code generator can be recognized by a parser for the intended resulting language, i.e. the code generator produces output sentences of the language $\mathscr{L}(G_{intended})$. The intended language is the language for which the code generator should produce sentences, for example, Java or C.
This chapter presents an approach based on constructing a grammar for templates containing the definition of the metalanguage and the object language of a template. The construction of a template grammar is generic and based on the combination of the metalanguage grammar and the (off-the-shelf) object language grammar, where only a combination grammar connecting both has to be defined manually.
The benefit of a template grammar is that not only the output code is syntactically correct, but also syntax errors are found in the template itself. Having a template grammar enables parsing the complete template, which ensures that all (sub)sentences are syntactically correct, without the need of compiling or interpreting generated code. Hence, this approach helps to avoid syntax errors, both in the metacode and in the object code, before the template is used for generating code.
Figure 5.1 shows the architecture used for syntax-safe template evaluation. The first stage is parsing the template using a template grammar resulting in a parse tree of the template. The second stage is the evaluation of templates. The evaluator uses the parsed template and input data as input and generates the output code. A syntax-safe template evaluator called *Repleo* is implemented. Repleo is a generic syntax-safe template evaluator system parameterized with the object language grammar to ensure the output is syntactically correct. The metalanguage of Repleo is unparser-complete, as discussed in the previous chapters. Chapter 6 discusses this evaluator.

5.1 Syntax-Safe Templates

During the discussion of the metalanguage for templates in Chapter 4, the object language of templates was ignored. The object language was considered as strings, i.e. sequences of alphabet symbols. Considering the object language as strings does not guarantee that the output sentences are well-formed with respect to their intended output language $\mathscr{L}(G_{intended})$. This section will discuss the requirements to ensure that a template cannot produce sentences that are not in $\mathscr{L}(G_{intended})$.

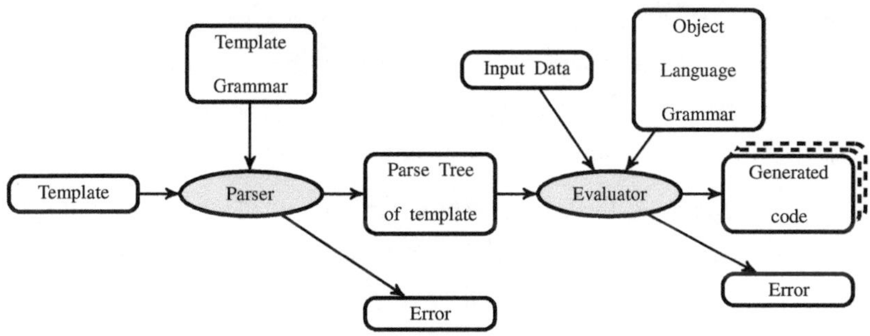

Fig. 5.1 Syntax-safe evaluation architecture.

In a template the following languages are involved: $\mathscr{L}(G_{object})$, $\mathscr{L}(G_{meta})$, $\mathscr{L}(G_{template})$ and $\mathscr{L}(G_{output})$. The sentences and structure of the template directly copied to the output sentence of the evaluator, i.e. the object code, are defined by the object language $\mathscr{L}(G_{object})$. The placeholders in the template are sentences of the (context-free) meta-language $\mathscr{L}(G_{meta})$ and they are interpreted by the template evaluator and not propagated to the output sentence. The template is a sentence of $\mathscr{L}(G_{template})$, which is based on the union of the grammars of G_{object}, G_{meta} and production rules connecting both. The sentences produced by a template form the output language $\mathscr{L}(G_{output})$.

For example, given the template `<: $x :>b<: $y :>`, where `$x` and `$y` are metavariables bound to `$x = a` respectively `$y = c`. Evaluating this template results in the sentence `abc`. Considering the different languages, the following statements must hold for the grammars describing this template:

- `abc` is a sentence of $\mathscr{L}(G_{output})$;
- `<: $x :>` and `<: $y :>` are sentences of $\mathscr{L}(G_{meta})$;
- `b` and `n1n2n3`, where `n1`, `n2` and `n3` are nonterminals, are sentences of $\mathscr{L}(G_{object})$. `n1n2n3` represents the structure defined by the object language grammar. The concrete implementation of grammar G_{object} is undefined as long as it produces a language with a sentence of the form `n1n2n3`. Furthermore, since the template contains a `b` on the place of `n2` the language $\mathscr{L}(n_2)$ must at least contain the sentence `b`;
- `<: $x :>b<: $y :>` is a sentence of $\mathscr{L}(G_{template})$.

$\mathscr{L}(G_{object})$, $\mathscr{L}(G_{meta})$, $\mathscr{L}(G_{template})$ and $\mathscr{L}(G_{output})$ were discussed from a descriptive point of view. Since the goal is syntax-safe templates, these languages will be discussed from a declarative point of view, where the languages describe the allowed sentences. First a new language $\mathscr{L}(G_{intended})$ is introduced. This language is the intended output language of a code generator, where $\mathscr{L}(G_{intended})$ should be a context-free (programming) language. It is undesirable that a metaprogram can produce sentences, which are not part of $\mathscr{L}(G_{intended})$; a metaprogram should be syntax-safe.

Definition 5.1.1 (Syntax-safety). A metaprogram p is called syntax-safe with respect to the intended language $\mathscr{L}(G_{intended})$ if p, independent of its input, always generates a sentence s which is a sentence of the intended language $\mathscr{L}(G_{intended})$. In other words program p is syntax-safe if $\mathscr{L}(G_{output}) \subseteq \mathscr{L}(G_{intended})$.

Syntax-safe template evaluation involves the construction of a $G_{template}$ describing the templates, which always result in generation of a sentence in $\mathscr{L}(G_{intended})$. A template is a sentence of $\mathscr{L}(G_{template})$, which is based on a combination of the grammars G_{object} and G_{meta}. The next lemma shows that $\mathscr{L}(G_{object})$ is at least equal to $\mathscr{L}(G_{output})$.

Lemma 5.1.1. *The output language of a template $\mathscr{L}(G_{output})$ is a superset of the object language $\mathscr{L}(G_{object})$.*

Proof. Given a template $template[s]$ without placeholders, then $s \in \mathscr{L}(G_{object})$. The object code is copied to the output of the template evaluator $start(s, \varepsilon) \Rightarrow s$, so s must be a sentence of the language $\mathscr{L}(G_{output})$. So all sentences of $\mathscr{L}(G_{object})$ must be in $\mathscr{L}(G_{output})$. Beside the templates without placeholders, the template may contain placeholders. Placeholders can be substituted by any sentence, which does not have to be specified by the object language, as a result $\mathscr{L}(G_{output}) \supseteq \mathscr{L}(G_{object})$. ∎

In case of a text-based template environment $\mathscr{L}(G_{object})$ is defined as all possible sentences using an alphabet (most times the set of ASCII characters) minus the syntax defined by $\mathscr{L}(G_{meta})$. Considering the example `<: $x :>b<: $y :>`, the placeholders `<: $x :>` and `<: $y :>` are not defined by the object language, otherwise the template evaluator cannot make a distinction between metacode and object code. The $\mathscr{L}(G_{object})$ used in text-based templates has no restrictions, since it is only defined as a sequence of alphabet symbols. The result is that the output language $\mathscr{L}(G_{output})$ of text-based templates is often a superset of the intended output language $\mathscr{L}(G_{intended})$. This $\mathscr{L}(G_{object})$ enables the template evaluator to generate a sentence that is not in the set of sentences produced by $\mathscr{L}(G_{intended})$ and thus can result in generating code containing syntax errors. For example in case of generating code for the PICO language, it is possible in a text-based template environment to generate an identifier starting with a number, which is not allowed by the PICO language.

In order to satisfy the requirements for syntax-safety, it is necessary to ensure that the object code in a template exist of (sub)sentences of $\mathscr{L}(G_{intended})$ and that the metacode is replaced by (sub)sentences of $\mathscr{L}(G_{intended})$. The approach to guarantee that placeholders are substituted by (sub)sentences of $\mathscr{L}(G_{intended})$ is discussed in Chapter 6.

In order to ensure the object code of a template is a (sub)sentence of $G_{intended}$, a template grammar $G_{template}$ is constructed defining all valid templates for $\mathscr{L}(G_{intended})$. The G_{object} part of $G_{template}$ should be equal to $G_{intended}$ and the start symbol of $G_{template}$ should also be equal to the start symbol of $G_{intended}$. Indeed, $\mathscr{L}(G_{template})$ should also contain the sentences without placeholders, i.e. sentences of $\mathscr{L}(G_{intended})$.

Merging both grammars is not sufficient, as a connection between both grammars must be made. Otherwise the sentences of the metalanguage are not allowed as sub sentences of the object language. A context-free language can be extended by adding new alternatives for nonterminals. When a template contains placeholders, G_{object} should be extended with the placeholder syntax of G_{meta} resulting in a $G_{template}$ in such way that the template is a sentence of that instantiated $G_{template}$.

The placeholder syntax defined in G_{meta} is added as an alternative for nonterminals of G_{object} in $G_{template}$. Hence, the placeholders in syntax-safe templates can only replace context-free parts, as it cannot cover multiple nonterminals. For example, in a text-based template it is possible to write the PICO template `BEG<: id() :>ND`, while in a template based on a context-free grammar it is only possible to write `BEGIN <: id() :> a := 1 END`. In the first case the placeholder overlaps multiple (non)terminal symbols, while in the second case the placeholder can be parsed as the nonterminal *DECLS*. The next theorem shows that a $G_{template}$ can be constructed ensuring that the object code and its output language is a (sub)sentence of $\mathscr{L}(G_{intended})$.

Theorem 5.1.1. *For every $\mathscr{L}(G_{intended})$ a template grammar $G_{template}$ containing placeholder syntax can be constructed, which ensures that the object code is a (sub)sentence of that $\mathscr{L}(G_{intended})$.*

Proof. Given a template $tmp = template[s]$, evaluating this template results in the output sentence $start(tmp, \varepsilon) \Rightarrow s$. The template is syntax-safe if $s \in \mathscr{L}(G_{intended})$, i.e. parsing s using $G_{intended}$ should return a parse tree. So $G_{template}$ must define a language, which is a subset or equal to the language of $G_{intended}$, otherwise it is possible to generate a sentence s

not in $\mathscr{L}(G_{intended})$.

A template can contain placeholders. They are not part of the syntax of the object language. In order to ensure syntax-safety, under a strict condition $G_{template}$ may be extended with the syntax of the placeholders. This condition states that all additional placeholder syntax is replaced by valid (sub)sentences of $G_{intended}$ during evaluation of the template. The metalanguage has two kernel placeholders: the subtemplate call placeholder and the match-replace placeholder. For both placeholder, extending nonterminals in $G_{template}$ is syntax-safe.

Assume that $G_{template}$ contains an object language production rule of the form $S \to n_1 n2$, where S is the start symbol and n_1 and n_2 are nonterminals. Consider the templates *tmps*:

```
template[
 <: n1() :> s2
]
n1[
 s1
]
```

where `s1` and `s2` may recursively contain placeholders. The evaluation

$$start(tmps, t) \Rightarrow s$$

is syntax-safe, when for every input data (sub)tree t accepted by the template the output $s \in \mathscr{L}(G_{intended})$. That is, when `<: n1() :>` replaces itself by sentence of $\mathscr{L}(n_1)$ and $s2 \in \mathscr{L}(n_2)$. Subtemplate `n1` must produce a sentence of $\mathscr{L}(n_1)$ to ensure that `<: n1() :>` replaces itself by sentence of $\mathscr{L}(n_1)$, which means that the production rule $TMPS \to$ "$n1$["n_1"]" is in $G_{template}$, where $TMPS$ is the nonterminal representing the list of (sub)templates. Since the subtemplate a produces a sentence of $\mathscr{L}(n_1)$ it is allowed to add the production rule

$$n_1 \to \text{“ <: } n1(\text{”}Expr\text{“}) \text{ :> ”}$$

in $G_{template}$, where $Expr$ is the nonterminal for the metalanguage expressions.

Assume that $G_{template}$ contains object language production rules $S \to n_1$ and $S \to n_2$, where S is the start symbol and n_1 and n_2 are nonterminals. Consider the template *tmps*:

```
template[
 <: match :>
   <: mp =:> s1
```

```
   <: mp' =:> s2
 <: end :>
]
```

where s_1 and s_2 may recursively contain placeholders. For every t accepted by the template, that is if t matches mp or mp', the evaluation $start(tmps,t) \Rightarrow s$ is syntax-safe, when $s \in \mathscr{L}(G_{intended})$. The match-replace selects either s_1 or s_2, which means that both s_1 and s_2 must be a sentence of $\mathscr{L}(G_{intended})$, i.e. a sentence of $\mathscr{L}(n_1)$ or $\mathscr{L}(n_2)$. In order to ensure that the template fulfills this requirement the following productions rules are added to $G_{template}$:

- $S \rightarrow$ " <: match" *Expr* " :> " *MatchRuleS*$+$ " <: end :> "
- *MatchRuleS* $\rightarrow$ " <: " *MP* " =:> " *S*

where *MP* is the nonterminal for the match-pattern syntax and *Expr* for the metalanguage expression syntax. The suffix *S* of the *MatchRule* nonterminal is to specify that only match-rules containing object code for the nonterminal *S* are allowed.
A $G_{template}$ constructed using these rules defines the language of templates resulting in a syntax-safe template evaluation for $G_{intended}$. If a template is a sentence of such a $G_{template}$ then its evaluation result is a sentence of $\mathscr{L}(G_{intended})$, since the applied placeholders are always replaced by a (sub)sentence valid for the nonterminal where they are applied. ■

After constructing a $G_{template}$ it is possible to build a parse tree of a template. A schematic view of such parse tree of a template is shown in Figure 5.2. G_{object} and $G_{template}$ have the same start symbol. Black sub-parse trees visualize the placeholders. The G_{meta} part of $G_{template}$ is used to parse them. A special case is the black part that contains a white subtree. At that point a placeholder contains a piece of object code, which is used as a pattern to replace the placeholder, as the case for the match-replace placeholders. The match-replace starts with a piece of metacode and fragments of object code are defined in the match-rules. Black and white parts may be arbitrarily nested. This nesting represents recursive nesting of placeholders, such as a match-replace placeholder applied inside a match-rule of another match-replace placeholder.
Having a $G_{template}$ enables the parsing of the entire template. The metalanguage and object language in a template are parsed simultaneously and misspellings in these languages are detected during the parsing phase. Syntax errors are found in the entire template. This helps to find syntax errors in the static part of the template before the template is evaluated,

Fig. 5.2 Schematic view of a parse tree of a template.

and thus input data is not necessary to detect these errors. A template only based on match-replace placeholders and subtemplates is already syntax-safe. When the template accepts the input data tree, it generates a sentence of $\mathscr{L}(G_{intended})$. An invalid input data tree will not result in output code, but will result in an error, because it is not accepted by the template.

5.2 The Metalanguage Grammar

In this section the implementation of template grammars in SDF [Heering *et al.* (1989)] is presented. The syntax of the placeholders is based on the metalanguage of Chapter 4. First, the syntax shared by all metalanguage constructs is discussed. After the shared syntax is presented, the syntax of the subtemplates, match-replace placeholder and substitution placeholder is given.

The template grammar is obtained by combining the object language grammar and placeholder grammar by adding the placeholder syntax as alternative to the object language nonterminals. SDF offers *module parameters* to specialize the placeholder syntax for a specific nonterminal, instead of redefining the placeholder syntax for every nonterminal, as proposed by Theorem 5.1.1. An SDF grammar module may have a number of (non)terminal parameters, which can be substituted during the import of a module by the actual required (non)terminal. When the placeholder grammar is added as an alternative for an object language nonterminal, this grammar is parameterized with that object language nonterminal to inject the placeholder syntax as alternative for it. The use of module parameters results in a compact definition of the grammar $G_{template}$. A template grammar is defined by a combination module importing the placeholder syntax for each object language nonterminal, which should be extended.

It should be possible to use another syntax formalism. When the grammar formalism does not support modularization and parameterization, one can choose to instantiate the placeholder injections using a code generator. The most important feature is that the chosen parser supports ambiguities as template grammars can be easily become ambiguous. An ambiguity occurs when a (sub) parse tree of a (sub) sentence can be constructed in multiple ways using the production rules of a context-free grammar. In the situation of the constructed template grammars ambiguities can have two causes: either the object language grammar itself is already ambiguous or the combination of object language grammar and metalanguage grammar introduces ambiguities.

5.2.1 *Shared Syntax*

The syntax definitions of the three placeholders have a number of shared syntax artifacts. This section discusses the syntax of the hedges, explicit syntactical typing of placeholders and meta-comment.

5.2.1.1 *Hedges*

Hedges are syntactical constructs used to indicate the transition between object language and metalanguage. The hedges make the transition between metacode and object code explicit, so humans can easily recognize the transistions. In text-template systems hedges are obligatory to recognize the placeholders. When a template is parsed and both object language and metalanguage are part of the template grammar, hedges are not longer necessary [Vinju (2006)]. The parser will recognize the placeholders as metacode as it cannot be parsed as a piece of object code. If the syntax of the metalanguage overlaps with the syntax of the object language ambiguities can occur. These ambiguities are efficiently eliminated when hedges are used that are not part of the object language. In the other cases disambiguation strategies should be defined in order to filter these ambiguities [Vinju (2006)].

It is essential that the hedges are a sequence of characters disjoint of the syntax of the object language to prevent ambiguities. Since the hedges are only used during the parsing phase and have no semantic meaning, the definition can be overridden by an alternative sequence of characters. The character sequences `<:` and `:>` are chosen for aesthetic reasons. These default hedges are defined in the SDF module of Figure 5.3.

5.2.1.2 *Syntactical Typing of Placeholders*

Template grammars can become ambiguous when placeholders can be parsed as multiple nonterminals. In Section 6.6 the origin of ambiguities are discussed in detail and a filter to handle them is presented. However, the use of an ambiguity filter reduces the performance of the template evaluator. Therefore a syntactical construction "`sort:Sort`" is included to force the parser to recognize a placeholder as a specified nonterminal. The `Sort` is replaced by the actual name of the nonterminal during parameterization of the placeholder syntax (see Section 2.6.2 for explanation). This construct can be used to disambiguate a placeholder when multiple types of placeholders fit on a position. For example, it is used in Figure 6.8 at line 24 to force that the placeholder `<: $stms sort:STATEMENT* :>` is parsed as the nonterminal `STATEMENT*`.
When multiple object language nonterminals are extended an overlap between the `PlaceHolderType`'s will occur. The parameterized nonterminal feature of SDF, supported by the `[[Sort]]` syntax, is used to avoid name clashes between different instances of the same imported placeholder.

5.2.1.3 *Meta-comment*

The last provided syntactical artifact is *meta-comment*: `<:%% meta-comment :>`. Meta-comment is not copied to the output code and its purpose is documenting template code, which is not relevant in the generated code. It is an alternative for the `LAYOUT` sort, which is a special kind of nonterminal in the SGLR [Visser (1997)] implementation in order to handle layout. The `LAYOUT` sort represents all symbols, which have no semantic meaning. The other layout artifacts are one-to-one copied to the output, necessary for output languages with layout criteria and to generate human readable output code.

5.2.2 *Subtemplates*

Two syntactical constructions are necessary for subtemplates. First subtemplates must be declared and identifiable, second a subtemplate call placeholder is necessary to instantiate a subtemplate. The subtemplate is declared via a label, followed by a fragment of code. The subtemplate call placeholder consists of a pair of hedges combined with the identifier of the subtemplate and an expression to provide a new input data context to the subtemplate. Figure 5.4 shows the grammar definition. The annotation `placeholder("subtemplate")` is used by the evaluator, see Chapter 6, to detect the placeholder.
In order to parse a template with subtemplate call placeholders, it is necessary to embed

```
module Common["Sort" Sort]

exports
 sorts BeginTag EndTag

 lexical syntax
   "<:"              -> BeginTag
   ":>"              -> EndTag

   "sort:" "Sort"    -> PlaceHolderType[[Sort]]

   BeginTag "%%" line:~[\n]* EndTag
                     -> LAYOUT
```

Fig. 5.3 Syntax shared by all placeholders.

```
module PlaceHolderSubTemplate["Sort" Sort]

imports Common["Sort" Sort]
imports basic/IdentifierCon
imports Expression

exports
  sorts Template

  context-free syntax
    IdCon "[" Sort "]" -> Template

    BeginTag IdCon"(" Expression ")"
             PlaceHolderType[[Sort]]? EndTag
                       -> Sort {placeholder("subtemplate")}
```

Fig. 5.4 Syntax for subtemplates.

the placeholder syntax in the object language. This grammar module defines the placeholder syntax with the generic result nonterminal `Sort`. The definition can be added as an alternative to an arbitrary object language nonterminal. The injection of the placeholder in the object language is achieved by importing the placeholder grammar, while parameterizing this module with an object language nonterminal. During parameterization `Sort` is internally replaced by the object language nonterminal, as a result the placeholder syntax becomes an alternative for that object language nonterminal.

The parameterizing of `Sort` is compliant with the proposed construction of template grammars in Theorem 5.1.1. The identifier nonterminal used to label the subtemplates gener-

```
module PlaceHolderMatchReplace["Sort" Sort]

imports Common["Sort" Sort]
imports Expression
imports MatchPattern

exports
  sorts MatchRule
  context-free syntax
    BeginTag "match" Expression
             PlaceHolderType[[Sort]]? EndTag
        MatchRule[[Sort]]+
        BeginTag "end" EndTag
             -> Sort {placeholder("matchreplace")}

    BeginTag MatchPattern "=" EndTag
        Sort
             -> MatchRule[[Sort]]
```

Fig. 5.5 Syntax for match-replace placeholder.

alizes from the fixed label in production rules of Theorem 5.1.1. This means the template evaluator should check whether the called subtemplate result in the correct grammatical sort. Syntax-safe evaluation is discussed in Chapter 6.

An example of the use of a subtemplate can be found in Figure 6.8. At lines 38-50 the subtemplate `expr` is declared. Amongst others, this subtemplate is called at line 23.

5.2.3 *Match-Replace*

The match-replace placeholder is a construction containing multiple match-rules. Each match-rule has a fragment of object code accompanied by a tree match-pattern. The match-replace replaces itself with a fragment of object code defined in the match-rule. This implies that the fragment of object code in a match-rule must be parsed as the same object language nonterminal as the match-replace substitutes.

The principle of extending the object language is the same as the subtemplate call placeholder. The match-replace placeholder is also injected as an alternative for an object language placeholder. Furthermore, it supports an expression to specify the context for the match-rules. This expression is evaluated before the match-rules are tried. Figure 5.5 shows the generic match-replace grammar module.

A match-rule contains a `MatchPattern` and a fragment of resulting object language code. The `MatchPattern` is a tree pattern containing possible metavariables. The syntax de-

```
module PlaceHolderSubstitution["Sort" Sort]

imports Common["Sort" Sort]
imports Expression

exports
  context-free syntax
    BeginTag Expression PlaceHolderType[[Sort]]? EndTag
                       -> Sort {placeholder("substitution")}
    "end"              -> IdCon {reject}
```

Fig. 5.6 Syntax for substitution placeholder.

pends on the particular tree representation, i.e. ATerms [van den Brand *et al.* (2000)]. The approach is not limited to ATerms and it can be used with another tree syntax like XML or JSON. The `MatchPattern` supports metavariables defined as a dollar sign followed by a label with the character class `[A-Za-z][A-Za-z\-0-9]*`.

The match-replace syntax definition is compliant with the proposed construction of template grammars in Theorem 5.1.1. The result code of a match-rule is of the same syntactical type as the injection of the match-replace, which is visible in the grammar definition. The `MatchRule` contains the `Sort` nonterminal and finally the match-replace is injected in the `Sort` nonterminal as alternative. The following chain of productions is recognizable: $Sort \Rightarrow MatchRule[[Sort]]+ \Rightarrow Sort$. This structure enforces that all possible results of match-replace are of the nonterminal `Sort`, i.e. it is not possible to mix different sorts in the match-rule set. The `MatchRule` nonterminal is augmented with the parameterized name `[[Sort]]`, so that the `MatchRule` nonterminal is unique for every object nonterminal extended with placeholder syntax.

Multiple examples of the use of the match-replace placeholder can be found in figure 6.8. For instance at lines 5-14 a match-replace placeholder is used.

5.2.4 *Substitution Placeholder*

A substitution placeholder consists of a couple of hedges and an expression to obtain the data to replace it. The syntactical pattern for the substitution placeholder is `<: Expr :>` or `<: Expr sort:SORT :>`, where the capitalized `SORT` is the nonterminal name. This last construction is used to force the parser to parse the placeholder as the given syntactical type to solve ambiguities. A generic syntax definition of the substitution placeholder is given in Figure 5.6.

The substitution placeholder is a superfluous construct as it can be expressed using subtemplates and match-replace placeholders. There are two reasons to discuss this placeholder. First, the substitution is an intuitive construct expected when using templates. Second, in a syntax-safe template evaluator implicit behavior can be added to it, which will be discussed in Chapter 6. The difference with the previous two discussed metalanguage constructs is that syntax-safety is not enforced by the grammar, but must be handled by the template evaluator.

A final note: For aesthetic and readability reasons the keyword `end` is used as closing tag of the match-replace placeholder. Since `end` can be parsed as nonterminal `IdCon` an ambiguity may occur on the closing tag of the match-replace placeholder given that it also can be recognized as a substitution placeholder. The `end` label is rejected as `IdCon` in order to remove the chance of this ambiguity. This reject restricts the use of the word `end` as label in the input data. One can choose to replace `end` with a sequence of characters, which cannot be parsed as an `IdCon` in order to remove this restriction.

5.3 Grammar Merging

The template grammar $G_{template}$ is instantiated by combining the G_{object} and G_{meta} via importing both grammars in a combination module and describing their connection. In order to connect the object language and the metalanguage, nonterminals of the G_{object} are extended with an extra alternative to connect the object language nonterminal with the root nonterminal of the metalanguage.

The presented placeholder syntax definitions are independent of the object language grammar. In order to inject the placeholder syntax in the object language grammar, the placeholder grammar modules are imported in the combination module and at the same time parameterized with a nonterminal of the object language grammar. At the moment that the placeholders are imported and parameterized with a nonterminal of the object language, the placeholder is injected as an alternative for that nonterminal. Since all three placeholder constructs are simultaneously applied to a nonterminal, the three previously defined placeholder modules are combined in a single module called `PlaceHolder`, which is shown in Figure 5.7. A small note must be made on the parameterization arguments: `"Sort"` must be the literal name of the `Sort` and is used as a keyword to fix the sort of substitution placeholders syntactically, since SDF has no syntax to do this automatically.

The last grammar module `StartSymbol`, shown in Figure 5.8, is of a more operational

```
module PlaceHolder["Sort" Sort]

imports PlaceHolderSubstitution["Sort" Sort]
imports PlaceHolderSubTemplate["Sort" Sort]
imports PlaceHolderMatchReplace["Sort" Sort]
```

Fig. 5.7 Combination of all placeholders to a single module.

```
module StartSymbol["Sort" Sort]

imports basic/IdentifierCon
imports utilities/fileIO/Directory
imports PlaceHolderSubstitution["Filename" Filename]
imports PlaceHolderSubstitution["SubDirectory" SubDirectory]
imports PlaceHolder["Template*" Template*]

exports
  context-free start-symbols
    TemplateSet

  sorts Template

  context-free syntax
    "[" Template* "]"                      -> TemplateSet
    "template" "[" File "," Sort "]"       -> Template
    "template" "[" Sort "]"                -> Template
    "template"                             -> IdCon {reject}
```

Fig. 5.8 Start symbol module.

nature. It defines a start symbol `TemplateSet` representing a list of (sub)templates. The template with the identifier `template` is the starting point of the evaluator and it contains object code for `Sort`, which is most likely equal to the start symbol of the object language. This start template may be accompanied by a file name to instantiate a file containing the generated code. File handling is necessary for using templates in the case studies of Chapter 7. The nonterminals `Filename` and `SubDirectory` belonging to the nonterminal `File` are extended with placeholders to enable parameterization. The `Template*` nonterminal is also extended with placeholder syntax to enable iteration.

All ingredients for the combination module to instantiate a template grammar are defined. The combination module is the only object language specific part of the $G_{template}$ definition. It imports the object language, it instantiates the `StartSymbol` module and it defines which nonterminals of the object language are injected with placeholder syntax.

```
module Template-Pico

imports Pico

imports StartSymbol["PROGRAM*" PROGRAM*]
imports PlaceHolder["NatCon" NatCon]
imports PlaceHolder["StrCon" StrCon]
imports PlaceHolder["TYPE" TYPE]
imports PlaceHolder["PICO-ID" PICO-ID]
imports PlaceHolder["EXP" EXP]
imports PlaceHolder["STATEMENT" STATEMENT]
imports PlaceHolder["ID-TYPE" ID-TYPE]
imports PlaceHolder["DECLS" DECLS]
imports PlaceHolder["PROGRAM" PROGRAM]
imports PlaceHolder["STATEMENT*" {STATEMENT ";" }*]
imports PlaceHolder["ID-TYPE*" {ID-TYPE "," }*]
```

Fig. 5.9 PICO combination module.

A side effect of the injection of placeholders in an object language is that the grammar $G_{template}$ often becomes highly ambiguous. The ambiguities are caused by the possibility to recognize multiple parameterized placeholders. The chance of ambiguities increases if more object language nonterminals are extended with placeholder syntax. Therefore automatic parameterization of placeholders with every object language nonterminal is undesired. The selection process of the nonterminals for parameterization of the placeholders must be done manually. In Section 6.6 this problem will be discussed in more detail. It is hard to automatically predict which sorts must be selected for the parameterization of placeholders. A similar problem is discussed in [Visser (2002)]: although the authors generate their connection rules, they consider it useful to have full control over the selection of the nonterminals.

Figure 5.9 shows the combination module for the PICO Language. This template grammar can parse the unparser template of Figure 4.7.
There is one requirement left for the object language grammar. Nonterminals in G_{object} must not be defined in G_{meta}, that is $N_{object} \cap N_{meta} = \emptyset$; otherwise undesirable and uncontrolled nonterminal injections occur. In practice this can be simply achieved by adding a unique prefix or suffix to the (non)terminals of a grammar, or a typical SDF specific solution consists of parameterization of all nonterminals of a language with its language name to create a namespace [Bravenboer *et al.* (2006b)].

The modularity of SDF allows specifying the metalanguage and object language grammars separately. The advantage of this approach is the ease of using off-the-shelf object language grammars [Klint *et al.* (2005)]. In case an off-the-shelf object language grammar is not available and full syntax checking of templates is not required, one can decide to use an *island grammar* [Moonen (2001)]. An island grammar only defines small parts of a language. The rest of the language is defined at a global level, for example as a list of characters.

5.4 Similar Approaches

SafeGen [Huang *et al.* (2005)] is an approach aiming for type safe templates. It uses an automatic theorem prover to prove the well-formedness of the generated code for all possible inputs.

This approach heavily depends on the assumptions that the input is a valid Java program and the knowledge of the Java type system. The template programmer can define placeholders (cursors) to obtain data from the Java input program. Those placeholders must contain constraints based on their use in the template. For example a placeholder in the `extends` section of a class in a template must guarantee the extended class is not final. A prover used to check the constraints ensures that the template cannot generate ill-formed code.

SafeGen depends on the knowledge that the input and output program is Java. This fact makes the environment incapable of generating code from an abstract high-level input data in another representation than the object language. Although the approach could give more and better guarantees about the generator, switching to another object language and input data representation is hard. A template grammar, such as described here, is more flexible in the choice of input data language and output language.

Another approach to achieve syntax-safe code generation is using *abstract parsing* [Kong *et al.* (2009)]. Abstract parsing is a statically analysis technique for checking the syntax of generated strings. It uses data-flow analysis and checks via a kind of parser if the data-flow produces a sentence conform the intended output language grammar. During runtime no further checking is required. This technique requires an analyzer for the data-flow to feed the parser. Abstract parsing is a generalization of the template grammar, as it can be used for every kind of metaprogram, when data-flow analysis is possible. In contrast with abstract parsing, syntax-safe templates do not need external data-flow analysis to achieve syntax-safety.

5.5 Conclusions

In this chapter an approach to define a grammar with syntax rules for all languages in a template is presented. Having such a grammar allows to detect syntax errors in the object code of a template while parsing the template, instead of dealing with syntax errors at compile time of the generated code. The whole template is parsed, and thus checked for syntax errors, including rarely generated code in conditional placeholders. Checking a template offers accurate error messages, instead of checking the generated code such as the output of the C preprocessor [Ernst *et al.* (2002)]. It is the first step to achieve more safety in template evaluation and helps to avoid syntax errors, like misspellings. The templates are syntactically not different from text-templates and as a result they provide the same user experience.

The modular grammar definition combined with parameterization allows to instantiate template grammars for different object languages with minimal redefinition and cloning. The advantage of this approach is the ease of using off-the-shelf object language grammars.

Parsing templates on its own is not sufficient to guarantee that the output of the template evaluator is a sentence of the output language. In Chapter 6 syntax-safe evaluation is discussed, including the requirements for it.

Chapter 6

Repleo: Syntax-Safe Template Evaluation

Parsing a template alone is not sufficient to achieve syntax-safe code generation. Via the introduction of the substitution placeholder and the free choice of identifiers for subtemplates, correctness of the parse tree of a template does not imply that the generated code will be syntactically correct. For example, a subtemplate call placeholder with identifier s is applied for nonterminal n_1, while the root nonterminal of the subtemplate with the identifier s is n_2 and thus not equal to n_1. Although the substitution placeholder breaks static verification of syntax-safety, it is a design choice to leave it in the metalanguage, as it is one of the "natural" constructs in a template metalanguage. Most (industrial) template evaluators offer the substitution placeholder. Figure 1.13, Figure 4.11, Figure 4.13 and Figure 4.15 show examples of applications of the substitution placeholder in related template evaluators. The substitution placeholder allows replacing it by unstructured strings stored in the input data. Therefore, it is necessary to dynamically verify that the string stored in the input data is allowed to replace the placeholder.

This chapter discusses the implementation of a syntax-safe template evaluator. The template grammar is used to obtain a parse tree of a template and to check the syntax of object code and metacode in one parse phase. The template evaluator uses the object language grammar while substituting the placeholders to guarantee that the output parse tree complies to the object language grammar. Syntax-safe evaluation is achieved by checking that a placeholder parsed as nonterminal A_{object} is replaced by a sub parse tree where the root is nonterminal A_{object}. *Repleo* is implemented to facilitate empirical validation of syntax-safe evaluation and to facilitate empirical validation of the usability of unparser-complete metalanguages (see Chapter 7).

First the syntax-safe evaluation function is discussed, followed by the specific evaluation for the substitution placeholder, match-replace placeholder and subtemplate call placeholder in Sections 6.2, 6.3 and 6.4. Syntax-safe evaluation also allows implicit subtemplates in order to express list rendering and tree rendering in a more compact fashion. This implicit subtemplate mechanism is introduced and the revisited substitution placeholder evaluation is discussed in Section 6.5. In addition to the discussion of the placeholders, the evaluator also has to resolve ambiguities and handle separators in Section 6.6 and 6.7. After the introduction of syntax-safe evaluation, a couple of examples of syntax-safe templates are presented, including a reimplementation of the PICO unparser using the additional semantic properties of the metalanguage in Section 6.10.

6.1 Syntax-Safe Evaluation

The operational semantics of syntax-safe evaluation are based on the semantics of the metalanguage discussed in Section 4.2. These operational semantics are extended, since the information in the parse tree allows defining implicit subtemplates, resulting in more concise templates.

The core of the syntax-safe evaluator is the same single tree traversal as discussed in Section 4.2, with a different signature:

$$seval : Template \times Templates \times MVars \to Tree,$$

where *Template* is the current template parse tree, *Templates* is a symbol table containing (sub)template parse trees, *MVars* is a symbol table containing metavariables and *Tree* is the parse tree resulting from the template evaluation. The function is called *seval* to emphasize the difference between the non syntax-safe template evaluator *eval* function. The *seval* function differs from the *eval* function in the following properties:

- The output of *seval* is a parse tree of the output language, the *yield* function is used to convert it to a string;
- *Template* and *Templates* are parse trees rather than strings; lexical analysis is performed during the template parsing;
- The symbol table *Templates* is a block-structured symbol table (see Section 4.2.2).

The *seval* function traverses the parse tree and checks whether the current node is a placeholder. At the moment a placeholder is found, the type of placeholder (substitution, match-replace or subtemplate call) is determined using the annotation and the accompanying *seval* evaluation sub function is invoked. The result of that sub function is a sub parse tree replacing the placeholder node, unless an error occurs. The final result of the evaluator function is a parse tree without placeholders, or an error message.

In Section 5.2 the grammars for the placeholders were presented. The production rules for the placeholders were extended by the annotation `placeholder(...)`, containing the kind of the placeholder, i.e. `substitution`, `subtemplate`, or `matchreplace`, which is used by *seval* to select the evaluation function. This annotation is an implementation choice simplifying placeholder detection in the parse tree. The traversal function matches on the annotation instead of the syntactical pattern of the placeholder.

When *seval* detects a placeholder in the parse tree, it is necessary to know to what object language nonterminal it is applied, i.e. the type of the parent node in the parse tree. Therefore, to obtain the object language nonterminal of the placeholder a helper function $getparentnt : Tree \rightarrow n$ is introduced. There are several ways to implement this function. For example, *seval* can be extended by an extra parameter holding the parent nonterminal, or the nonterminal of the placeholder can be parameterized by the parent nonterminal. A specific technical solution is used in the *Repleo* implementation; this solution is based on the assumption that the SGLR parser implementation is used. The SGLR parser implementation produces verbose parse trees, where every node is augmented with the production rule used for instantiating it. The *getparentnt* function uses this production rule to obtain the parent nonterminal. It returns the producing nonterminal from the production rule, which is equal to the parent node in the parse tree.

6.2 Substitution Placeholder

The substitution placeholder allows one to have unstructured data in the form of a string in the input data tree and to use it for replacing a substitution placeholder. A mechanism is necessary to verify that it is valid to substitute the placeholder in the template with the string from the input data.

A sub parse tree with root n_{object} can safely replace a substitution placeholder of nonterminal n_{object}. The expression specified in the substitution placeholder can result in a string or a tree. In Section 6.5 the behavior is discussed when the result of the expression evaluation is a tree. In case the expression evaluator yields a string, it is necessary to convert the string to the corresponding parse tree and check whether its root is n_{object}. The check is implemented using a parser for the object language. When the parsing succeeds and the root nonterminal of the (sub) parse tree is n_{object}, the parse tree can safely substitute the placeholder. In case the string of the input data cannot be parsed or the root nonterminal differs from n_{object}, i.e. the string is not a sentence of $\mathscr{L}(G(n_{object}))$, an error message is generated.

The following equation specifies the behavior of the syntax-safe substitution evaluation. For ease of presentation, the concrete object syntax notation is used in the equation. Inspired by [Visser (2002)], the notation [[...]] is used to specify concrete syntax, which is internally represented as a parse tree.

$$\frac{\begin{array}{c} getparentnt([[<: expr :>]]) \mapsto n \\ evalexpr([[expr]], bst_{vars}) \mapsto s \\ parse_{G(n)}(s) \mapsto t \end{array}}{seval([[<: expr :>]], bst_{tmps}, bst_{vars}) \mapsto t}$$

$$\frac{\begin{array}{c} getparentnt([[<: expr :>]]) \mapsto n \\ evalexpr([[expr]], bst_{vars}) \mapsto s \\ parse_{G(n)}(s) = ERROR \end{array}}{seval([[<: expr :>]], bst_{tmps}, bst_{vars}) \mapsto ERROR}$$

6.3 Match-replace Placeholder

The evaluation of match-replace placeholders does not differ from the evaluation scheme discussed in Section 4.2.4. Only at the start of the evaluation of the match-replace, the (sub) parse tree belonging to the match-replace is added to the (sub)templates symbol table in a fresh scope. The label for the subtemplate is equal to the nonterminal of the match-replace prefixed with a _. The prefix _ is not allowed for manual declared (sub)templates, so the labels of the implicit placeholders do not conflict with the labels of manually declared (sub)templates.

The use of scopes is necessary to remove conflicts if multiple implicit subtemplates are added to the symbol table with the same name, i.e. the same nonterminal of the match-replace. This mechanism facilitates that the last added implicit subtemplate is selected, when multiple match-replace placeholders for the same nonterminal are nested.

The formalized behavior specification is presented below. It is almost equivalent to the equation of Section 4.2.4, except that it uses parse trees instead of strings. Furthermore, the sub parse tree of the match-replace is stored on the subtemplate stack.

$$\frac{\begin{array}{c} t_1 = [[<:\text{ match }:>[mr_1,\ldots,mr_i]\ <:\text{ end }:>]] \\ getparentnt(t_1) \mapsto n \\ startblk(bst_{vars1}) \mapsto bst_{vars2} \\ startblk(bst_{tmps1}) \mapsto bst_{tmps2} \\ add(bst_{tmps2}, \_n, t_1) \mapsto bst_{tmps3} \\ lookup(bst_{vars2}, \$\$) \mapsto t_2 \\ findmatch(t_2, [mr_1,\ldots,mr_i], bst_{vars2}) \mapsto \langle t_3, bst_{vars3} \rangle \\ seval(t_3, bst_{tmps3}, bst_{vars3}) \mapsto t_4 \end{array}}{seval([[<:\text{ match }:>[mr_1,\ldots,mr_i]\ <:\text{ end }:>]], bst_{tmps1}, bst_{vars1}) \mapsto t_4}$$

6.4 Subtemplate Placeholder

Syntax-safe evaluation requires that the subtemplate call placeholder is replaced by a sub parse tree with root nonterminal n_{object} which is equal to the n_{object} where the subtemplate call placeholder is applied. The behavior of the subtemplate call placeholder is not changed with respect to the operation definition in Section 4.2.3. A subtemplate is selected based on its identifier. However, the free choice of an identifier for subtemplates results in the risk that the subtemplate is not of the correct syntactic sort to replace the subtemplate call placeholder.

In order to guarantee syntax-safety, a sub parse tree with the correct root nonterminal must replace the subtemplate call placeholder. Hence, it is only allowed to insert the result of an evaluated subtemplate when its root nonterminal matches the nonterminal where the subtemplate call placeholder is applied. An extra condition is added to the original operation semantics to check whether the root nonterminal of the subtemplate matches the nonterminal of the calling placeholder. An error is generated in case no suitable subtemplate can be found.

$$\frac{\begin{array}{c} getparentnt([[\text{<: } idcon(expr) \text{ :>}]]) \mapsto n_1 \\ lookup(bst_{tmps}, idcon) \mapsto t \\ getparentnt(t) \mapsto n_2 \\ n_1 = n_2 \\ evalexpr([[expr]], bst_{vars1}) \mapsto bst_{vars2} \\ seval(t, bst_{tmps}, bst_{vars2}) \mapsto t' \end{array}}{seval([[\text{<: } idcon(expr) \text{ :>}]], bst_{tmps}, bst_{vars1}) \mapsto t'}$$

$$\frac{\begin{array}{c} getparentnt([[\text{<: } idcon(expr) \text{ :>}]]) \mapsto n_1 \\ lookup(bst_{tmps}, idcon) \mapsto t \\ getparentnt(t) \mapsto n_2 \\ n_1 \neq n_2 \end{array}}{seval([[\text{<: } idcon(expr) \text{ :>}]], bst_{tmps}, bst_{vars}) \mapsto ERROR}$$

6.5 Substitution Placeholder Revisited

In the discussion of the metalanguage in Chapter 4 the concept of subtemplates is introduced to enable unfolding to render lists and trees, or to enable the reduction of code clones in the templates. The disadvantage of using the match-replace and subtemplates to express the rendering of lists and trees is its verbosity. Furthermore, the structure of the generated code is less clear, since a subtemplate placeholder is called at the place where the list or tree must be rendered. The availability of syntax-safe templates enables to define implicit subtemplates, providing a more natural way to express unfolding. It uses the syntactical type of the match-replace placeholder to automatically add an implicit subtemplate to the subtemplates symbol table and the syntactical type of the substitution placeholder to invoke the subtemplate.

The concept of implicit subtemplates is shown by the following figures. Figure 6.1 shows a snippet of the original PICO unparser with a subtemplate `decls`. This subtemplate can be re-factored to an implicit subtemplate. Figure 6.2 shows the integration of the subtemplate `decls` in the first match-replace placeholder. The subtemplate call `<: decls($tail) :>` is replaced by a substitution placeholder `<: $tail :>`. Since the match-replace placeholder will be parsed as `Decls` and the placeholder `<: $tail :>` will also be parsed as

`Decls`, this mechanism will render a list of declarations. The `[ head ]` match rule can also be omitted as specified in the original PICO unparser of Chapter 4, since the syntax-safe evaluator provides a generic separator handler (see Section 6.7).

```
template[
<: match :>
 <: program( decls($decls), $stms ) =:>
  begin declare
  <: decls( $decls ) :>;
  <: stms( $stms ):>
  end
<: end :>
]

decls[
<: match :>
  <: [] =:>
  <: [ $head ] =:>  <: idtype($head) :>
  <: [ $head, $tail ] =:> <: idtype($head) :>, <: decls($tail) :>
<: end :>
]
```

Fig. 6.1 Original snippet of PICO abstract syntax tree unparser.

```
template[
<: match :>
 <: program( decls($decls), $stms ) =:>
  begin declare
  <: match :>
   <: [] =:>
   <: [ $head, $tail ] =:> <: idtype($head) :>, <: $tail :>
  <: end :>;
  <: stms( $stms ):>
  end
<: end :>
]
```

Fig. 6.2 Implicit subtemplate example.

Implicit subtemplates use the property that the object language nonterminal can be used as a label for a subtemplate. As mentioned in Section 6.3, the sub parse tree of a match-replace placeholder is added to symbol table containing the subtemplates. The match-replace placeholder acts as an implicit subtemplate, where the identifier is the object language nonterminal prefixed by an underscore. A substitution placeholder in the object code fragments of the match rules can call the implicit subtemplate. This placeholder becomes an implicit subtemplate caller, when its expression results in a subtree of the input data instead of a string. At the moment the expression returns a tree, an implicit subtemplate is selected based on the syntactical type of the substitution placeholder. The last added implicit subtemplate with the same syntactical type as the substitution placeholder is used for evaluation. The current input data context is set to the subtree selected by the expression of the substitution placeholder. If no implicit subtemplate can be found, an error will be generated. The additional rules for the behavior of the substitution placeholder calling an implicit placeholder are shown below.

$$\frac{\begin{array}{c} getparentnt([[<: expr :>]]) \mapsto n \\ evalexpr([[expr]], bst_{vars1}) \mapsto t \\ startblk(bst_{vars1}) \mapsto bst_{vars2} \\ add(bst_{vars2}, \$\$, t) \mapsto bst_{vars3} \\ lookup(bst_{tmps}, \_n) \mapsto t_1 \\ seval(t_1, bst_{tmps}, bst_{vars3}) \mapsto t_2 \end{array}}{seval([[<: expr :>]], bst_{tmps}, bst_{vars1}) \mapsto t_2}$$

$$\frac{\begin{array}{c} getparentnt([[<: expr :>]]) \mapsto n \\ evalexpr([[expr]], bst_{vars1}) \mapsto t \\ startblk(bst_{vars1}) \mapsto bst_{vars2} \\ add(bst_{vars2}, \$\$, t) \mapsto bst_{vars3} \\ lookup(bst_{tmps}, \_n) = \varepsilon \end{array}}{seval([[<: expr :>]], bst_{tmps}, bst_{vars1}) \mapsto ERROR}$$

6.6 Ambiguity Handling

Adding placeholders to the grammar of an object language to obtain a template grammar can lead to undesired ambiguities. An ambiguity occurs when a (sub) parse tree of a (sub) sentence can be constructed in multiple ways using the production rules of a context-free grammar. In the situation of the constructed template grammars ambiguities can have two causes: either the object language grammar itself is already ambiguous or the combination of object language grammar and metalanguage grammar introduces ambiguities. Ambiguities are a problem when parsing (source) code, because it can lead to misinterpretation.

Although those ambiguities are unwanted when analyzing source code, they do not matter when generating source code, as will be shown in this section.
Instantiating template grammars, by adding placeholders to an object language grammar, can introduce new ambiguities. Placeholders are added as alternative for different object language nonterminals, but the syntax of these placeholders is equal. The parser cannot distinguish syntactically the desired derivation when different placeholders fit, hence the introduction of the explicit syntactical typing for placeholders via the optional syntax of the nonterminal `PlaceHolderType[[Sort]]`. Adding placeholders as alternatives for object language nonterminals can result in two kinds of ambiguities:

- Multiple sibling alternative placeholders can be used to parse the sentence;
- The placeholders are defined in chain rules and multiple chain rules can be used to parse the sentence.

The following examples illustrate these two causes. The first example is based on different possible sibling alternatives for a nonterminal. This kind of ambiguity is introduced when a grammar has the following two production rules: $n_1 \rightarrow n_3, n_2 \rightarrow n_3$, where both n_1 and n_2 are extended with a placeholder. Consider the grammar of Figure 6.3. The grammar becomes ambiguous when placeholder syntax is added to the nonterminals `A` and `B`. Figure 6.4 shows the ambiguous parse tree of the template `<: v1 :>`. The placeholder can be either parsed as child of the nonterminal `A` or as child of the nonterminal `B`. It depends on the value stored in the input data for the node `v`, whether the final evaluated template results in the branch for nonterminal `A` or the branch for nonterminal `B`.
During evaluation, the final selection of which alternative succeeds depends on the content of the input data. Consider the following two inputs:

(1) `v( "a" )`

(2) `v( "b" )`

Both inputs will result in a valid parse tree for the object language. The first input yields the left branch of the ambiguity; the second input the right branch.
The second cause for ambiguities is the presence of chain rules in the grammar when parent and child nonterminal both are extended with a placeholder. A production rule is a *chain rule*, when it has the following form $n_1 \rightarrow n_2$. Consider the grammar of Figure 6.5 and define placeholders for the nonterminals `A` and `B`; the grammar becomes ambiguous. Figure 6.6 shows this ambiguity inside the parse tree of the term `<: "a" :>`. The placeholder can parsed either as an placeholder for the nonterminal `A` or `B`. Considering Figure 6.5,

after evaluation `PlaceHolder[[A]]` will return a sub parse tree with `A` as root and `"a"` as child, while evaluating `PlaceHolder[[B]]` will return a sub parse tree with `B` as root, `A` as child of `B` and `"a"` as terminal. When both branches of the ambiguity are evaluated, both branches of the ambiguity will contain the same sub parse tree.

```
context-free start-symbols C
context-free syntax
    A | B          -> C
    "a"            -> A
    "b"            -> B
```

Fig. 6.3 Grammar with two alternatives.

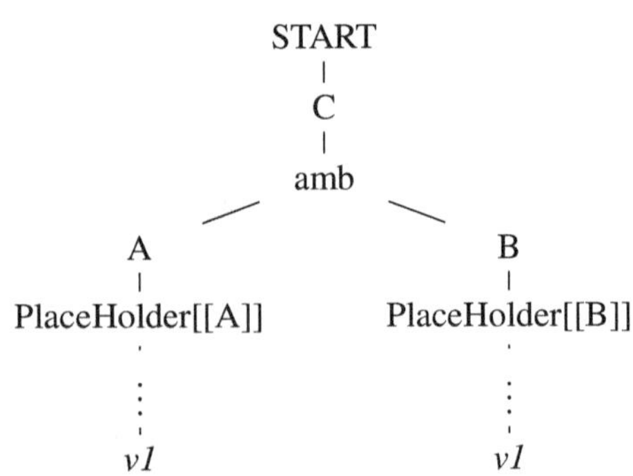

Fig. 6.4 Parse tree of ambiguous template.

A parser used to parse a template should be based on an algorithm supporting ambiguities, as by nature a template grammar is probably ambiguous. The support of ambiguities is the reason for the use of a(n) (S)GLR based parser. This kind of parsers constructs a collection of (sub) parse trees in case of an ambiguity. The SGLR parser automatically constructs a parse tree. A special `amb` node is introduced by SGLR in case of an ambiguity. This `amb` node contains the list of possible valid (sub) parse trees. Other parser algorithms supporting ambiguities such as the Cocke-Younger-Kasami algorithm [Nijholt (1991)], the Earley algorithm [Earley (1970)] and more recently GLL [Scott and Johnstone (2010)] can be used. Parser algorithms like LL, LR and LALR [Aho *et al.* (1986)] cannot be used, as they do not support ambiguities.

```
context-free start-symbols B
context-free syntax
  A        -> B
  "a"      -> A
```

Fig. 6.5 Grammar with chain rules.

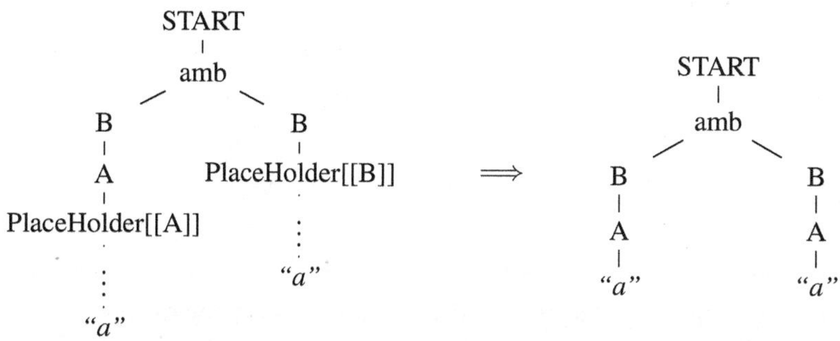

Fig. 6.6 Chain rule ambiguity and evaluation result.

Ambiguities belonging to the mix of object language and metalanguage must not be solved during parsing, but stored in the parse tree. These ambiguities represent different syntactically legal alternatives for the output code. It is undesired to remove legal alternatives during parsing if not explicitly defined in the templates, as removing legal alternatives would limit the applicability of a template.

A disambiguation filter based on rewriting [Vinju (2005)] is used to resolve the ambiguities during template evaluation. In order to deal with ambiguities the evaluator tries to evaluate the different alternatives of the ambiguities with the same context, i.e. bst_{tmps} and bst_{vars}. The alternatives are evaluated one by one and at the moment an alternative successfully evaluates; it is used to replace the ambiguity node. The steps are shown by the equations below. This filter is part of the *seval* traversal function and matches on ambiguity nodes.

$$\frac{seval(t_1, bst_{tmps}, bst_{vars}) \mapsto t}{seval(amb(t_1, \ldots, t_k), bst_{tmps}, bst_{vars}) \mapsto t}$$

$$\frac{\begin{array}{c} seval(t_1, bst_{tmps}, bst_{vars}) = ERROR \\ seval(amb(t_2, \ldots, t_k)) \mapsto t \end{array}}{seval(amb(t_1, t_2, \ldots, t_k), bst_{tmps}, bst_{vars}) \mapsto t}$$

$$\frac{seval(t_1, bst_{tmps}, bst_{vars}) = ERROR}{seval(amb(t_1), bst_{tmps}, bst_{vars}) \mapsto ERROR}$$

It is not necessary to evaluate every alternative of the ambiguity when a successful evaluation is found [Bravenboer *et al.* (2007)]. Evaluating different ambiguity alternatives could result in different structures of the parse trees, but the leaves of those trees contain the same lexical characters. The yielded strings of different ambiguity alternatives are identical. This and since after evaluation the resulting parse tree is converted to a string, allows stopping evaluating the ambiguity alternatives after one successful result is found. The evaluator generates an error when it is not possible to evaluate any of the ambiguity alternatives successfully.
Although ambiguities could not always be avoided during the construction of a template grammar, one should carefully select the object language nonterminals to extend with placeholders syntax to prevent undesired ambiguities. The algorithm presented above can resolve the remaining template related ambiguities, but this solution comes with a performance penalty.

6.7 Separator Handling

SDF supports lists with separators. When a template is evaluated containing separated lists, it is not automatically guaranteed that the separated lists in the generated code are syntactical correct. Figure 6.7 shows an example that generates code with a syntax error. The comma at the second match-rule is parsed as separator. Following the evaluation rules of the match-replace, this template will generate a terminated list $(t,t,t,)$ instead of a separated list, while a separated list (t,t,t) is required. In a text-based context one can solve this problem by introducing a third rule between line 2 and 3: `<: [ $head ] =:> <: $head $>`. This solution is also chosen in the text-based PICO unparser of Figure 4.7.

```
  <: match :>
2 <: [] =:>
  <: [ $head , $tail ] =:> <: $head :>, <: $tail :>
4 <: end :>
```

Fig. 6.7 Separated list generation.

In case of syntax-safe templates based on SDF, where a verbose parse tree is available this fix is not necessary. The evaluator uses the information in the parse tree to fix the separators and guarantee that the separator in a separated list is correctly applied. The filter checks whether a separated list conforms to the pattern $n_1 s n_2 \ldots s n_k$, where n represents an element and s the separator. It adds or deletes separators in case they are missing or redundant. This solution is also used in the ASF evaluator [Bergstra *et al.* (1989)].

6.8 Repleo

In order to perform practical validation of the ideas a prototype called *Repleo* is implemented based on the presented template grammars and evaluation strategy. The Repleo evaluator is generic with respect to the object language of a template grammar. It can be used for every template grammar constructed following the method of Chapter 4.
The implementation is separated in two components: the SGLR parser including the template grammars defined in SDF and the template evaluator. The template evaluator is written in Java and composed around a tree traversal, i.e. the *seval* function. The traversal calls the SGLR parser to parse strings from the input data in case a substitution placeholder is detected. The evaluation process is stopped when an error occurs to prevent generation of syntactical incorrect code. The error handling uses the exception mechanism provided by Java. When an error is detected an error message is thrown, which contains the reason of the error and source code location in the template.

6.9 Other Syntax-Safe Template Approaches

First, the approach of Heidenreich et al. [Heidenreich *et al.* (2009)] is based on abstract syntax of templates. Heidenreich et al. designed a syntax-safe template approach based on metamodels. Metamodels define the abstract syntax grammar of the template language and models are instantiations of these templates, comparable to an abstract syntax tree of a template. These metamodels even allows one to go beyond syntax-safety and perform some static semantic checking. However, reasoning on the level on abstract syntax of templates ignores some practical syntactical related issues, like layout and syntactical ambiguities.
Wachsmuth [Wachsmuth (2009)] presented an alternative approach. He discusses an approach to extend a target language grammar with metalanguage artifacts in order to obtain a template grammar, which guarantees syntax-safe generation of code. It is similar to the constructing a template grammar discussed in Theorem 5.1.1. The approach of Wachsmuth statically enforces syntax correctness, since substitution placeholders are not supported

and thus all output code is already defined in the template. Hence the relation with Theorem 5.1.1. This approach does not allow having substitution placeholders replacing themselves by string values from the input data. Substitution placeholders are not necessary for unparser-completeness (see Theorem 4.2.1). However, a metalanguage without substitution placeholders is less flexible in use, since the behavior of the substitution placeholder must be captured in a combination of match-replace like placeholders and subtemplates (see Section 4.2.5).

6.10 Case Studies

This section discusses examples of syntax-safe templates. The first case study is the reimplementation of the PICO unparser of Section 4.3. The goal of this reimplementation is to show the benefits of implicit subtemplates.

In order to show that syntax-safe templates are not limited to academic toy languages, three case studies are presented based on the industrially used object languages Java (general purpose programming language), XHTML (website markup language), and SQL (database query language). The choice of these object languages is based on their contemporary use in three-tier (web) applications; Java for the business layer, SQL for the database layer and XHTML for the presentation layer. Finally, a template based on an object language supporting multiple languages is presented. This example shows an object language based on Java with embedded SQL.

6.10.1 *PICO Unparser*

Syntax-safe evaluation provides implicit subtemplates and separator handling. This reduces the amount of syntax necessary to implement list generation and tree generation comparing to the text-based templates of Chapter 4. Figure 6.8 shows the reimplementation of the PICO unparser using the syntax-safe evaluator. Most match-replace placeholders are nested, only the `expr` code is defined in a subtemplate, since it is called on three places in the template and replacing these calls with the code of the subtemplate `expr` will result in cloning. After refactoring, the definition of the PICO unparser is 9 lines shorter than the text-based template PICO unparser implementation (see Section 4.3).

```
template[
<: match :>
<: program( decls($decls), $stms ) =:>
  begin declare
  <: match $decls :>
  <: [] =:>
  <: [ decl( $id, $type ), $tail] =:>
  <: $id :> : <: match $type :>
                <: natural =:> natural
                <: string  =:> string
                <: nil-type =:> nil-type
              <: end :>,
  <: $tail sort:ID-TYPE* :>
  <: end :>
  ;
  <: match $stms :>
  <: [] =:>
  <: [ $head, $tail] =:>
    <: match $head :>
      <: assignment( $id, $expr ) =:>
          <: $id :> := <: expr( $expr ) :>
      <: while( $expr, $stms ) =:>
          while <: expr($expr) :> do
                  <: $stms sort:STATEMENT* :>
          od
      <: if( $expr, $thenstms, $elsestms ) =:>
          if <: expr($expr) :> then
                  <: $thenstms sort:STATEMENT* :>
          else
                  <: $elsestms sort:STATEMENT* :>
          fi
    <: end :>;
    <: $tail sort:STATEMENT* :>
  <: end :>
  end
<: end :>
]
expr[
<: match $expr :>
 <: natcon( $natcon ) =:> <: $natcon sort:EXP :>
 <: strcon( $strcon ) =:> <: $strcon sort:EXP :>
 <: id( $id ) =:> <: $id sort:EXP :>
 <: sub( $lhs, $rhs ) =:>
           <: $lhs sort:EXP :> - <: $rhs sort:EXP :>
 <: concat( $lhs, $rhs ) =:>
           <: $lhs sort:EXP :> || <: $rhs sort:EXP :>
 <: add( $lhs, $rhs ) =:>
           <: $lhs sort:EXP :> + <: $rhs sort:EXP :>
<: end :>
]
```

Fig. 6.8 PICO abstract syntax tree unparser (syntax-safe).

6.10.2 *Java*

The first example of a template with an industrially used object language is a Java template. This template generates data model classed in Java, i.e. Java classes with fields accompanied with getters and setters. The template is shown Figure 6.10. The template grammar used for parsing this template is shown in Figure 6.9.

```
module Template-Java

imports Java
imports StartSymbol["CompilationUnit*" CompilationUnit*]
imports PlaceHolder["ID" ID]
imports PlaceHolder["Type" Type]
imports PlaceHolder["Modifier" Modifier]
imports PlaceHolder["ClassBodyDec*" ClassBodyDec*]
imports PlaceHolder["BlockStm*" BlockStm*]
```

Fig. 6.9 Java template grammar.

```
class <: model2name1 :> {

<: model3cons1vis1 :> <: model2name1 :>(){}

<: match model4fields1 :>
  <: [] =:>
  <: [ field( $field ), $tail ] =:>
    private <: $field2type1 :> <: $field1name1 :>;

    <: $field2type1 :> <: "get" + $field1name1 :>(){
      <: match $field1log3 :>
        <: true =:> System.out.println("get" +
                                   <: "\"" + $field1name1 +
                                      "\"" :>+"() is called.");
      <: end :>
      return <: $field1name1 :>;
    }

    void <: "set" + $field1name1 :>(
                                     <: $field2type1 :> value ){
      <: $field1name1 :> = value;
    }
    <: $tail :>
<: end :>
}
```

Fig. 6.10 A Java template.

```
1  model(
   number(104),
3  name("Customer"),
   cons(vis("public")),
5  fields([
     field(
7        name("firstName"),
         type("String"),
9        log(true)
     ),
11   field(
         name("lastName"),
13       type("String"),
         log(false)
15   )
   ])
17 )
```

Fig. 6.11 Input Data example for Java Template of Figure 6.10.

Syntax errors in a template based generation system can be caused by errors in the template or by invalid input data. Table 6.1 shows a couple of errors that could be made in the template of Figure 6.10 and errors that could be made in the input data shown in Figure 6.11. First, the object code of a template contains syntax errors and the generated code inherits these errors (errors A and B). Second, the data obtained from the input data to substitute a placeholder does not syntactically fit into the object code of the template (errors C, D and E). These errors are prevented in case of using syntax-safe templates. The first set of errors (C, D, and E) are detected during parsing the template, the second class of errors (A and B) will be reported during the evaluation of the template.

Table 6.1 Possible errors in template and input data.

	Substitute line	**by**	**creating error**
A	1	`clss <: model2name1 :> {`	class misspelled.
B	12	`1System.out.println("get"`	`1System` is not a valid identifier.
C	1	`class <: model1number1 :> {`	number not allowed as identifier.
D	Input, 3	`name("Shop-Client")`	identifier contains a dash.
E	Input, 4	`vis("abstract" )`	modifier abstract not allowed.

6.10.3 *XHTML*

Templates are a common technique to render (X)HTML for web pages in web applications. XHTML (Extensible Hypertext Markup Language) is a markup language based on XML and the Hypertext Markup Language (HTML). The syntax of XHTML is more strict than HTML, and can be specified using a context-free syntax formalism. The instantiation of a combination grammar for XHTML templates is shown in Figure 6.12. Based on the same input data of Figure 6.11, a template to generate a basic XHTML form is defined in Figure 6.13.

```
module Template-XHtml

imports XHtml
imports StartSymbol["XHtml" XHtml]
imports PlaceHolder["PCDATA" PCDATA]
imports PlaceHolder["CDATA" CDATA]
imports PlaceHolder["Quoted-CDATA" Quoted-CDATA]
imports PlaceHolder["XHtml-form-content-item*"
                    XHtml-form-content-item*]
```

Fig. 6.12 XHTML template grammar.

A screen shot of the output after evaluation of the XHTML template is shown in Figure 6.14. For every field in the input data an input field is generated in the web form.
The use of a template grammar for the template prevents syntax errors in the object code. An example of such an error is a space between < and `input` at line 15 in Figure 6.13. The syntax-safe evaluation results in the guarantee that the output is always a syntactically valid XHTML document. It can even be used to prevent injection attacks. This application of syntax-safe evaluation is discussed in Section 7.5.

6.10.4 *SQL*

SQL is a language in the domain of information systems for expressing database queries. The Listing 6.15 shows the combination module definition for parsing templates for SQL select statements.

```
<!DOCTYPE HTML PUBLIC "-//W3C//DTD XHTML 1.0 Strict//EN"
"http://www.w3.org/TR/xhtml1/DTD/xhtml1-strict.dtd">

<html>
 <head>
  <title><: model2name1 + " form" :></title>
 </head>
 <body>
  <form action="/commit" method="post">
   <: match model4fields1 :>
    <: [] =:>
    <: [ field( $field ), $tail ] =:>
     <p>
      <: $field1name1 :> <br />
      <input type="text"
         name=<: "\"" + $field1name1 + "\"" :> size="20">
     </p>
     <: $tail :>
   <: end :>
    <p>
     <input type="submit" value="Submit">
     <input type="reset" value="Reset">
    </p>
  </form>
 </body>
</html>
```

Fig. 6.13 XHTML Template.

Fig. 6.14 Output after evaluation of the XHTML template.

```
module Template-Sql

imports Sql
imports StartSymbol["SqlId" SqlId]
imports PlaceHolder["SqlId*" {SqlId ","}*]
```

Fig. 6.15 SQL combination module.

The next example shows an SQL select statement template in Figure 6.16. This template can also be evaluated using the input data of Figure 6.11. The result of the evaluation of the SQL template is

```
SELECT  (firstName, lastName) FROM Customer
```

```
SELECT
(
<: match model4fields1 :>
  <: [] =:>
  <: [ field( $field ), $tail ] =:>
    <: $field1name1 :> , <: $tail :>
<: end :>
)
FROM <: model2name1 :>
```

Fig. 6.16 SQL Template.

6.10.5 *Multi-language Templates*

Sometimes program fragments contain multiple programming languages, like a third generation language with an embedded language. The language containing foreign language artifacts is called the *host language* and the embedded language is called *guest language*. Usually these guest language fragments are embedded in strings, and considered as data in the host language. A compiler of the host language is not equipped to check the correctness of the embedded guest language code. The aim of this section is to show that a syntax-safe template, where the object language is based on multiple sublanguages, generates correct sentences with respect to all the sublanguages of the object language. First StringBorg is discussed, an approach for guaranteeing that multiple languages in a program are syntactical correct.

StringBorg [Bravenboer *et al.* (2007)] is an approach solving the limitation of a compiler not supporting multiple languages. This system is able to check a host language with embedded guest language code. Quotations (<| ... |>) are used to switch from the host language, to the guest language(s), and anti-quotations (&{ ... }) to go back to the host language. StringBorg prevents that guest language artifacts from being syntactically incorrect and the approach especially aims at providing protection against injection attacks. A common example is a language, like Java, containing database queries expressed in SQL. Figure 6.17 shows a Java listing with embedded SQL using StringBorg to ensure syntactical correctness of both languages.

```
class CustomerDao {
  public Collection getCustomers(){
    Collection items = new java.util.ArrayList();
    SQL q = <| SELECT (firstName,lastName)
                FROM Customer |>;
    ResultSet rs = con.query(q.toString());
    try {
      for (; rs.next(); ) {
        Customer item = new Customer();
        item.setfirstName(
          rs.getString("firstName"));
        item.setlastName(
          rs.getString("lastName"));
        items.add(item);
      }
    } catch (SQLException e) {
      e.printStackTrace();
      System.exit(1);
    }
    return items;
  }
}
```

Fig. 6.17 Java with SQL code inside quotations.

The consequence of using quotations is that the code cannot be compiled and/or executed without a tool interpreting these quotations. It is desirable to keep the build environment with as less as possible tools, since all these tools must be maintained. An approach introducing static syntax-safety for guest language fragments is presented. This approach does not add new constructs to the syntax of the original host language by defining a grammar configured to detect guest languages without the quotations. The quotations are defined as function signatures in the host language. This approach uses the assumption that most guest language sentences are specified in an API function call. For example, most Java environments use JDBC[1] to establish a connection to a database. The guest language syntax is embedded in the host language grammar by adding a specialized function signature for the generic function signature in the grammar. This approach facilitates syntactical correctness of all generated code, including the embedded languages. It does not add new language constructs to the host language, so no extra tooling is necessary to compile and execute the code. However, StringBorg is more flexible with respect to the places where guest language fragments can be defined. Syntax-safe templates also do not prevent against dynamic injection attacks when running the generated code, but only finds syntactical errors in the static defined code.

The grammar of Figure 6.18 shows the embedding of SQL in Java. It inserts a special grammar rule for the function `prepareStatement`. It is necessary that the function `prepareStatement` cannot be parsed as a normal function call. A reject rule is specified at line 9 to specify `prepareStatement` as a preferred keyword [van den Brand *et al.* (2002)]. The `Java-Sql` grammar is able to parse Java with embedded SQL code in the `prepareStatement` function without adding new language constructions. The connection between the host language and the guest language should be based on API calls or other natural transition points. Some effort is needed to define a grammar module for this connection and to maintain it when the API changes. However API's such as JDBC do not change often or maintain backward compatibility [Andersen (2006)].

```
   module Java-Sql
 2 imports Sql
   imports Java
 4 exports
     sorts SqlMethod SqlExpr MethodName
 6   context-free syntax
       SqlMethod "(" SqlExpr ")"     -> Expr {prefer}
 8     SqlMethodName                 -> SqlMethod
       SqlMethodName                 -> ID {reject}
10     AmbName "." SqlMethodName     -> SqlMethod
       "prepareStatement"            -> SqlMethodName
12     "\"" Query "\""               -> SqlExpr
```

Fig. 6.18 Combining Java and SQL.

Syntax-safety for all language fragments is also crucial for templates. Syntax errors in

[1]http://java.sun.com/javase/technologies/database/ (accessed on December 18, 2011)

guest language fragments of a template can easily remain undetected until run-time. The compiler of the host language does also not check the guest language fragments. From a grammar perspective the `Java-Sql` can be seen as a new language, in other words the union of languages results in a new language. This new language can be extended with placeholders in the same way as the original languages. The syntax-safe template evaluator will guarantee that its output is a sentence of this new language, i.e. all the sublanguages of the output are syntactical correct. Figure 6.19 shows the template grammar for `Java-Sql` templates.

```
module Template-Java-Sql

imports Java-Sql
imports StartSymbol["CompilationUnit*" CompilationUnit*]
imports PlaceHolder["ID" ID]
imports PlaceHolder["Type" Type]
imports PlaceHolder["Modifier" Modifier]
imports PlaceHolder["ClassBodyDec*" ClassBodyDec*]
imports PlaceHolder["BlockStm*" BlockStm*]

imports PlaceHolder["SqlId" SqlId]
imports PlaceHolder["SqlId*" {SqlId ","}*]
```

Fig. 6.19 Java-SQL template grammar.

Figure 6.20 shows a `Java-Sql` template. This template can also be evaluated using the input data of the Listing 6.11. The result after evaluating the template is listed in Figure 6.21. The generated code can be compiled without a special preprocessor and both host language code and guest language code are guaranteed to be syntactically correct. The template evaluator detects syntax errors in both languages, since the grammar contains production rules for both. For example, an error is generated when an identifier fits in a Java placeholder but not in an SQL placeholder. This property forces to use the greatest common divisor of the character classes of the Java identifiers and SQL identifiers in the input data. The advantage of using an object language grammar containing production rules for embedded languages is that sentences of these sublanguages constructed during code generation are syntax-safe. It is not an obstacle to use an object language based on multiple unified context-free languages, since syntax-safe template evaluation only requires that the object language is context-free.

```
class <: model2name1 + "Dao" :> {
 public Collection <: "get" + model2name1 + "s" :>(){
   Collection items = new java.util.ArrayList();
   ResultSet rs = con.prepareStatement(
    "SELECT (<: match model4fields1 :>
              <: [] =:>
              <: [ field( $field ), $tail ] =:>
                <: $field1name1 :> , <: $tail :>
              <: end :>) FROM <: model2name1 :>");
   try {
     for (; rs.next(); ) {
       <: model2name1 :> item = new
<: model2name1 :>();
       <: match model4fields1 :>
        <: [] =:>
        <: [ field( $field ), $tail ] =:>
         item.<: "set" + $field1name1 :>(
          rs.getString(<:"\""+$field1name1+"\"":>));
         <: $tail :>
        <: end :>
     items.add(item);
     }
   } catch (SQLException e) { ... }
   return items;
 }
}
```

Fig. 6.20 Java-SQL template.

```
class CustomerDao {
  public Collection getCustomers(){
    Collection items = new java.util.ArrayList();
    ResultSet rs = con.prepareStatement(
        "SELECT (firstName, lastName)
         FROM Customer");
    try {
      for (; rs.next(); ) {
        Customer item = new Customer();
        item.setfirstName(
          rs.getString("firstName"));
        item.setlastName(
          rs.getString("lastName"));
        items.add(item);
      }
    } catch (SQLException e) { ... }
    return items;
  }
}
```

Fig. 6.21 Result of evaluation of Java-SQL template.

6.10.6 *Embedded Languages*

Embedding one computer language in another computer language is not a new phenomenon. Most times the embedded languages are considered as strings. Several approaches go beyond handling these embedded languages as strings.
MetaBorg [Bravenboer *et al.* (2006a)] is a system to embed a guest language in a host language. It translates the guest language fragments into host language fragments. MetaBorg does not use explicit hedges to indicate the transitions between host language and guest language. The requirements for MetaBorg differ, as the only concern is the syntactical correctness of the embedded code. StringBorg is the successor of MetaBorg.
Another approach to embed a language is domain specific embedded compilers [Leijen and Meijer (1999)]. This is a technology to express a domain specific language, such as HASKELL/DB, in a high order typed language like Haskell. HASKELL/DB is a proprietary language to express database queries in Haskell. These queries are translated to SQL. The HASKELL/DB fragments are checked for syntax correctness and type correctness. The type safety is obtained by introducing *phantom types* for the guest language. Phantom typing is a technique to create annotations containing type information for the nonterminals in the parse tree of the HASKELL/DB code. This allows the Haskell type system to check the type correctness of the embedded language. The use of a proprietary language for SQL makes this concept less easy to use and maintain than a system based on the concrete syntax of SQL.

6.11 Conclusions

Syntax-safe templates provide a mechanism to detect syntax errors during the generation of the code, instead of dealing with syntax errors at compile time. It prevents that placeholders in a template are replaced by syntactical incorrect sentences. The output code of a syntax-safe template evaluator is a sentence of the intended output language.
The evaluation strategy is not dependent on the object language and does not need to be changed when another object language is used. It is even possible to use object code containing multiple languages.
The presented ideas are implemented in a prototype called *Repleo*. This prototype is used to validate the presented approach in a couple of case studies, discussed in Chapter 7.

Chapter 7

Case Studies

Three case studies are presented in this chapter to show the use of the unparser-complete metalanguage and the usability of the syntax-safe template evaluator in a practical setting. The syntax-safe template evaluator *Repleo* is used for implementing these case studies. Two case studies show a reimplementation of an existing code generator. The reimplemented code generators use a separated model transformation stage, resulting in less code and better maintainable code than the original implementations. The use of separated model transformation stage is also enforced by the unparser-complete metalanguage of Repleo. The maintainability is achieved by less code clones in the code generator specification and less entanglement of metacode and object code. The third case study shows the benefits of syntax-safe templates in the context of dynamic web page generation. Syntax-safe templates provide a solution against cross-site scripting attacks.

The first case study, see Section 7.3, is a reimplementation of ApiGen [de Jong and Olivier (2004)]. ApiGen is an application to generate a Java API for creating, manipulating and querying tree-like data structures represented as ATerms. It covers the generation of Java code based on the *Factory* pattern and *Composite* pattern [Gamma *et al.* (1995)]. The second case study, see Section 7.4, is the reimplementation of NunniFSMGen. NunniFSMGen is a tool to generate finite state machines from a transition table. It covers the generation of behavioral code based on the *state* design pattern [Gamma *et al.* (1995)] for different output languages. These two case studies show that the use of a two-stage architecture results in better separation of concerns. The third case study, presented in Section 7.5, shows that syntax-safety can improve the safety of dynamic code generation in web applications. It covers code generation during the usage of an application, where syntax-safety is used to reduce the possibility of security bugs. This chapter ends with an overall conclusion. First, the different implementation architectures of code generators used by the case studies are presented.

7.1 Code Generator Architectures

This section discusses three code generator architectures: the single-stage architecture, the two-stage architecture and the model-view-controller architecture.

7.1.1 *Single-Stage Generator*

The single-stage generator architecture is the less advanced approach to implement a code generator. All processing and calculations are performed in a single module, without the use of an intermediate representation. The code generator directly emits code when parsing the input model. Figure 7.1 shows a visual representation of the single-stage architecture.

This architecture comes with serious drawbacks and should only be considered in simple and small cases. First, the single-stage architecture has the drawback that the code is less maintainable and less reusable, as all code and responsibilities are entangled in a single component. Intermediate results and functions are not available for reuse. The same calculations are performed every time they are necessary. Caching results of calculations will break the single-stage architecture, as the cached result is a kind of intermediate representation.

Another side effect of this architecture is that code cloning can easily occur. At the moment the same calculations are necessary at different moments, it will result in a code clone. The single-stage architecture does not allow combining these code clones in a model transformation stage.

Last, debugging is also more difficult; since everything is done in one phase and translation steps cannot be tested in isolation.

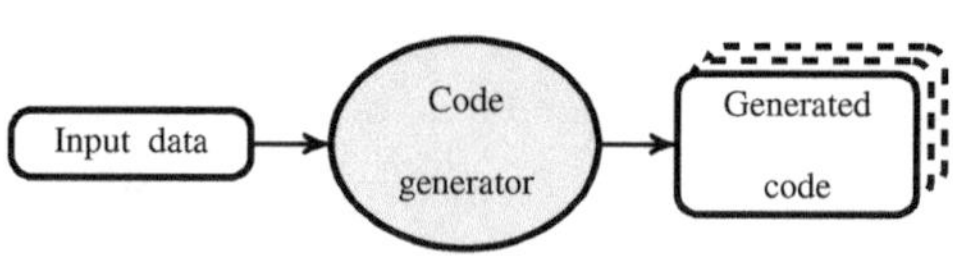

Fig. 7.1 Single-stage architecture.

7.1.2 *Two-Stage Generator*

The two-stage architecture accommodates multiple output steps, where the input data is first translated to an intermediate representation before the final output code is generated. The code generation process is separated in a model transformation stage and the code emitting stage. The intermediate representation is used by the code emitter stage. In the case studies, this code emitter stage is implemented as a set of templates in combination with a template evaluator. The model transformation stage is considered as one mapping, but depending on the necessary refining, it can be implemented using a number of sub mappings. Figure 7.2 shows the corresponding two-stage architecture.

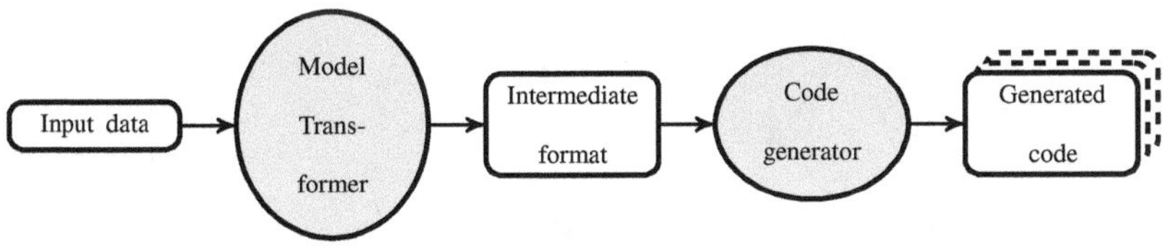

Fig. 7.2 Two-stage architecture.

In a two-stage generator, the translation of input model to output code is distributed over two components, namely a model transformation and code emitter(s). In case multiple code emitters are used for generating the output code, an equivalent single-stage generator has to be implemented as a set of separated code generators. It is likely, that this set of code generators share code clones, since the same distance between the levels of abstraction of the input data and output code needs to be bridged. Compared to the single-stage architecture, the use of a two-stage architecture allows one to reduce the number of code clones in the generator code by specifying the non-output language specific calculations in the model transformation. It should be the aim to design the intermediate representation at a level of abstraction that it is not output language specific. When the intermediate representation does not contain output language specific information, it is possible to use it for multiple output languages. On the other hand, the intermediate representation should be close enough to the level of abstraction of the output code. At that point of abstraction, the code emitters act as a render component with minimal calculations, while the intermediate representation is still not output language specific. Although the intermediate representation should not contain output language specific artifacts, the intermediate representation can already be paradigm specific or has specific requirements of target language concepts, which an output language should support. For example, the intermediate representation represents a design pattern that can only be implemented using an object-oriented programming language.

The use of a two-stage approach is already a common architecture for implementing compilers [Aho *et al.* (1977, 1986, 1989)]. For example, the GCC compiler[1] processes the input code and translates it to a representation belonging to the *register transfer language*. The register transfer language is the intermediate representation of GCC and is used to separate the compiler front-ends from the compiler back-ends. The intermediate representation is translated to assembler by the back-end of GCC. The register transfer language representations are still independent of the final target processor, so it can be used for different compiler back-ends for different processors.

7.1.3 *Model-View-Controller Architecture*

The *model-view-controller* architecture (MVC) [Krasner and Pope (1988)] describes a decomposition of an application in three parts: *model*, *controller* and *view*, with their specific responsibility. It aims for separation of concerns to improve re-usability and maintainability of applications. The model is responsible for actually executing the calculations for the application domain and is distinct of the controller and view part of the application. The controller is used to send messages to the model, and provides the interface between the model with its associated views and the interactive user interface devices. The view deals with everything graphical on screen, printer, files and other devices, i.e. the output of the application. It uses data from the model component to render the output screen.
An MVC based application consists of a model and can have one or more views and controllers associated with it. The re-usability of the model is improved when it does not have knowledge of the views and controllers of the application, only the views and controllers need to have knowledge about their model explicitly. Figure 7.3 provides a visual sketch of the MVC architecture.
The original discussion of the MVC architecture considers an end-user application, where the view is a (graphical) user interface and the controllers handle direct user input via keyboard or mouse. Beside the original context, the MVC architecture also fits for applications generating code, like web applications. In MVC based web applications, the controller handles the requests and the views return generated HTML pages, PDF documents, etcetera. Often this view component of a web application is implemented using templates.

[1] http://gcc.gnu.org (accessed on December 18, 2011)

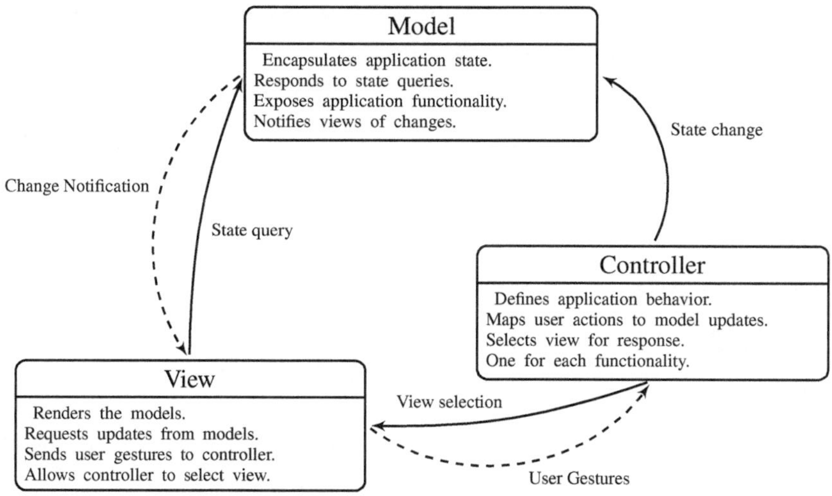

Fig. 7.3 Model-view-controller architecture.

7.2 Metrics

The three case studies discussed in this chapter will be compared using volume metrics. These metrics quantify the volume differences of the re-implementations in comparison with the original code generators. The volume is measured using the lines of code metric. This metrics gives a rough indication of the size of the code.

The lines of code metric does not give accurate information about the amount of text in the source code, therefore the number of tokens is also counted. Instead of characters, tokens are counted, as they abstract from the length of identifiers. Independent of its length each identifier is parsed as one token, otherwise the length of the identifiers could influence the comparison.

By nature, metaprograms contain a lot of non-alphanumeric characters to switch from object code to metacode and vice versa. These characters have a negative impact on the readability of the code. In order to quantify the readability of the code the number of non-alphanumeric characters used in the code is measured.

The grammar for quantifying the amount of text contains the following lexical classes (see the grammar of Figure 7.4 for the definition of them):

- `ID` - represents identifiers and keywords in Java, C, SDF, ASF and shell scripts;
- `Bracket` - represents brackets, and initializes a token per bracket;

- `NonID` - represents non-alphanumeric character sequences, excluding brackets;
- `WS` - represents sequences of white space characters.

The grammar of Figure 7.4 is used to parse the source code of the code generator implementations. The result of the parser is a parse tree with a root node `Tokens` and for each token a child node. A function iterates over this list to count the occurrences of the different kinds of nodes. The number of non-alphanumeric characters is the sum of the number of `Bracket` tokens and `NonID` tokens. They are parsed as different nonterminals, since `Bracket` detects single characters and `NonID` detects the longest match for a character sequence.

These metrics have a lot in common with the Halstead complexity metrics [Halstead (1977)], based on the number of (distinct) operands and (distinct) operators. Unfortunately, these metrics could not be used directly as templates contain metacode and object code. It is not clear how to define operands and operators in a metaprogramming situation. Considering the object code fragments as operands is not sufficient as depending of the execution stage they are considered as operand or operator. The metrics used in this chapter are at a basic lexical level, which not consider the differences between metalanguage and object language.

```
module Tokens

exports
  sorts Text Bracket NonID ID WS
  context-free start-symbols Text
  context-free syntax
     (Bracket | NonID | ID | WS)*          -> Text

  lexical syntax
    [A-Za-z0-9\*\'\$]+                     -> ID
    [\"\{\}\[\]\<\>\(\)]                   -> Bracket
    ~[\"\{\}\[\]\<\>\(\)\ \t\n\rA-Za-z0-9\*\'\$]+
                                           -> NonID
    [\ \t\n\r]+                            -> WS

  context-free restrictions
    NonID -/- ~[\"\{\}\[\]\<\>\(\)\ \t\n\rA-Za-z0-9\*\'\$]
    WS -/- [\ \t\n\r]
    ID  -/- [A-Za-z0-9\*\'\$]
```

Fig. 7.4 Grammar for the token counter.

7.3 ApiGen

This case study covers the reimplementation of the Java back-end of ApiGen [de Jong and Olivier (2004); van den Brand *et al.* (2005)]. ApiGen is a tool to generate a Java or C application programming interfaces (API) for creating, manipulating and querying tree-like data structures represented as ATerms [van den Brand *et al.* (2000)]. The API generated by ApiGen is based on the *Factory* pattern and *Composite* pattern [Gamma *et al.* (1995)]. The reimplementation of ApiGen makes use of the two-stage architecture and syntax-safe templates.

7.3.1 *Introduction*

ApiGen finds its origin in the *ASF+SDF Meta-Environment* [van den Brand *et al.* (2001)], an interactive development environment for program analysis and transformations. The ASF+SDF Meta-Environment provides various language processing components, such as a parser and a term rewrite engine. Data between these components is exchanged via ATerms, where these components expect that ATerms belong to a certain regular tree grammar. This regular tree grammar was not explicitly defined, but dictated by manually specified functions in an API accepting the ATerm. Synchronizing these manually defined API's for the various components is a complex maintenance issue [de Jong and Olivier (2004)].

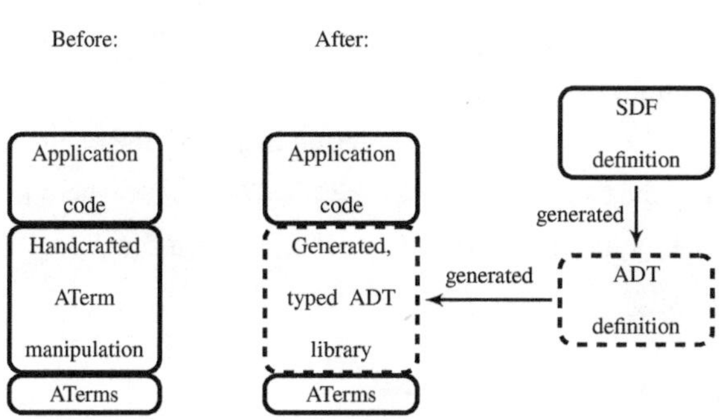

Fig. 7.5 Overview of an application before and after introduction of a generated API.

ApiGen solves this maintenance problem by generating an API for ATerms from a regular tree grammar or concrete syntax definition (SDF). It translates a regular tree grammar, specified in a format called *annotated data-type* or in short *ADT*, to an API for manipulating, reading and creating ATerms belonging to the language of the regular tree grammar.

Generating an API from the ADT removes the need of error-prone handcrafted ATerms. The generated API also provides more safety when manipulating trees, since the node objects are not typed as a generic node, but typed as its alternative, which is a subclass of its producing nonterminal. A schematic overview is shown in Figure 7.5. This figure also shows that an ADT can be derived from an SDF specification. The translation of SDF to ADT is out of the scope of this case study and the original tool `sdf2-to-adt` is used to generate an ADT from an SDF grammar.

7.3.2 *Annotated Data Type*

The ADT format is a formalism to define a set of legal ATerms, comparable to schema formalisms such as Document Type Definition and XML Schema for XML documents [Bex *et al.* (2004)]. The format can be classified as a regular tree grammar formalism, allowing trees with *infinite arity* [Murata *et al.* (2005)]. Trees with infinite arity may contain symbols used with different arities, while the symbols in the previously discussed trees have a fixed arity. The ADT format finds it origin as an intermediate representation between an SDF definition and the generated API for manipulating parse trees belonging to that SDF definition. In accordance with the structure of these parse trees, three types of rules are supported:

- Production rules: `constructor(n, c, ATerm)`, where `n` is the nonterminal, `c` the alternative and `ATerm` the corresponding pattern. The couple of `n` and `c` must be unique in an ADT definition;
- Lists: `list(n, n')`, where `n` is the nonterminal and `n'` the element type;
- Separated lists: `separated-list( n, n', [ATerm+])`, where `n` is the nonterminal and `n'` the element type and `ATerm+` is a list of allowed separators.

```
[
  home(
    name("Arnoldus"),
    voice(020114556)
  ),
  work(
    name("University"),
    fax(020114520)
  )
]
```

Fig. 7.6 An instance of a phone book ATerm.

The running example for this case study is a phone book data-structure, see Figure 7.6 for an example. It contains a list of entries, where the type of an entry can be person or company. Both person and company have the fields name and phone number. The phone number can be either a voice number or a fax number. Figure 7.7 shows the ADT definition for this phone book data-structure.

```
[
  list(PhoneBook, Entry),
  constructor( Entry, Home,
               home(<person(Name)>,<phone(PhoneNumber)>) ),
  constructor( Entry, Work,
               work(<company(Name)>,<phone(PhoneNumber)>) ),
  constructor( Name, Name, name(<string(str)>) ),
  constructor( PhoneNumber, Voice, voice(<integer(int)>)),
  constructor( PhoneNumber, Fax, fax(<integer(int)>))
]
```

Fig. 7.7 The ADT definition for the phone book example.

It should be noted that the ADT formalism does not support the explicit definition of start symbols. Instead of defining a start symbol, ApiGen generates for all nonterminals a function to parse trees using that nonterminal as start symbol.

7.3.3 *From ADT to an API*

The code generated by ApiGen contains two different components:

- A data structure based on the regular tree grammar.
- A *factory* to create and manipulate trees stored in that data structure.

These components of the generated API are based on the *composite* pattern and *factory* pattern as documented in [Gamma *et al.* (1995)].

7.3.3.1 *Data Structure*

The data structure implementation provides a type structure to represent a tree in the form of objects connected to each other via a *has-a* relationship. The nonterminals in the regular tree grammar are implemented as abstract classes and the production rules are implemented as concrete subclasses of that nonterminal.

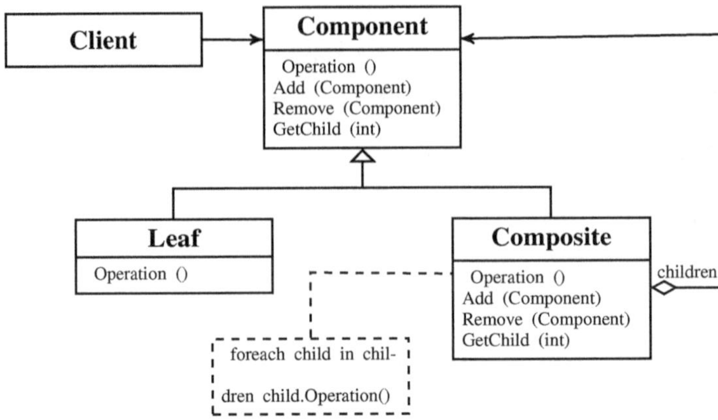

Fig. 7.8 Composite design pattern.

ApiGen generates the classes based on the composite pattern, see Figure 7.8, on top of the generic Java ATerm library. The connection between the ATerm Library and the concrete classes representing the nodes contains a number of inheritance levels. Two classes `AbstractType` and `AbstractListType` are generated to form the bridge between the generated API and the ATerm library. The first extends the class `ATermApplImpl` and the second the class `ATermListImpl`, which are members of the ATerm library representing an ATerm node and ATerm list node. The `AbstractType` and `AbstractListType` contain the default methods provided by every subclass of the generated API. The next layer generated by ApiGen is the abstract classes representing the nonterminals of the ADT. For each nonterminal an abstract class with the name of the nonterminal is generated. This generated abstract class extends `AbstractType` or in case the nonterminal represents a list, the abstract class extends `AbstractListType`. The nonterminal class contains the definition and default behavior of the accessor methods for that nonterminal. Figure 7.9 shows the core of the generated class for the nonterminal `PhoneNumber`.

The final layer generated by ApiGen is the concrete classes for the different alternatives of a nonterminal. For each alternative a class with the name of the alternative is generated. This class extends the abstract class of the nonterminal belonging to the alternative, where all the accessor methods are implemented. These classes are used to instantiate trees belonging to the tree language defined by the ADT. Figure 7.10 shows the concrete class for the alternative `Fax` of the nonterminal `PhoneNumber` generated by ApiGen. In case of the alternative for `Voice` the same listing is generated, where `Fax` is replaced by `Voice`.

```
abstract public class PhoneNumber extends AbstractType {

  public PhoneNumber( ... ) {
     super( ... );
  }

  public boolean isEqual(PhoneNumber peer) {
    return super.isEqual(peer);
  }

  public boolean isSortPhoneNumber() {
    return true;
  }

  public boolean isVoice() { return false; }

  public boolean isFax() { return false; }

  public boolean hasInteger() { return false; }

  public int getInteger() {
     throw new UnsupportedOperationException(
             "This PhoneNumber has no integer");
  }

  public PhoneNumber setInteger( int integer) {
     throw new IllegalArgumentException(
             "Illegal argument: integer");
  }

}
```

Fig. 7.9 Snippet of the PhoneNumber class.

7.3.3.2 *Factory*

The second generated component is a factory, see Figure 7.11, to instantiate trees based on the generated data structure. This generated factory provides methods to create, parse, manipulate and export trees conforming to the ADT. It is obligatory to use a factory for instantiating ATerm based trees in order to provide *maximal subterm sharing*; a mechanism to ensure that only one instance of any subterm exists in memory. The Java ATerm library provides this factory by the implementation called "`ATermFactory`". In case an API for an ATerm based tree language is generated, a factory must be created supporting the instantiation of trees for that tree language. Therefore, ApiGen generates a layer on top of the `ATermFactory` containing `make` methods to instantiate (sub)trees using the classes of the generated data structure.

```
public class Fax extends PhoneNumber {

  public Fax( ... ) { super( ... );  }
  private static int index_integer = 0;

  public shared.SharedObject duplicate() { ... }

  public boolean equivalent(shared.SharedObject peer)
    { ... }

  protected aterm.ATermAppl make(
      aterm.AFun fun, aterm.ATerm[] args,
      aterm.ATermList annos) {
    return
      getPhonebookFactory()
         .makePhoneNumber_Fax(fun, args, annos);
  }

  public aterm.ATerm toTerm() {
    if (term == null) {
      term = getPhonebookFactory().toTerm(this);
    }
    return term;
  }

  public boolean isFax() { return true;  }

  public boolean hasInteger() { return true;  }

  public phonebook.types.PhoneNumber setInteger(int
integer) {
    return (phonebook.types.PhoneNumber) super.setArgument(
      getFactory().makeInt(integer), index_integer);
  }

  public int getInteger() {
    return ((aterm.ATermInt)
                getArgument( index_integer )).getInt();
  }

  public aterm.ATermAppl setArgument(aterm.ATerm arg, int i)
    { ... }

  protected int hashFunction() { ... }

}
```

Fig. 7.10 Snippet of the Fax alternative for the PhoneNumber nonterminal.

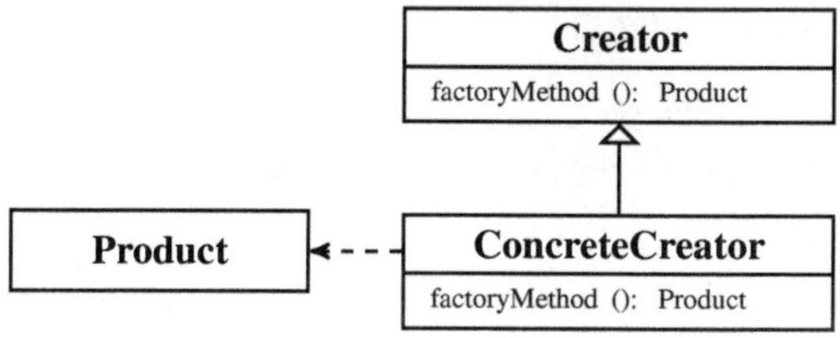

Fig. 7.11 Factory design pattern.

The generated factory provides special `make` methods for the nodes defined in the ADT. These `make` methods abstracts from the ATerm library, as it is not necessary to know the underlying ATerm representation to create trees defined by the ADT. When called, these `make` methods instantiate nodes based on the classes of the generated data structure and encapsulate the administration to achieve maximal subterm sharing. Maximal subterm sharing is a technique to reduce the memory footprint of terms by only storing unique terms in memory. In case of list types, the factory class also provides the list operations `reverse`, `concat` and `append`. The factory class also contains methods to instantiate a tree from a string, to serialize it from a tree to a string, and cast methods to transform a tree to a generic ATerm representation and vice versa. Figure 7.12 shows a snippet of the generated factory for the phone book example.

```
public phonebook.types.phonenumber.Voice
    makePhoneNumber_Voice(int _integer) {
  aterm.ATerm[] args = new aterm.ATerm[] {
      factory.makeInt(_integer)
  };
  return makePhoneNumber_Voice(
      fun_PhoneNumber_Voice, args, factory.getEmpty());
}

public phonebook.types.phonenumber.Voice
    makePhoneNumber_Voice(int _integer,
    aterm.ATermList annos) {
  aterm.ATerm[] args = new aterm.ATerm[] {
      factory.makeInt(_integer)
  };
  return makePhoneNumber_Voice(
          fun_PhoneNumber_Voice, args, annos);
}
```

Fig. 7.12 Snippet of the generated factory.

7.3.4 *Original Code Generator*

The original Java implementation of ApiGen is based on the two-stage architecture. The first stage is the ADT reader. It reads an ADT specification, containing the specification of the tree structure, from file. The ADT is an ATerm and as a result a generated API implements the in-memory representation of an ADT. The ADT reader calls the factory to instantiate the in-memory representation of an ADT file. Besides reading the ADT file, the first stage also executes a couple of model transformations. For example, the constructor rules in the ADT contain an ATerm pattern belonging to that node. The model transformation extracts the ATerm placeholders to collect the fields for that constructor rule. Figure 7.13 shows the field collection method of the model transformation. It is a recursive function traversing an ATerm pattern and instantiating a field object for every ATerm placeholder occurring in the pattern. For example the fields `company` and `phone` with their respective arguments `Name` and `PhoneNumber` are extracted from the ATerm pattern of the `work` alternative

```
work(<company(Name)>,<phone(PhoneNumber)>)
```

The second stage of ApiGen is responsible for generating the output code. A code emitter is written for every kind of class generated by ApiGen. ApiGen contains seven code emitter classes: `FactoryGenerator`, `AbstractListGenerator`, `AbstractTypeGenerator`, `ListTypeGenerator`, `SeparatedListTypeGenerator`, `TypeGenerator` and `AlternativeGenerator`. The emitter classes are implemented as `println` generators, which results in a mix of Java used as object code and Java used as metacode. Figure 7.14 shows the `genMakeMethod` method of the `FactoryGenerator` class. This method is responsible for generating the `make` methods of the factory class, as shown in Figure 7.12.

For each alternative declared by the constructor rules in the ADT a set of `make` methods are generated. Considering the code snippet of Figure 7.14, the following actions are executed. The first statements, in lines 3-9, construct the identifiers used in the generated code by calling a number of helper functions. At line 11-12, the output code is instantiated by printing a string to the output buffer, internally redirect to the output file. The `if`-statement is used to select the generation of a forwarded `make` method in case an imported ADT module defines the factory. Helper functions such as `buildActualTypedAltArgumentList` are used to reduce code clones in the generator self. At line 31 an `if`-statement is used to ensure the separator token is only generated when the alternative has fields.

```
private void extractFields(ATerm t) {
  AFun fun;
  ATermAppl appl;
  ATermList list;
  switch (t.getType()) {
    case ATerm.APPL :
      appl = (ATermAppl) t;
      fun = appl.getAFun();
      for (int i = 0; i < fun.getArity(); i++) {
        extractFields(appl.getArgument(i));
      }

      break;
    case ATerm.LIST :
      list = (ATermList) t;
      for (int i = 0; !list.isEmpty(); i++) {
        extractFields(list.getFirst());
        list = list.getNext();
      }
      break;
    case ATerm.PLACEHOLDER :
      ATerm ph = ((ATermPlaceholder) t).getPlaceholder();
      if (ph.getType() == ATerm.LIST) {
        ...
        addField(fieldId, fieldType);
      } else if (ph.getType() == ATerm.APPL) {
        ...
        addField(fieldId, fieldType);
      } else {
        throw new
          RuntimeException("illegal field spec: " + t);
      }
      break;
    default :
      break;
  }
}
```

Fig. 7.13 Extraction of fields from ATerm pattern.

```
private void genMakeMethod(Type type,
  Alternative alt, boolean forwarding, String moduleName) {
  JavaGenerationParameters params =
                  getJavaGenerationParameters();
  String altClassName =
                  AlternativeGenerator.qualifiedClassName(
                      params, type, alt);
  String makeMethodName = "make" + concatTypeAlt(type, alt);
  String funVar = funVariable(type, alt);

  print("    public " + altClassName
                  + ' ' + makeMethodName + "(");
  printFormalTypedAltArgumentList(type, alt);
  println(") {");
  if (!forwarding) {
    print(
    "       aterm.ATerm[] args = new aterm.ATerm[] {");
    printActualTypedArgumentList(type, alt);
    println("};");
    println("       return " + makeMethodName +
      "(" + funVar + ", args, factory.getEmpty());");
  } else {
    ...
  }
  println("    }");
  println();

  print("    public " + altClassName
                          + ' ' + makeMethodName + "(");
  printFormalTypedAltArgumentList(type, alt);
  if(type.altFieldIterator(alt.getId()).hasNext())
                                            print(", ");
  println("aterm.ATermList annos) {");
  if (!forwarding) {
    ...
  } else {
    ...
  }
  println("    }");
  println();
}
```

Fig. 7.14 Small part of the ApiGen code emitter.

Although, the original ApiGen implementation is based on a two-stage architecture, the distribution of responsibilities for the model transformation and code emitter is not optimal. Some model transformations are executed during code generation. For example Figure 7.15 shows a model transformation task inside the `AlternativeGenerator` class at line 4. This method `genAltFieldIndexMembers` is called for every type defined in the ADT. The type object contains all fields possible for that type. When this method is called, the statement at line 4 fetches all fields for the current alternative of the type. This filtering should be done at model transformation phase, for example the class `Alternative` should provide a list of its associated fields. Although this filtering seems innocent, it is a call back to the model, so a wrong implementation of the `altFieldIterator` could change the model. The `altFieldIterator` is a member of the type `Type` and it has direct access to the private fields of `Type`. It is possible to change the values of these private fields, resulting in a change of the model during code generation. Furthermore, `genAltFieldIndexMembers` cannot be expressed in Repleo, as a compare operator and a mechanism to store values is necessary.

```
1  private void genAltFieldIndexMembers(Type type,
                                        Alternative alt) {
3    Iterator<Field> fields =
                   type.altFieldIterator(alt.getId());
5    int argnr = 0;
     while (fields.hasNext()) {
7     Field field = fields.next();
      String fieldId = getFieldIndex(field.getId());
9     println("  private static int " + fieldId
             + " = " + argnr + ";");
11    argnr++;
     }
13 }
```

Fig. 7.15 Example of model transformation in code emitter.

7.3.5 *Reimplemented Code Generator*

ApiGen is reimplemented using the two-stage architecture with a strict separation between the model transformation stage and code emitter stage. The model transformation is defined as a set of rewrite rules using a term rewriting system (ASF+SDF) and the code emitter is implemented using syntax-safe templates. Term rewriting provides a powerful computational paradigm to express these transformations, as they are tree rewrite rules. Figure 7.16 shows the architecture of the reimplementation. The rectangular shapes denote (intermediate) files and the circular shapes denote the transformation engines. The model transformation reads the ADT input model and computes the intermediate representation, also an ATerm. The second stage consists of a set of templates accepting the intermediate representation as input data.

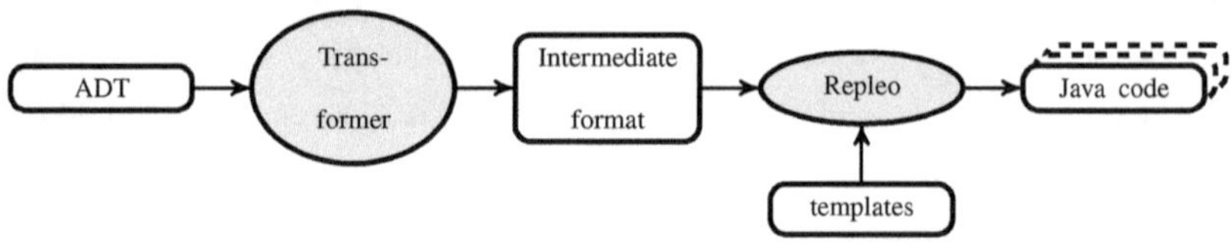

Fig. 7.16 Generation scheme: from ADT to code.

The code generated from the ADT definition exists of a data structure based on the composite pattern and a factory to instantiate trees. The intermediate representation already implements these design patterns. It contains a list of types, categorized into `type` and `list`. These types represent the nonterminals and are implemented as abstract classes, see Figure 7.9. The concrete classes of these abstract classes are defined by the alternatives of these types, see Figure 7.10.

The intermediate representation of the phone book example is shown in Figure 7.18. One can notice cloning of fields between the level of the type node and alternative nodes. The unparser-complete metalanguage is not capable to calculate the fields for an alternative; as a result the field nodes are stored multiple times in the input data. Since this intermediate representation is also used for the generation of the factory class, the alternatives contain an ATerm pattern corresponding with the node.

The model transformation is responsible for translating the ADT input model to the intermediate representation. Considering the ADT of Figure 7.7 and the intermediate representation of Figure 7.18, the model transformation has collected all constructor rules for a type in a single node, where the different constructor rules are represented as alternatives for that type. Besides collecting the types, the model transformation extracts the fields from the ATerm pattern specified in each constructor rule. Additionally the ATerm pattern is translated to the pattern used in the factory class, i.e. the placeholders are replaced with generic ATerm placeholders.

Figure 7.17 shows the extraction of fields for an ATerm pattern belonging to an alternative for a type. It is the reimplementation of the code of Figure 7.13 using ASF+SDF. A traversal is configured to traverse the ATerm pattern in an ADT production rule, where this rewrite rule declares a match on an ATerm placeholder. The identifiers having a dollar-sign prefix are declared as variables. The traversal stops when it detects an ATerm placeholder, specified by the pattern `< $IdCon($IdCon') >`. At a match it returns an instantiated field for the intermediate representation. Note, the `$NatCon` is a helper argument in order to provide an index number to the field.

```
getFieldsForAlt(< $IdCon($IdCon') >, < $FieldAlt*, $NatCon >) =
<
$FieldAlt*,
field( unparse-to-string($IdCon),
       getTypeImplementation($IdCon'),
       $NatCon ),
$NatCon + 1
>
```

Fig. 7.17 Extraction of fields from ATerm pattern.

The second stage is responsible for the actual code generation and is implemented using syntax-safe templates. Seven templates are defined. The original implementation comes also with seven emitter classes, where the templates share the same tasks. Figure 7.19 shows a snippet of the template generating the factory class. This snippet is responsible for generating the `make` methods, see Figure 7.12 for the result when using the input data of Figure 7.18. These methods are generated for each alternative of each type. The loop over the alternatives is expressed by two match-replace placeholders. This example also uses the built-in metalanguage functions `_lc` and `_cc`. These are shorthand notations for transforming a string to lowercase or camel-case, i.e. the first letter is capitalized. From a Puritan point of view, these functions should not be available in the metalanguage. The different layouts of identifiers should be stored in the input data. In practice, this would lead to a lot of variants of lexical layouts of identifiers in the input data, while most string manipulations are necessary to comply with the layout convention of the object language[2]. The availability of these functions makes it possible to express the layout requirements in the template, instead of having them in the input data.

[2]It is possible to express the semantics of the string manipulation functions in a couple of subtemplates in combination with match-replace placeholders. The implementation would be a variant of the template given in Section 4.2.5.

```
[
type(
  "Entry",
  [
   alternative( "Home" , 2, "home(<term>,<term>)",
    [
     field( "person", notreserved("Name"), 0 ),
     field( "phone", notreserved("PhoneNumber"), 1 )
    ]),
   alternative( "Work" , 2, "work(<term>,<term>)",
    [
     field( "company", notreserved("Name"), 0 ),
     field( "phone", notreserved("PhoneNumber"), 1 )
    ])
  ],
  [
   field( "person", notreserved("Name") ),
   field( "phone", notreserved("PhoneNumber") ),
   field( "company", notreserved("Name") )
  ]
 ),
type(
  "Name",
  [
   alternative( "Name" , 1, "name(<str>)",
    [
     field( "string", reserved(str), 0 )
    ])
  ],
  [
     field( "string", reserved(str) )
  ]),
type(
  "PhoneNumber",
  [
   alternative( "Voice" , 1, "voice(<int>)",
    [
     field( "integer", reserved(int), 0 )
    ]),
   alternative( "Fax" , 1, "fax(<int>)",
    [
     field( "integer", reserved(int), 0 )
    ])
  ],
  [
   field( "integer", reserved(int) )
  ]
),
list( "PhoneBook", notreserved("Entry") )
]
```

Fig. 7.18 The intermediate representation of the phone book.

```
...
template[
...
<: match :>
<: [ type($type,$alternatives,$fields), $types ] =:>
 <: match $alternatives :>
 <: [ alternative($altname,$arity,$pattern, $altfields),
                                  $alternatives ] =:>
 public <:$apiname:>.types.<:_lc($type):>.<:_cc($altname):>
   <: "make" + $type + "_" + _cc($altname) :>
                          ( <: genArguments( $altfields ) :> ) {
   aterm.ATerm[] args =
             new aterm.ATerm[] { <: genArray( $altfields ) :>
};
   return <: "make" + $type + "_" + _cc($altname) :>(
           <: "fun_" + $type + "_" + _cc($altname) sort:Expr:>,
                                   args, factory.getEmpty());
  }

 public <:$apiname:>.types.<:_lc($type):>.<:_cc($altname):>
             <: "make" + $type + "_" + _cc($altname) :>
               (<: genArguments( $altfields ) :>,
                                   aterm.ATermList annos) {
  aterm.ATerm[] args =
               new aterm.ATerm[] { <: genArray( $altfields ) :> };
  return <: "make" + $type + "_" + _cc($altname) :>
    ( <: "fun_" + $type + "_" + _cc($altname) sort:Expr:>,
                                             args, annos);
 }
 ...
 <: $alternatives sort:ClassBodyDec*:>
 <: [ ] =:>
 <: end :>
<: $types sort:ClassBodyDec*:>
...
<: [] =:>
<: end :>
...
]
...
```

Fig. 7.19 Small part of the ApiGen code emitter.

7.3.6 *Difference Old and New Implementation*

The original implementation and reimplementation is compared on architectural level and code level. On architectural level, both implementations are based on the two-stage architecture. The original implementation does not have a concrete syntax for the intermediate representation. It uses a class structure for the objects to store the derived information. The

separation between the two-stages is not strict as the code emitters call the model transformation during the generation of the code. Calling the model transformation from the code emitter is impossible in the reimplemented ApiGen. Only a one-way link between the model transformation and the templates exists. For example, the restricted metalanguages forces to specify the calculation performed in the code emitter method of Figure 7.15 in the model transformation stage.
The original ApiGen implementation is written in Java, while the reimplementation uses ASF+SDF for the model transformation and syntax-safe templates for the code emitters. The model transformation is a function reading the ADT, which is a tree, with as output the intermediate representation, which is also a tree. Tree rewriting can be expressed compactly using a term rewriting system, especially since the used term rewriting system ASF+SDF has native support for traversal functions [van den Brand *et al.* (2003)]. The model transformation phase in the reimplementation is specified with a total of 21 functions based on 54 (sub) equations. The original model transformation implementation is more verbose and has a total of 3112 lines of code (without blank lines) spread over 34 files. An example of the reduction of lines of code is the refactoring of the snippet of Figure 7.13 to the reimplementation shown in Figure 7.17.
In the original implementation the code emitter stage is implemented using `println()` statements. The use of templates in the reimplementation results in a smaller implementation in volume. The template evaluator covers common tasks, like file handling and separator handling.

The Table 7.1 shows the result of measuring the old implementation of ApiGen and the reimplementation. All 57 files of the original ApiGen implementation[3] are measured. The total number of files of the reimplementation is 14, including grammar definitions, model transformations, shell script and templates.
Considering Table 7.1, the number of lines of code of the reimplementation is almost a third of the original implementation and the number of tokens is reduced 2.5 times. The reduction of the volume of the code is a result of three differences between the original implementation and the reimplementation. First the model transformation is expressed in a term rewriting formalism instead of Java. Second, the original implementation uses a generated API for the ADT format, while the reimplementation only contains a grammar definition for it. The last reason is that original implementation contains code for output file handling, which is encapsulated by the template evaluator in the reimplementation.

[3]The original implementation also provided a C code emitter. These classes are removed from the project.

The ratio's between lines of code and tokens is not improved. The number of tokens per line of code in the reimplementation is even higher than the original implementation. Also the number of non-alphanumeric tokens per line is increased by 43% in the reimplementation. The original implementation of ApiGen has a limited number of methods containing string constants with object code. The authors of ApiGen have aimed for the reduction of code clones on the level of the object code specification. Having less strings results in a lower level of non-alphanumeric tokens. At first sight, the original implementation seemed better readable than the reimplementation. However, at the moment that one notices that the reimplementation contains Java code in string constants, it will be harder to read and harder to understand the code it generates. The object code in ApiGen is specified as small chunks and one must analyze the flow graph of the code generator to understand how the output code is constructed [Christensen *et al.* (2003)].

Table 7.1 Metrics of ApiGen and the reimplementation.

Metric	**Original**	**Reimplementation**
Lines of Code	8,789	2,975
Lines of Code (without blank lines)	7,296	2,361
Tokens	84,230	33,254
Alphanumeric tokens	25,986	7,572
Non-alphanumeric tokens	33,704	15,669
White space tokens	24,540	10,013
Average number of tokens per line	11.5	14.08
Average number of non-alphanumeric tokens per line	4.62	6.64

7.3.7 *Evaluation*

The separation of concerns between the model transformation and the code emitters is improved in the reimplementation. The connection from the code emitter stage to the model transformations is also absent. The use of formalisms better suitable for the intended task, i.e. term rewriting for the model transformation and templates for the code emitters, results in a more compact definition of the code generator and it results in better maintainability [Spinellis (2001)]. The number of lines of code of the reimplementation is almost a third of the original implementation and the number of tokens is reduced 2.5 times, without removing functionality.

7.4 NunniFSMGen

NunniFSMGen is a tool to translate a specification of a finite state machine into an implementation for Java, C or C++. It uses the state design pattern [Gamma *et al.* (1995)] to implement the state machine in the different output languages.
First an overview of the original approach of NunniFSMGen is given. Next the reimplementation of NunniFSMGen is presented. The reimplementation of NunniFSMGen uses a parser, model transformation and templates. At the end the original implementation is compared to the new template based implementation.

7.4.1 *Finite State Machines*

Before discussing the input format of NunniFSMGen, a formal definition of finite state machines is given. Hereafter the input format of NunniFSMGen is related to the formal concept of finite state machines [Aho *et al.* (1986)].

Definition 7.4.1 (Deterministic finite state machine). A deterministic finite state machine is a 5-tuple $M = \langle \Sigma, Q, q0, \delta, F \rangle$, where:

Σ is the input alphabet,
Q is a finite, non-empty set of states,
$q0$ is an initial state and $q0 \in Q$,
δ is the state-transition function: $\delta : Q \times \Sigma \rightarrow Q$,
F is the set of final states, a (possibly empty) subset of Q.

Example 7.4.1. Let `M` be a finite state machine, where

$\Sigma = \{\text{activate}, \text{deactivate}, \text{hotenough}, \text{maintenance}\}$,
$Q = \{\text{STANDBY}, \text{WARMINGUP}, \text{ERROR}, \text{MAINTENANCE}\}$,
$q0 = \text{STANDBY}$, $F = \{\}$

and the transition function:

$$\delta(\text{STANDBY}, \text{activate}) = \text{WARMINGUP}$$
$$\delta(\text{STANDBY}, \text{hotenough}) = \text{ERROR}$$
$$\delta(\text{STANDBY}, \text{maintenance}) = \text{MAINTENANCE}$$
$$\delta(\text{STANDBY}, \text{deactivate}) = \text{STANDBY}$$
$$\delta(\text{WARMINGUP}, \text{activate}) = \text{WARMINGUP}$$

$$\delta(\text{WARMINGUP}, \text{deactivate}) = \text{STANDBY}$$
$$\delta(\text{WARMINGUP}, \text{hotenough}) = \text{STANDBY}$$
$$\delta(\text{WARMINGUP}, \text{maintenance}) = \text{MAINTENANCE}$$
$$\delta(\text{ERROR}, \text{activate}) = \text{ERROR}$$
$$\delta(\text{ERROR}, \text{deactivate}) = \text{ERROR}$$
$$\delta(\text{ERROR}, \text{hotenough}) = \text{ERROR}$$
$$\delta(\text{ERROR}, \text{maintenance}) = \text{MAINTENANCE}$$
$$\delta(\text{MAINTENANCE}, \text{activate}) = \text{STANDBY}$$
$$\delta(\text{MAINTENANCE}, \text{hotenough}) = \text{MAINTENANCE}$$
$$\delta(\text{MAINTENANCE}, \text{maintenance}) = \text{MAINTENANCE}$$
$$\delta(\text{MAINTENANCE}, \text{deactivate}) = \text{MAINTENANCE}$$

This state machine describes the behavior of a central heating system (see Figure 7.20 for a graphical representation). It is an example state machine distributed along with the source code of the original NunniFSMGen implementation.

7.4.2 *NunniFSMGen Input Model*

The input model used by NunniFSMGen is not a 5-tuple of a state machine as defined in Paragraph 7.4.1, but a transition table. The transition table is a set of transition rules of the form `startingState event nextState action`. The tuple of `startingState` and `event` is equal to the left-hand side of the transition rules of Definition 7.4.1. The name `event` is chosen instead of `token` to indicate it is an event driven state machine. The right-hand side of the transition rule corresponds to the `nextState`. An additional feature is to specify a method call hooked to a transition using the `action` field. This method call is invoked when the state machines uses that transition rule. If the `nextState` is a dash `-`, then a transition rule will not cause a change of state. The dash `-` can also be used in the `action` field to specify that no action is required when the transition is executed. The action can also contain an exclamation mark `!`. The exclamation mark defines that the action must throw an exception and that the state machine will go the *error state*. The states and alphabet are declared implicitly by means of the transition rules.

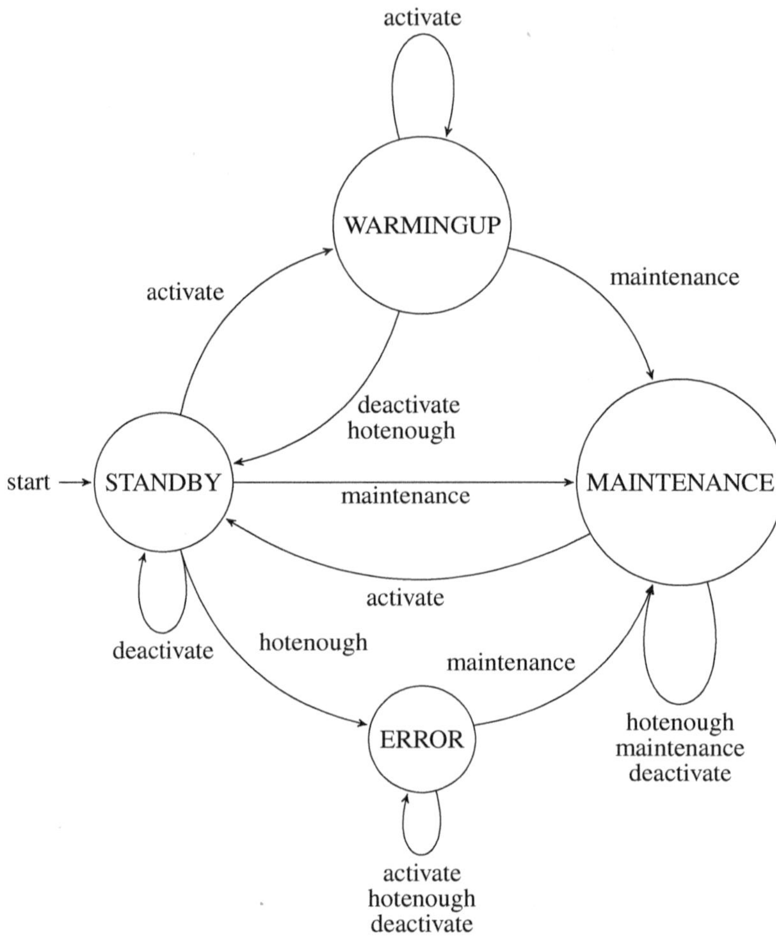

Fig. 7.20 Graphical representation of the central heating state machine.

The transition table also supports the declaration of parameters to specify (optional) properties, such as the error state. The following properties are available:

- `Context`: Name of the FSM. All resulting classes are named after this name using it as prefix.
- `InitialState`: The initial state of the FSM.
- `ErrorState`: The error state of the FSM. This is a required field in case an error action '`!`' is specified.

- `Package`(only Java): Name of the package of the generated code.
- `EventParamType`(optional): parameter type passed on event methods.
- `Copyright`(optional): a file containing a copyright text to be included at the top of each generated file.

The optional properties of the transition table are not available in the reimplementation of NunniFSMGen.

The grammar of the transition table format is shown in Figure 7.21. Constructor information is specified to translate the parse tree of the state tables to abstract syntax trees. The character classes of the lexical sorts are equal to Java strings, and as a result, it is possible to define a state table resulting in syntactical incorrect output code.

The original implementation of NunniFSMGen does not use an advanced grammar for parsing the state table. The grammar of the state table of the reimplemented NunniFSMGen prevents syntax errors as it does only allow character classes which are accepted by the identifier character classes of the target languages. The advantage of checking the input data is earlier detection of errors in the generation process. For example, the nonterminal `Id` is defined by the character class shared by all output languages of NunniFSMGen. When the character class of one output language is richer than the other output language(s), it is possible that code generated for the first output language is well-formed, while the code generated for the next output language is syntactically incorrect. The allowed identifiers are limited by defining *reject* rules for `Id` to prevent collisions with keywords of the output languages, such as the `if`. Instead of using *reject* rules in the transition table grammar, a prefix could be added to the identifiers in the generated code. This approach is not used to have a clear mapping between the transition table and the generated code.

In accordance with the state machine definition of Definition 7.4.1, NunniFSMGen requires that a transition rule is defined for each pair existing in the Cartesian product of states and events, even when transition and action are empty. In other words, the number of transition rules $|transition\ rules|$ must be equal to $|states| * |events|$. A NunniFSMGen transition table for the central heating system of Example 7.4.1 is shown in Figure 7.22. The abstract syntax tree of this transition table is given in Figure 7.23. It is obtained by desugaring the parse result of the transition table. The model transformation presented in Section 7.4.3 uses this abstract syntax tree as input.

```
module FSMGen

hiddens
  context-free start-symbols Rules
exports
  sorts Rules Rule NextState Action
  context-free syntax
    Rule*                      -> Rules {cons("rules")}
    "Context" Id               -> Rule {cons("context")}
    "InitialState" Id          -> Rule {cons("initial")}
    "ErrorState" Id            -> Rule {cons("error")}
    "Package" PackageName      -> Rule {cons("package")}
    "Copyright" FileName       -> Rule {cons("copyright")}
    "EventParamType" Id        -> Rule {cons("paramtype")}
    Id Id NextState Action     -> Rule {cons("transition")}
    Id                         -> NextState {cons("nextstate")}
    "-"                        -> NextState {cons("nonextstate")}
    Id                         -> Action {cons("action")}
    "-"                        -> Action {cons("noaction")}
    "!"                        -> Action {cons("erroraction")}

    "if"                       -> Id {reject}

exports
  sorts Id
  lexical syntax
        [a-zA-Z\_][a-zA-Z\_0-9]* -> Id
  lexical restrictions
        Id -/- [a-zA-Z\_0-9]
```

Fig. 7.21 Context-free grammar for NunniFSMGen transition table.

```
Context       Heater
InitialState  STANDBY
ErrorState    ERROR
Package       examples.heater

STANDBY       activate      WARMINGUP     warmup
STANDBY       deactivate    –             –
STANDBY       hotenough     ERROR         !
STANDBY       maintenance   MAINTENANCE   maintain
WARMINGUP     activate      –             –
WARMINGUP     deactivate    STANDBY
heateroff
WARMINGUP     hotenough     STANDBY
heateroff
WARMINGUP     maintenance   MAINTENANCE
heateroff
ERROR         activate      –             –
ERROR         deactivate    –             –
ERROR         hotenough     –             –
ERROR         maintenance   MAINTENANCE   –
MAINTENANCE   activate      STANDBY
initialize
MAINTENANCE   deactivate    –             –
MAINTENANCE   hotenough     –             –
MAINTENANCE   maintenance   –             –
```

Fig. 7.22 Transition table for the central heating system of Example 7.4.1.

```
rules([
  context("Heater"),
  initial("STANDBY"),
  error("ERROR"),
  package("examples.heater"),
  transition("STANDBY","activate",
      nextstate("WARMINGUP"),action("warmup")),
  ...
  transition("MAINTENANCE","maintenance",
                       nonextstate ,noaction)
])
```

Fig. 7.23 Part of the abstract syntax tree of the transition table of Example 7.4.1.

7.4.3 *State Machine Implementation*

NunniFSMGen translates a transition table into an implementation based on the state design pattern [Gamma *et al.* (1995)]. The state design pattern is given in Figure 7.24. NunniFSMGen implements the state pattern using the transition table, where the events are the handles and the states are implemented as concrete states. The UML class diagram of the central heating system of the Java code generated by NunniFSMGen is shown in Figure 7.25. The generated state machine slightly differs from the original state pattern. First, the context class `HeaterFSM` overrides a class `Heater`. The class `Heater` contains the implementation of the action methods and is used by the states to invoke the action methods at a state transition. The inheritance of the class `Heater` allows editing of the action method bodies in the `Heater` class. The second difference with the original state design pattern is the object `o` in the argument of the event handlers. This argument is an optional object, which can be used by the action methods as context information. On class level the following functionality is provided by the generated classes:

- `HeaterFSM (Context)`
  It defines the abstract methods to handle events and is the interface for components using the state machine.

  It defines a private `changeState` method replacing the current state object by a new one.
- `HeaterState (State)`
  It defines an interface for all classes that represent different operational states.
- `HeaterSTANDBYState (ConcreteStates)`
  Each subclass implements a behavior associated with a state.
  It handles the different events invoked via the `Context` object. The handle call has the `Context` object as argument and when a transition is defined, the `changeState` method is called with an object of the new concrete state. If an action is defined, this action is called before the `changeState` method is invoked.

Next to Java, NunniFSMGen also supports C++ and C. The implementation of the state machines in C++ and C are almost similar to the Java one, except that the C implementation of the state machine uses a struct to store the state object. Furthermore, C has no native support for exception handling, this is simulated by a return value. It is possible to support other output languages, as long as these languages have constructs to implement the state design pattern.

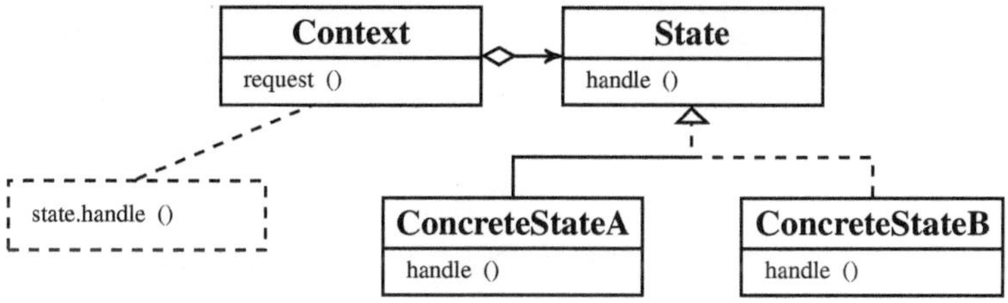

Fig. 7.24 State design pattern.

7.4.4 *Original Code Generator*

The original implementation of NunniFSMGen is a print statement based generator written in Java. Its main class contains a simple parser for the input file, constructing a one-to-one in memory representation of the transition table without any kind of rewriting or transformation. For each output language a code generator class is implemented containing all the generator logic and object code. Such a code generator class can be classified as a single-stage code generator, since the different code generator classes share a lot of mutual shared code not factorized out in a model transformation. The model transformations are entangled between object code artifacts. During the initialization of the code generator, only the set of events and the set of states are calculated. An example of the entanglement model transformation is the generation of the particular code for an event. These print statements are combined with the calculation of all events for a given state.
NunniFSMGen supports different configurations for an event:

- No transition, no action;
- No transition, with action;
- Transition to new state without action;
- Transition to new state with action;
- Transition to `errorState` with error action.

Considering the original implementation of NunniFSMGen, the different implementations of the required behavior are selected via a set of conditions. Since NunniFSMGen exists of three almost independent single-stage code emitters, the set of conditions are cloned between the different code emitters. The NunniFSMGen code emitters for C++ and Java are almost identical except for the object code. In case of the code emitter for C, the metacode is almost the same, however the C implementation of the exception handling differs from the C++ and Java version.

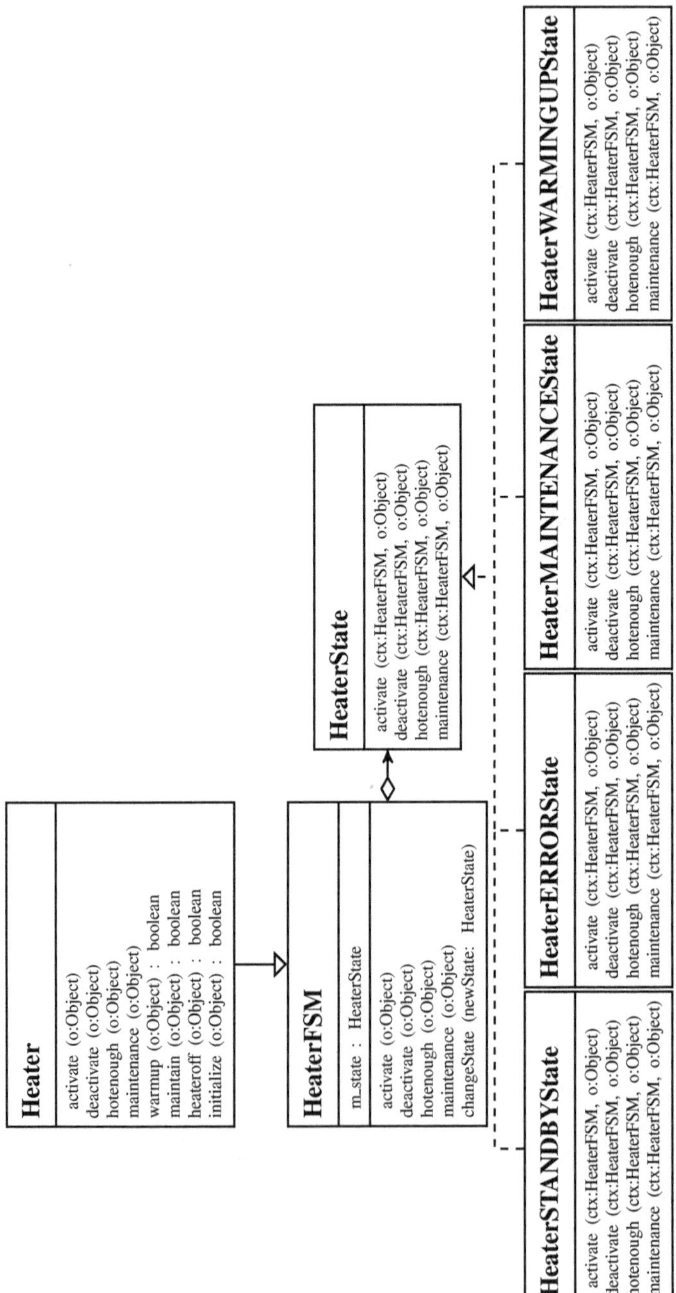

Fig. 7.25 Classes generated from the heater transition table.

7.4.5 *Reimplemented Code Generator*

The reimplementation of NunniFSMGen is based on a two-stage architecture using a parser, model transformation phase and templates. The architecture of the reimplemented NunniFSMGen is shown in Figure 7.26. The input model parser and model transformation are output language independent, while the templates contain the output language specific code. For each output language, i.e. C, C++ and Java, a set of templates is defined. The mutual shared code in the templates is limited to the metacode responsible for traversing the input data tree. All templates use the same abstract representation of the state machine as input data. Tailored model transformations for a specific output language are unnecessary. As a result the model transformation is not longer entangled in the output language specific part of the code generator.

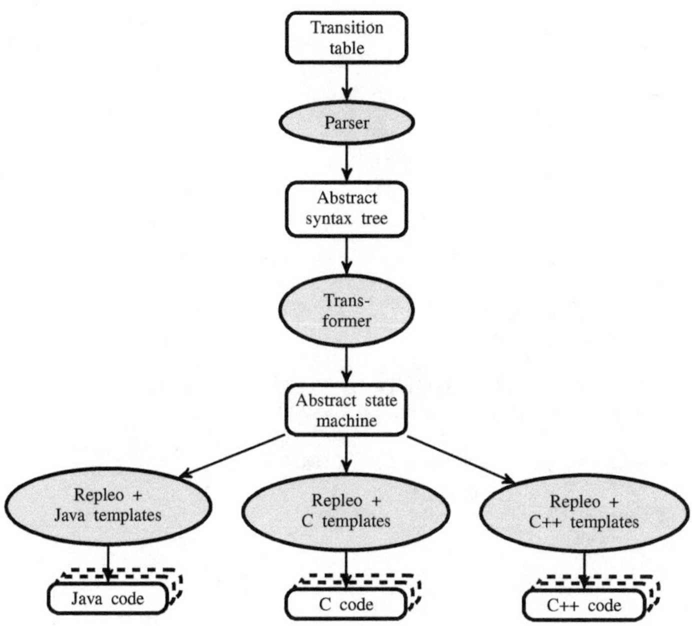

Fig. 7.26 Architecture of the reimplemented NunniFSMGen.

The transition table cannot be used directly for generating the code. The state pattern has a hierarchical structure, where each state implements handlers for each event, while the transition table is a list of vectors pointing from the `startState` to the `nextState`. A model transformation is necessary to map the vector based transition table to a hierarchical format. This format is an abstract implementation of the state design pattern. It is used as input for the code emitters to generate the actual implementation of the state machine. Figure 7.27 shows the regular tree grammar of this hierarchical format. The core elements are `initialstate`, the set of `events`, the set of `actions` and the list of `transitions`. The first three elements directly map on elements of the 5-tuple of the formal definition of a state machine. The element `transition` defines the transition for a state for every possible event.

```
hiddens
  start-symbols AFSM

exports
  sorts AFSM Context InitialState ErrorState
        Package CopyRight ParamType Transitions
        Events Actions Transition Event
        NextState Action State

  syntax
    afsm( Context, InitialState,
          ErrorState, Package, CopyRight,
          ParamTypem, Transitions, Events,
          Actions )
                                        -> AFSM
    context( Id )                       -> Context
    initialstate( Id )                  -> InitialState
    errorstate( Id )                    -> ErrorState
    package( PackageName )              -> Package
    copyright( FileName )               -> CopyRight
    paramtype( Id )                     -> ParamType
    transitions( Transition* )          -> Transitions
    transition( State, events( Event* )
                                        -> Transition
    event( Event, NextState, Action )
                                        -> Event
    events( Id* )                       -> Events
    actions( Id* )                      -> Actions
    Id                                  -> State
    Id                                  -> Event
    Id                                  -> NextState
    Id                                  -> Action
    StrCon                              -> Id
    StrCon                              -> FileName
    StrCon                              -> PackageName
```

Fig. 7.27 Regular tree grammar of abstract implementation of the state design pattern.

A model transformation is specified to transform the abstract syntax tree of the transition table to the abstract implementation of the state design pattern. This transformation is based on the following, here informally defined, rules:

- Propagate all properties to the output model;
- Collect all unique events from the transition rules and store them in the set `events`;
- Collect all unique actions from the transition rules and store them in the set `actions`;
- Make for each unique state a new `transition` rule and add for each event a triple containing the `event`, the `nextState` and the `action`. Collect all these rules in the set `transitions`.

This model transformation is implemented in ASF using seven equations and 18 sub-equations. The abstract implementation of the state design pattern of the central heating system is shown in Figure 7.28.

```
afsm(
  context("Heater" ),
  initial("STANDBY"),
  error("ERROR"),
  package("examples.heater"),
  copyright(""),
  paramtype(""),
  transitions([
   transition( "STANDBY", events([
     event( "activate",
                 nextstate("WARMINGUP"), action("warmup") ),
     event( "deactivate", nonextstate, noaction ),
     event( "hotenough", nextstate("ERROR"), erroraction ),
     event( "maintenance", nextstate("MAINTENANCE"),
                                 action("maintain") ) ])),
     ...
  ]),
  events([ "activate", "deactivate",
           "hotenough", "maintenance" ]),
  actions([ "warmup","maintain","heateroff", "initialize" ])
)
```

Fig. 7.28 Abstract implementation of the state design pattern of the heater transition table of Example 7.4.1.

The code emitters are implemented using syntax-safe templates (see Figures 7.29, 7.30 and 7.31). The use of syntax-safe templates has some consequences over the use of a text-based generator. For example, the C and C++ grammars have a couple of *plus list* nonterminals, which requires that at least one item must be inserted in that list. A placeholder representing such a plus list should at least generate one element. The placeholders and template evaluator traversal are context-free, so they have no notion of the surrounding elements. The template evaluator cannot determine whether the list is empty or not. Therefore a plus list placeholder must return at least one element. For example, the semi-colon defined at Line 46 of Figure 7.29.

Another consequence of using a syntax-safe approach, and thus also for syntax-safe templates, is the cloning of the object code in lines 9-21 of Figure 7.31. The if-statement in the object code is defined twice, first with an else part and second without the else part. Syntax-safe templates require that the if-statement is a complete grammar element. The else part is not defined as an optional nonterminal in the used C grammar, thus the object code must be defined twice.

The metavariable `$root` is used in these snippets to obtain global information, like the FSM context name, while processing a subtree of the input data. Finally, the Java template of Figure 7.30 shows how multiple files are generated for every concrete state by the match-replace placeholder surrounding the template `template`.

```
template[
 ...
<: match $events1events1 :>
  <: [event( $event , $nextstate , $action )] =:>
<: eventcode() :>
  <: [event( $event , $nextstate , $action ),$eventlist] =:>
<: eventcode() :>
<: $eventlist :>
<: end :>
 ..
]

eventcode[
void <: $root1afsm1context1 + $state + "State" :>::<: $event :>
    ( <: $root1afsm1context1 + "FSM" :> *ctx ,
                void *o ) throw (LogicError) {
  <: match $action :>
    <: erroraction =:>
      ctx->changeState(
         <: $root1afsm1context1 + $root1afsm1error5
             + "State" :>::instance() );
      throw LogicError();
    <: action($actionname) =:>
      try {
         ctx-><: $actionname :>( o );
      }
      catch( LogicError &e ) {
        ctx->changeState(
          <: $root1afsm1context1 + $root1afsm1error5
              + "State" :>::instance() );
      throw;
      }
      <: nextstatetmp($nextstate)  :>
    <: noaction =:>
      <: nextstatetmp($nextstate) :>
  <: end :>
}
]

nextstatetmp[
 <: match :>
   <: nextstate($nextstatename) =:>
     ctx->changeState(
        <: $root1afsm1context1 + $nextstatename
           + "State" :>::instance() );
   <: nonextstate =:> ;
 <: end :>
]
```

Fig. 7.29 C++ version of the template implementation.

```
<: match afsm1transitions6 :>
  <: [ transition( $state , $events), $transitions ] =:>
template[
<: $root1afsm1context1 + $state + "State.java" :>,
class <: $root1afsm1context1 + $state + "State" :>
          extends <: $root1afsm1context1 + "State" :>
{
...
}
]
<: $transitions :>
<: [] =:>
<: end :>
```

Fig. 7.30 Java snippet of the template implementation.

```
eventcode[
static int <: $root1afsm1context1 + $state + "State" + $event :>
       ( struct <: $root1afsm1context1 + "FSM" :> *fsm,
         void * o ) {
  int ret = 0;
  <: match $action :>
    ...
    <: nextstate($nextstatename) =:>
      if ( ret < 0 )
          fsm->changeState( fsm,
             &<: "m_" + $root1afsm1context1
                  + $root1afsm1error5 + "State" :> );
      else
          fsm->changeState( fsm,
             &<: "m_" + $root1afsm1context1
                  + $nextstatename + "State" :> );
    <: nonextstate =:>
      if ( ret < 0 )
          fsm->changeState( fsm,
             &<: "m_" + $root1afsm1context1
                  + $root1afsm1error5 + "State" :> );
    ...
  <: end :>
  return ret;
}
]
```

Fig. 7.31 C snippet of the template implementation.

7.4.6 *Difference Old and New Implementation*

On architectural level, the new implementation of NunniFSMGen is based on a two-stage architecture, where the old implementation almost directly generates code from the transition table in a single-stage architecture. The reimplementation offers better separation of concerns by separating the model transformation from the code generation. The first stage parses and rewrites the transition table to get an abstract implementation of the state design pattern. The second stage is responsible for generating the concrete code for the different output languages. It is expected that the more strict separation of concerns reduces the work for adding a new output language compared to the work for adding a new output language in the original implementation. In the original implementation also the model transformation has to be reimplemented. Furthermore, the original code generator contains code clones between the different code emitters for the different output language. Introducing a model transformation stage for the mutual shared code solved the code clones while leaving the case specific code in the templates.

At code level, the original implementation shows a lot of entanglement of different code artifacts in a single compilation unit. The original implementations contain statements for the model transformation, statements for the code generation phase and strings containing the object code in a single compilation unit. The object code syntax has a lot in common with the metalanguage syntax, which makes it hard to distinguish the different code artifacts. The cocktail of these different code fragments is confusing and is hard to read, as a result hard to maintain. When looking to the templates of the new implementation, it is still a hard to understand component of the code generator. However, the template based implementation shows a better syntactical difference between the metacode and object code. The object code is not encapsulated in single line strings, so the object code is not obfuscated by brackets and quotes, making it easier to read and understand.

The Table 7.2 shows the metrics for the old implementation of NunniFSMGen and the reimplementation. All the nine files of the original NunniFSMGen are measured and only the license blocks are stripped from the code. The set of files measured of the reimplementation are the grammar definitions, model transformations and templates. Total number of files of the reimplementation is 19.

Considering Table 7.2, the number of lines of codes without blanks is almost halved. The number of tokens of the reimplementation is more than halved with respect to the original implementation. The average number of non-alphanumeric characters per line is not altered. In comparison with the original implementation of ApiGen, the code emitter classes of NunniFSMGen show a lot of string constants containing object code. These string constants contain a lot of brackets and quotes, the result is that the ratio of non-alphanumeric tokens per line is not lower in the original implementation.

Table 7.2 Metrics of NunniFSMGen and the reimplementation.

Metric	Original	Reimplementation
Lines of Code	1,602	1,005
Lines of Code (without blank lines)	1,430	738
Tokens	22,024	10,438
Alphanumeric tokens	5,820	2,393
Non-alphanumeric tokens	9,189	4,762
White space tokens	7,015	3,283
Average number of tokens per line	15.4	14.14
Average number of non-alphanumeric tokens per line	6.43	6.45

7.4.7 *Evaluation*

The original implementation of NunniFSMGen contains a single-stage generator for each output language. The reimplementation is based on a two-stage architecture, where the output language is selected via the set of templates in the second stage. The model transformation is the same for all output languages and only output language specific code is defined in the templates. The result is that the size of the reimplementation is almost halved with respect to the original implementation of NunniFSMGen. It is expected that the more strict separation of concerns reduces the work for adding a new output language than adding a new output language in the original implementation, where the model transformation also has to be reimplemented. On code level, the use of templates results in better readable object code, since object code is not embedded in `println` statements, which obfuscate the code by splitting it in substrings.

Beside the improved maintainability, the use of grammars and the use of the syntax-safe template evaluator improve the correctness of the generated code of the reimplemented NunniFSMGen. Syntax errors are earlier detected in the reimplemented code generator, so users of the code generator are not confronted with syntax errors in the generated code.

7.5 Dynamic XHTML generation

Beside just-in-time compilation [Krall (1998)], run-time code generation plays an important role in contemporary applications communicating via the Internet, i.e. web applications. These web applications generate (X)HTML pages on request, which are interpreted by the browser to render the user interface of the application. Since the emergence of web applications a lot of web application frameworks, such as Java Spring Framework[4], Ruby on Rails[5], Django[6], PHP Zend[7], and so on, have been developed. These web application frameworks have in common that they are delivered with a kind of text-based template evaluator to render the HTML output.

The problem of these web applications is to ensure that the fixed HTML code in the templates does not contain syntax errors, which otherwise will result in errors in the browser. Dynamic code generation and the ability of browsers to execute code, like cascade style sheets (CSS) [8] and JavaScript [Goodman and Eich (2000)], can also result in security breaches.

This case study covers code generation during the use of an application instead of using code generation for the development of the application. It is about dynamic XHTML generation in web applications. XHTML [Pemberton *et al.* (2002)] is a more restrictive version of HTML, so that it can be defined by a context-free grammar. This case study shows the use of syntax-safe templates to reduce the possibility of security bugs in applications generating code during run-time. A small shout-wall web application is implemented, where the security is enforced in a declarative manner by grammar definitions and syntax-safe template evaluation. First cross-site scripting is discussed. After that the implementation of the shout-wall web application is presented followed by the approach to ensure the web application is no longer vulnerable for cross-site scripting.

7.5.1 *Cross-site Scripting*

Cross-site scripting (XSS) is the class of web application vulnerabilities in which an attacker causes a victim's browser to execute untrusted JavaScript, CSS or (X)HTML tags with the privileges of a trusted host [Wassermann and Su (2008)]. This untrusted code can collect data, change the look and/or change the behavior of the original web site. It is the

[4]http://www.springsource.org (accessed on December 18, 2011)
[5]http://rubyonrails.org(accessed on December 18, 2011)
[6]http://www.djangoproject.com (accessed on December 18, 2011)
[7]http://www.zend.com (accessed on December 18, 2011)
[8]http://www.w3.org/TR/CSS1/ (accessed on December 18, 2011)

number four of the top 25 security bugs in web applications in 2011[9]. Even contemporary large web-services, like Google, YouTube, Twitter and Facebook, have to deal with cross-site scripting. The main cause of cross-site scripting is the evolution of (X)HTML (and sub-languages) over the past decades. The way (X)HTML has evolved resulted in a liberal interpretation of the (X)HTML language. Browsers, such as Firefox and MS Internet Explorer, even interpret (X)HTML code containing a lot of errors. As a result, the evaluation function of the browser executes JavaScript or CSS embedded in the most exotic constructions, like hex encoding or code with embedded tabs or new lines[10].

The first requirement for a web application to be vulnerable for XSS is to have some untrusted (user) input, which is used for rendering the output. This security bug is already present natively in a basic web application having a commit form and a result view containing the committed data. An attacker can post some untrusted code between `script` or `style` tags in the commit form, which is interpreted by a browser rendering the result page.

A common architecture for implementing these web applications is the model-view-controller architecture. The controller describes the behavior of the web application and is usually some application specific (business) logic written in a general purpose (script) language on top of a web framework, such as Django, Java Spring Framework or Ruby on Rails. The controller handles the web requests and returns the view to the web browser. The web framework performs web application domain specific tasks such as URL mapping, load balancing and so on. The information necessary for processing these web requests is stored in the model; usually implemented as a relational database. This database contains information loaded at deployment of the web application, submitted via the web or inserted via another external source. The view renders the web page and is most times implemented as a text-template system querying the objects provided by the controller.

The problem of cross-site scripting arises when data is literally stored in the database and literally inserted in the rendered web page. An attacker can, for example, submit a piece of JavaScript

```
<script>alert("Hello World");</script>
```

on a reaction form on a web site. The JavaScript code is stored in the database and rendered on all the web pages of all viewers of that web site. This results in an annoying pop-up message, see Figure 7.32.

[9] http://cwe.mitre.org/top25/ (accessed on December 18, 2011)
[10] http://ha.ckers.org/xss.html (accessed on December 18, 2011)

Fig. 7.32 JavaScript pop-up message.

Most web frameworks already offer prevention against this naive form of cross-site scripting. The first solution is to scan the input committed via a web form before it is inserted in the database, so the database only contains *trusted* data. The problem of this approach is that it assumes that the database only contains trusted data. This is a valid solution as long as the database itself is not vulnerable for attacks, but that is in practice not a realistic assumption. Besides that, alternative sources of data, such as RFID tags or URL parameters, are often seen by developers as trusted data and directly stored in the database, while this data can contain malicious code [Rieback *et al.* (2006)]. At the end, one cannot trust any data stored in the database, and at the level of the web page generator one should consider all the data as untrusted to prevent cross-site scripting attacks.

The second solution against cross-site scripting provided by web frameworks is based on the assumption that the data necessary to render the web page can indeed not be trusted. Most attacks can easily be *disarmed* by replacing the characters < and > to a non executable equivalent, `<` and `>`, before inserting it in the final (X)HTML code. Contemporary template evaluators provided by web frameworks escape potential hazardous characters before the data is inserted in the web page by default. However, sometimes it is not feasible to use this escaping of characters as it is required to render layout information, like bold and italic tags, or it is even required to render a subset of JavaScript such as a JSON tree. At that point the escape mechanism must be turned off for that placeholder. As a result the web page generator is vulnerable for cross-site scripting attacks.

In case character replacement cannot be used, a specific cross-site scripting filter or check can be defined. These filters are most times manually written in the same general purpose language as used for implementing the controller component of the web application. These implementations contain a lot of unrelated details and the filter specification is scattered over the code. An example of a small hand-written filter is given in Figure 7.33[11]. It removes <script> tags, javascript: calls and onXxxxx attributes, like onLoad or onClick.

```
public static String sanitize(String string) {
  return string
    .replaceAll("(?i)<script.*?>.*?</script.*?>", "")
    .replaceAll("(?i)<.*?javascript:.*?>.*?</.*?>", "")
    .replaceAll("(?i)<.*?\\s+on.*?>.*?</.*?>", "");
}
```

Fig. 7.33 Hand-written cross-site scripting filter.

7.5.2 *Preventing Cross-site Scripting*

Syntax-safe templates can be used to prevent cross-site scripting. In short, this solution uses syntax-safe templates to parse the XHTML web-page including placeholders. The object code is already checked for well-formedness with respect to the XHTML grammar. The placeholders in the template are typed with the object language nonterminal they represent. This object language nonterminal is used to check that these placeholders are replaced by a valid (sub)set of the XHTML language during rendering the web page. Most times the language produced by the nonterminal of the placeholder is too broad to prevent cross-site scripting. Most tags of XHTML accept the complete XHTML language in their body. Section 5.2.1.2 introduced explicit syntactical typing of placeholders, which can be used to limit the language the placeholder can produce. The syntax-safe evaluator prevents inserting malicious code in the generated XHTML page, when the subset of the XHTML language produced by the nonterminal of the placeholder is disjoint from the set of browser executable code.

This solution to prevent injection of malicious code in the XHTML is based on filtering the data before it is inserted. Filtering can be based on the principle of *black-listing* or *white-listing* [Wassermann and Su (2008)]. In case of white-listing, the set of allowed sentences is specified, in case of black-listing every sentence is allowed except the harmful ones, which are rewritten or removed by the filter. The problem of filtering is that browsers handle XHTML liberally and not in a uniform way. Covering the prevention of all manners of triggering the JavaScript and CSS evaluator is hard and different per browser. Wassermann et al. [Wassermann and Su (2008)] have reviewed the source code and documentation of

[11] http://www.rgagnon.com/javadetails/java-0627.html (accessed on December 18, 2011)

common browsers to obtain a list of ways to write executable JavaScript or CSS code. This list depends on the inspected version of the browser and for closed-source browsers this list is probably not complete. Without knowing which sentences are triggering the browser evaluation engine, it is hard, if not impossible, to ensure that cross-site scripting is prevented.

A white-list system is preferable over a black-listing approach. White-list filters only include trusted syntax instead of excluding untrusted syntax. In case of a black-list filter there is always a chance that some untrusted syntax is not excluded. A white-list filter does not allow more syntax than necessary. White-listing is less susceptible for browser updates, as new ways of expressing executable JavaScript or CSS are most likely not allowed, except if this new way is a subset of the white-listed sentences grammar. Testing, verifying or even proving that the nonterminal only produces a language without harmful sentences is more feasible than proving the completeness of black-list filters as context-free grammars are compact.

The white-list filter in the syntax-safe template approach is based on a context-free grammar for XHTML. The XHTML grammar used in this case study is a strict implementation of the XHTML specification [Pemberton *et al.* (2002)] and more strict than the HTML syntax accepted by most browsers. Using this grammar for the object language, it is precisely defined which language a nonterminal can produce. When this language of a nonterminal does not contain sentences resulting in triggering the JavaScript or CSS evaluator, it can be safely extended with placeholder syntax. The result of using syntax-safe templates combined with this XHTML grammar is that cross-site scripting protection is handled by the template evaluator instead of by hand-written error-prone filters.

7.5.3 *Example Web Application: Shout Wall*

This case study discusses an example web application, which demonstrates preventing cross-site scripting attacks by using syntax-safe templates. This web application is a "shout wall" or "guest book" where a visitor can post a message and a name. The following requirements are defined for this example web application:

- For a post, the message field is mandatory and the name field is optional.
- Both fields, name and message, must contain human readable text, XHTML tags are not allowed.
- Beside human readable text, the message field may contain a JSON tree between `script` tags.

The last rule, allowing JSON data in the message field is for demonstration purposes. This requirement makes it impossible to use a naive character replacement to prevent cross-site scripting. Instead of rewriting characters, it must be verified that only well-formed JSON, without any executable JavaScript artifacts, is inserted in the output code.

The "shout wall" web application is implemented using the model-view-controller architecture. The controller class is listed in Figure 7.34 and extends the Java *servlet* API [Hunter and Crawford (2001)]. A servlet class may respond to *HTTP* requests. For this application, persistent storage of the data is not required and thus the model is also declared in the controller class by the field `messages`, which is initialized as an empty list. The model is based on ATerms (see Section 2.6.3), the input data tree format used by Repleo. The ATermLibrary is used to ensure the ATerms are well-formed.

The controller class implements two methods of the Java servlet API. The first method handles the *get* requests and returns a web page based on an instantiated template. The template evaluator is invoked when the `doGet` is called. During evaluation of the template it will throw an exception if a parse error occurs. A parse error is the result of a string in the input data for the field message or name, which is not defined by the object language grammar. If a (parser) exception occurs the latest added message is removed from the input data list and the web page is rendered again with a flag to display an error message. This second template evaluator call in the catch block is not enclosed in a try-catch statement, because the web application returns in a valid state when the last added message is removed. The web application is started in a valid state, i.e. a well-formed template and empty list of messages, only adding messages to the list can result in an exception, so it is always the last added message causing the exception.

The second method in the controller class handles the *post* request. It collects the data from the post request and stores it in a message object. The `ATmake` method of the ATerm factory is used to construct the message object to prevent ATerm injection.

The controller class does not contain any specific logic to prevent HTML injection attacks. Data committed by the user is directly stored in the model without any filtering. The only behavior responsible for the protection against cross-site scripting is the try-catch block in the controller. The controller expects that the template evaluator discover the attack resulting in an exception.

```
import java.io.*;
...

public class XssServlet extends HttpServlet {
  private ATermList messages;
  private aterm.pure.PureFactory termFactory = null;
  private WebPageGenerator pagegenerator;

public XssServlet() {
  termFactory = SingletonFactory.getInstance();
  pagegenerator = new WebPageGenerator();
  messages = termFactory.makeList();
}

public void doGet(HttpServletRequest req,HttpServletResponse res)
        throws ServletException, IOException {
  res.setContentType("text/html");
  PrintWriter out = res.getWriter();
  ATerm inputdata = termFactory.make(
    "data(error(noerror),messages(<term>))", messages);
  String html = "";
  try {
    html = pagegenerator.generate(inputdata);
  } catch (Exception e1) {
// remove evil message from messages
    this.messages = messages.getNext();
    inputdata = termFactory.make(
      "data(error(detected),messages(<term>))", messages);
    html = pagegenerator.generate(inputdata);
  }
  out.println(html);
  out.close();
}

public void doPost(HttpServletRequest req,HttpServletResponse res)
    throws ServletException, IOException {
  String message = req.getParameter("message");
  if (!message.trim().equals("")) {
    String name = req.getParameter("name");
    ATerm messageNode =
      termFactory.make("message(<str>,<str>)", name, message);
    this.messages =
      termFactory.makeList(messageNode, this.messages);
  }
  this.doGet(req, res);
}
}

}
```

Fig. 7.34 Java Controller of the “shout wall” web application.

The last discussed component of the "shout wall" web application is the view. The requirement for the view is that it only returns a well-formed XHTML page, otherwise it must throw an error. The template for the "shout wall" is shown in Figure 7.35. It contains XHTML code for the submit form and two match-replace placeholders; one for displaying an error message and one for rendering the messages list. The generation of this messages list is potentially vulnerable for cross-site scripting since substitution placeholders are used. Table 7.3 shows the metrics of the two files of the shout wall web application.

Table 7.3 Metrics of the Shout Wall web application.

Metric	**Shout Wall**
Lines of Code	168
Lines of Code (without blank lines)	149
Tokens	1,980
Alphanumeric tokens	649
Non-alphanumeric tokens	812
White space tokens	519
Average number of tokens per line	13.29
Average number of non-alphanumeric tokens per line	5.45

The view is implemented using syntax-safe templates, as a result the template is parsed and the placeholders have a syntactical type. This syntactical type is used by the evaluator to substitute the placeholders only with sentences belonging to the language of that syntactical type, otherwise an error is generated. This behavior of syntax-safe template evaluation is used to provide the protection against cross-site scripting attacks. An error during the evaluation process indicates that the input data contains a sentence that is not allowed to replace the substitution placeholder.

The requirements state that the message field may contain human readable text or a JSON tree, and that the name field is optional and must be human readable text. Human readable text without XHTML tags is provided by the XHTML grammar as the `PCDATA` nonterminal. PCDATA may contain every character except the characters <, > and `&`. The substitution placeholder responsible for generating the name is enforced to the syntactical type `PCDATA*`, where the star list sort allows to substitute it with no text. This protection against cross-site scripting attacks is easy to implement and indeed already supported by most web template systems. They provide automatic escaping for the three forbidden characters.

```
template[
<!DOCTYPE html PUBLIC "-//W3C//DTD XHTML 1.0 Strict//EN"
"http://www.w3.org/TR/xhtml1/DTD/xhtml1-strict.dtd">
<html xml:lang="en" xmlns="http://www.w3.org/1999/xhtml">
<head>
<title>Cross-site scripting prevention example</title>
</head>
<body>
<form action="/XssServlet.java" method="post">
<h1>Write your message on the wall</h1>
<br /><br />
<b>Message (PCDATA or JSON):</b><br />
<textarea name="message" cols="50" rows="7" class="textbox">
</textarea>
<br /><br />
<b>Name (only PCDATA):</b><br />
<input type="text" name="name" size="48" class="textbox">
<br /><br />
<input type="submit" value="Submit" class="textbox">
<br /><br />
</form>

<: match data1error1 sort:XHtml-flow-item* :>
 <: detected =:>
 <b style="color:red" >You tried to post some forbidden text!</b>
<br /><br />
 <: noerror =:>
<: end :>

<: match data2messages1 :>
 <: [ message($name, $text) , $t ] =:>
  <b>message:</b><br />
  <p><: $text sort:PCDATA-JSON :> </p> <br />
  <b>name:</b> <i><: $name sort:PCDATA* :></i> <br /><br />
  <: $t :>
 <: [ ] =:>
<: end :>

</body>
</html>
]
```

Fig. 7.35 XHTML template of the “shout wall” web application.

In order to show that syntax-safe templates are more advanced than simple escaping of some characters in a string, it is required that the text of the message may contain human readable text *or* a JSON tree. Escaping dangerous characters cannot be used anymore as JSON trees between script tags contain these characters. A grammar must be defined for JSON only producing valid JSON sentences that do not execute in the browser. A JSON grammar in SDF conforming to the JSON standard [Crockford (2008)] is presented in Figure 7.36. This JSON grammar defines a subset of the original JSON language specification by limiting the class of characters allowed for `JSStrings`. The greater-than and smaller-than characters are explicitly disabled; otherwise it is possible to embed a cross-site scripting attack inside a JSON tree.

```
module JSON

exports
  sorts JSON JSONTUPLE JSString JSStrChar

  context-free syntax
   "{" { JSONTUPLE "," }* "}"  -> JSON
   "[" { JSON "," }* "]"       -> JSON
   JSString                    -> JSON
   JSString ":" JSON           -> JSONTUPLE

  lexical syntax
    ~[\0-\31\n\t\"\\\<\>]      -> JSStrChar
    [\"] chars:JSStrChar* [\"] -> JSString
```

Fig. 7.36 JSON Grammar.

The JSON grammar is not a part of the XHTML grammar. Both grammars are mixed by defining the grammar module of Figure 7.37. This grammar module adds the nonterminal `PCDATA-JSON` as alternative to the `XHtml-Inline` of the XHTML grammar. The `PCDATA-JSON` nonterminal produces the language of sentences containing the set of JSON trees between `script` tags and the set of sentences provided by `PCDATA*`. The production rule adding `PCDATA-JSON` to the XHTML grammar is annotated with `avoid` to specify that it should never be used if another production rule can be applied. The priority of the added nonterminal `PCDATA-JSON` is lower than the original alternatives for `XHtml-Inline`.
The substitution placeholder is explicitly specified for the text part message by the syntactical type `PCDATA-JSON`. The template evaluator is allowed to replace it by human readable text *or* JSON trees. The syntax-safe template evaluator using the grammar handles the protection against JavaScript and/or CSS injection.

7.5.4 *Unhackability*

In order to verify the *unhackability* of the shout wall, the shout wall website is published on-line including the source code. A number of web security experts are asked to find security breaches in the implementation. Two bugs were found in the first shout wall implementation. First, that an input term containing a repeating pattern "`{ "a",`" caused a crash of the web server. This was a result of a stack overflow in the parser and is solved by fixing the stack overflow handling.

```
module XHtml-Json

imports XHtml
imports JSON

exports
  sorts PCDATA-JSON
  context-free syntax
    PCDATA-JSON                  -> XHtml-Inline {avoid}
    PCDATA*                      -> PCDATA-JSON
    "<script" ">" JSON "</script>"
                                 -> PCDATA-JSON
```

Fig. 7.37 Adding JSON as alternative for XHtml-Inline.

The second security issue was a cross-site scripting problem. The problem is inherent in the JSON language specification [Crockford (2008)], which allows strings of the character class

```
~[\0-\31\n\t\"\\]
```

This character class allows the symbols < and >, JavaScript encapsulated in a string is valid conform this grammar, however Firefox 3.0.19 interprets this as JavaScript code stored in JSON strings instead of handling it as data. This security breach is solved by limiting the character class for `JSStrChar` by disallowing the symbols < and > in the grammar of Figure 7.36. After these two errors were detected, no further security issues were found.

As discussed, the use of grammars in a syntax-safe template does not prevent all injection attacks. However, having formalisms for grammar definitions and syntax-safe templates provides a compact implementation of web applications. The use of languages at a higher level of abstraction, such as grammar definitions, prevents making silly errors resulting in security breaches. It is easier to examine the allowed sentences of a grammar than inspecting manually written parsers and filters. When a security breach is found, it is easier to repair it in a grammar, since grammars are compact and the formalism has a declarative nature.

7.5.5 *Preventing Injections at the Door*

A similar solution to prevent cross-site scripting and/or injection attacks is *syntax embeddings* presented by Bravenboer et al. [Bravenboer *et al.* (2007)]. This approach prevents injection attacks in sentences of an embedded language, for example SQL, manipulated in some host language, for example Java. It uses a grammar based on the host language extended with syntax of the embedded language to achieve the safety. An API is generated from this grammar to provide the appropriate unparsing, escaping, and checking of lexical values. The source code containing embedded syntax is translated to a file without embedded syntax by replacing this foreign syntax with calls to the generated API.

Syntax embedding and templates share the concept of combining grammars, however, there is a difference of the manipulated language. In case of syntax embeddings the language in the strings is the object language, and in case of templates the object language is surrounding the metalanguage. This manifests itself in the construction of the grammars. The grammars used for syntax embeddings are based on a metalanguage grammar where object language nonterminals are injected as alternatives, while in template grammars the object language grammar is extended with metalanguage constructs.

7.5.6 *Evaluation*

Cross-site scripting attacks are nowadays the number one security bug in web applications. Syntax-safe templates can provide a solution to prevent cross-site scripting without introducing a lot of boilerplate and checking code. Grammars are used to specify allowed (sub) sentences in the template instead of implementing the checks and filters for the input data in the controller component. Filters and checks implemented in a general purpose language contain a lot of detail, which make it hard to write, to maintain, to test and to validate these manually implemented filters and checkers, especially for complex languages. Obviously, the level of protection against injection attacks is dependent on the quality of the used grammars. However, a context-free grammar definition is easier to write and maintain than manually implemented checkers based on imperative constructs.

Beside the improved security during evaluation, parsing both XHTML and metalanguage provides easier development of templates. An IDE for editing syntax-safe templates can use the parse tree to report syntax errors directly in the editor. Syntax errors in the object code and metacode are already detected before any web-page is generated.

7.6 Conclusions

The compact metalanguage, as designed in Chapter 4, enforces to use the two-stage architecture. It is not possible to express all model transformations using the unparser-complete metalanguage, as it is not possible to express calculations and store intermediate values. This compact metalanguage complies with the recommendation of Parr [Parr (2004)] to a metalanguage to enforce strict separation of model and view.

The benefits of the two-stage architecture based on templates are reflected in the reduced number of lines of code of the two case studies ApiGen and NunniFSMGen. The reimplemented code generators are at least half the size of the original implementations. The NunniFSMGen case study showed that the choice of the output language is made at the template level, while the input data model is not changed. It is expected that the increased separation of concerns in the reimplementation result in easier adding a new output language to the reimplemented NunniFSMGen than adding a new output language to the original implementation.

Table 7.4 shows the volume of all re-implemented code generators. Both case studies show a reduction of code between the old implementation and the new implementation. The reduction is accomplished first by using languages better suited for implementing code generators, i.e. a term rewrite formalism and unparser complete metalanguage. Second, by reducing the number of code clones in the generator by improving the separation of concerns between the model transformation stage and code emitter stage.

Table 7.4 Metrics of the different case studies.

Metric	**ApiGen (old)**	**Apigen (new)**	**NunniFSMGen (old)**	**NunniFSMGen (new)**
Lines of Code	8,789	2,975	1,602	1,005
Lines of Code (without blank lines)	7,296	2,361	1,430	738

The third case study shows that syntax-safety increases the safety of dynamic code generation in web applications. Cross-site scripting is prevented using grammars instead of introducing boilerplate code and/or checking code. Only 168 lines of code are used to implement the shout wall application.

Chapter 8

Conclusions

This book discussed the theory and application of templates in the context of code generation. Code generators can be implemented using different approaches and techniques, including templates. A template is a text that contains placeholders. During evaluation of the template, these placeholders are replaced to obtain an output text. Contemporary template evaluators are text-based, not offering protection against syntax errors in the template and syntax errors in the code they instantiate.

The central theme of this book is increasing the (technical) quality of code generators based on templates. Both the technical quality of the code generator implementations as the technical quality of the generated code are involved. This book provides three main contributions. First, the maintainability of template based code generators is increased by specifying unparser-completeness. Unparser-completeness defines the computational power a metalanguage should at least, and at most, offer. This enforces separation of concerns between model and view [Parr (2004)], and unparser-complete metalanguages are strong enough to use in every code generator setting, see Sections 8.1 and 8.2. Second, syntactical correctness of the templates and generated code can be ensured, see Sections 8.3 and 8.4. Protection against syntax errors in the template provides a shorter development cycle, as code does not need to be generated to detect syntax errors in the object code. Third, the presented theory and techniques are validated by case studies, discussed in Section 8.5. The three case studies showed that unparser-completeness lead to improved separation of concerns. The limited computational power of unparse-complete metalanguages enforces a strict separation of concerns between the model transformer and the code emitters. The last case study also showed that syntax safe template evaluation provides out-of-the-box protection against code injection attacks.

The next sections discuss the contributions per chapter.

8.1 Unparser Completeness

Chapter 3 discussed the requirements for a metalanguage in the setting of code generation. The metalanguage should prevent programming in the view, and it should be expressive enough to instantiate every semantically correct sentence of the output language. The relations between concrete syntax, abstract syntax trees and their grammars are discussed. The mapping of abstract syntax trees to concrete syntax, i.e. the unparser, showed the required properties. Unparsers have two specific properties: parsing and desugaring its output results in the original abstract syntax tree of the used input, and unparsers can instantiate all semantically correct sentences of the output language.

The main contribution of this chapter is that a linear deterministic top-down tree-to-string transducer is strong enough to implement unparsers. A metalanguage for implementing unparsers should at least be powerful enough to express a linear deterministic top-down tree-to-string transducer, otherwise some sentences of the output language cannot be instantiated. This tree-to-string transducer is less strong than a Turing-complete language, and thus prevents programming in the view.

8.2 A Template Metalanguage

An unparser-complete metalanguage is presented in Chapter 4. This metalanguage provides two kernel constructs: subtemplates and match-replace placeholders. Also three derived constructs are introduced: substitution placeholders, iteration placeholders and conditional placeholders. These constructs are abbreviations for combinations of subtemplates and match-replace placeholders.

To prevent writing model transformations in templates, an unparser-complete metalanguage cannot change the input data and it does not support complex expressions. This enforces a clear separation of model and view.

The unparser-complete metalanguage is compared with metalanguages of other template systems: ERb, Velocity, JSP and StringTemplate. ERb, JSP and Velocity offer a Turing-complete metalanguage, while StringTemplate only supports basic functionality, like subtemplates, substitution, iteration and conditions. An unparser for the PICO language is implemented for each template environment to compare their metalanguages on the level of expressiveness.

The StringTemplate implementation of the PICO unparser has the fewest lines of code, but in contrast with the unparser-complete metalanguage presented in this book, StringTemplate cannot directly accept all regular trees. It can only handle unordered trees. An extra transformation is necessary to convert the input data from an ordered tree to an unordered tree accepted by StringTemplate.
ERb, Velocity and JSP come with a Turing-complete metalanguage. However, they do not provide a block scoping mechanism for the metavariables. A workaround was necessary for proper handling of metavariable scopes to implement the PICO unparser. This workaround resulted in additional boilerplate code. Furthermore, rich metalanguages increase the chance of undesired programming in templates, which can result in tangling of concerns. An example of such a risk is the specification of model transformations inside a template.

8.3 Syntactical Correctness of Templates

In Chapter 5 the topic is the syntactical correctness of templates. A grammar describing the metalanguage, object language and the connection between both can be constructed. Syntax errors in the object code and metacode of a template are detected while parsing the template instead of dealing with syntax errors at compile time of the generated code. The complete template is parsed, and thus checked for syntax errors. The syntax of the templates is not different from text-templates, as a result they provide the same user experience.
The template grammar is obtained by combining the object language grammar and metalanguage grammar by adding the placeholder syntax as alternative to the object language nonterminals. The construction of such a template grammar is generic. Only a combination grammar connecting both languages has to be defined manually. The advantage of this approach is the ease of using off-the-shelf object language grammars.

8.4 Syntax-Safe Evaluation

Only parsing templates is not sufficient to guarantee that the output of the template evaluator is a sentence of the output language. After parsing, it is still possible that a template evaluator, unaware of the output language, can replace the placeholders with not allowed sentences. Chapter 6 presents a syntax-safe template evaluation mechanism to prevent that placeholders in a template are being replaced by syntactical incorrect constructs. This guarantee is achieved by checking that the root nonterminal of the sub parse tree replacing a placeholder is equal to the object language nonterminal where the placeholder is applied. The presented evaluation strategy is independent of the object language and does not need to be changed when another object language is used. It is even possible to use object code containing multiple languages, like Java with embedded SQL. An implementation of this template evaluation strategy, called *Repleo*, is provided to validate the practical applicability of syntax-safe templates.

8.5 Case Studies

Chapter 7 presented three case studies using templates to validate the applicability of unparser-complete metalanguages and syntax-safe templates. The first case study was about the reimplementation of ApiGen. ApiGen is code generator for creating Java API's from a tree grammar to create, manipulate and query tree-like data structures. It covers the generation of Java code based on the factory pattern and composite pattern. The second case study discussed the reimplementation of NunniFSMGen. NunniFSMGen is a tool to generate finite state machines from a transition table. It covers the generation of behavioral code based on the state design pattern for different output languages. The last case study presented a web application using templates to render XHTML code on demand of an incoming request. The web application example is a 'shout wall', where someone could leave a message.

The first two case studies showed that unparser-completeness in combination with the use of a two-stage architecture results in an improved separation of concerns between the model transformation and code emitters. The compact metalanguage, as designed in Chapter 4, enforced the two-stage architecture, as it is not possible to express all model transformations in the templates. Albeit the metalanguage is not Turing-complete, this property does not pop-up as a limitation for these case studies. This is also not expected, as unparser-completeness guarantees that the metalanguage can be used to instantiate all semantically correct sentences of a context-free languages. Also, the NunniFSMGen case study showed that the intermediate representation between the model transformation and templates could be used for all output languages. It was not necessary to implement output language specific model transformations. The benefits of the two-stage architecture are also reflected in the reduced number of lines of code. The reimplemented code generators are two or three times as small as the original implementations.

The last case study shows that syntax-safety increases the safety of dynamic code generation in web applications. By nature, web applications have a big chance to be vulnerable for cross-site scripting, i.e. injection malicious code in the HTML output via user input. Grammars are used to specify the allowed (sub) sentences in the XHTML template instead of implementing the checks for the input data in the controller component of a web application. This case study showed that cross-site scripting is prevented without introducing boilerplate code and checking code.

Bibliography

Aho, A. V., Ganapathi, M. and Tjiang, S. W. K. (1989). Code generation using tree matching and dynamic programming, *ACM Transactions on Programming Languages and Systems* **11**, 4, pp. 491–516.

Aho, A. V., Johnson, S. C. and Ullman, J. D. (1977). Code generation for expressions with common subexpressions, *Journal of the ACM* **24**, 1, pp. 146–160.

Aho, A. V., Sethi, R. and Ullman, J. D. (1986). *Compilers: principles, techniques, and tools* (Addison-Wesley Longman Publishing Co., Boston, MA, USA), ISBN 0-201-10088-6.

Alpuente, M., Falaschi, M., Ramis, M. J. and Vidal, G. (1994). A compositional semantics for conditional term rewriting systems, in *ICCL '94: International Conference on Computer Languages* (IEEE Computer Society Press, Piscataway, NJ, USA), pp. 171–182.

Andersen, L. (2006). *JDBC(tm) 4.0 Specification*, Sun Microsystems, Inc., URL http://jcp.org/aboutJava/communityprocess/final/jsr221/index.html.

Arnoldus, B. J., Bijpost, J. W. and van den Brand, M. G. J. (2007). Repleo: a Syntax-Safe Template Engine, in *GPCE '07: Generative Programming and Component Engineering* (ACM Press, New York, NY, USA), ISBN 978-1-59593-855-8, pp. 25–32.

Arnoldus, B. J., van den Brand, M. G. J. and Serebrenik, A. (2011). Less is more: unparser-completeness of metalanguages for template engines, in *Proceedings of the 10th ACM international conference on Generative programming and component engineering*, GPCE '11 (ACM, New York, NY, USA), ISBN 978-1-4503-0689-8, pp. 137–146.

Baader, F. and Nipkow, T. (1998). *Term rewriting and all that* (Cambridge University Press, New York, NY, USA), ISBN 0-521-45520-0.

Backus, J. W., Bauer, F. L., Green, J., Katz, C., McCarthy, J., Naur, P., Perlis, A. J., Rutishauser, H., Samuelson, K., Vauquois, B., Wegstein, J. H., van Wijngaarden, A. and Woodger, M. (1960). Report on the algorithmic language ALGOL 60, *Communications of the ACM* **3**, 5, pp. 299–314.

Bergsten, H. (2002). *Javaserver Pages* (O'Reilly & Associates, Inc., Sebastopol, CA, USA), ISBN 059600317X.

Bergstra, J. A., Heering, J. and Klint, P. (1989). *Algebraic specification* (ACM Press, New York, NY, USA), ISBN 0-201-41635-2.

Bex, G. J., Neven, F. and van den Bussche, J. (2004). DTDs versus XML schema: a practical study, in *WebDB '04: International Workshop on the Web and Databases* (ACM Press, New York, NY, USA), pp. 79–84.

Borovanský, P., Kirchner, C., Kirchner, H., Moreau, P. E. and Vittek, M. (1996). ELAN: A logical framework based on computational systems, in *RWLW '96: First International Workshop on Rewriting Logic and its Applications*, Vol. 4 (Electronic Notes in Theoretical Computer Science), pp. 35–50.

Bracha, G. (2004). Generics in the Java Programming Language, Tech. rep., http://java.sun.com/j2se/1.5/pdf/generics-tutorial.pdf (accessed on December 18, 2011).

van den Brand, M. G. J., Klint, P. and Vinju, J. J. (2003). Term rewriting with traversal functions, *ACM Transactions on Software Engineering and Methodology* **12**, pp. 152–190.

van den Brand, M. G. J., Moreau, P. E. and Vinju, J. J. (2005). A generator of efficient strongly typed abstract syntax trees in Java, *IEE Proceedings Software* **152**, 2, pp. 70–78, URL http://www.asfsdf.org/pub/Meta-Environment/ApiGen/submitted-20-11-2003.pdf.

van den Brand, M. G. J., van Deursen, A., Heering, J., de Jong, H. A., de Jonge, M., Kuipers, T., Klint, P., Moonen, L., Olivier, P. A., Scheerder, J., Vinju, J. J., Visser, E. and Visser, J. (2001). The ASF+SDF Meta-environment: A Component-Based Language Development Environment, in *CC '01: Compiler Construction* (Springer-Verlag, London, UK), ISBN 3-540-41861-X, pp. 365–370.

van den Brand, M. G. J., de Jong, H. A., Klint, P. and Olivier, P. A. (2000). Efficient annotated terms, *Software: Practice and Experience* **30**, 3, pp. 259–291.

van den Brand, M. G. J., Scheerder, J., Vinju, J. J. and Visser, E. (2002). Disambiguation Filters for Scannerless Generalized LR Parsers, in *CC '02: Compiler Construction* (Springer-Verlag, London, UK), ISBN 3-540-43369-4, pp. 143–158.

van den Brand, M. G. J. and Visser, E. (1996). Generation of formatters for context-free languages, *ACM Transactions on Software Engineering and Methodology* **5**, 1, pp. 1–41.

Bravenboer, M., Dolstra, E. and Visser, E. (2007). Preventing injection attacks with syntax embeddings, in *GPCE '07: Generative Programming and Component Engineering* (ACM Press, New York, NY, USA), ISBN 978-1-59593-855-8, pp. 3–12.

Bravenboer, M., de Groot, R. and Visser, E. (2006a). MetaBorg in Action: Examples of Domain-Specific Language Embedding and Assimilation Using Stratego/XT, in *GTTSE '05: Generative and Transformational Techniques in Software Engineering*, *Lecture Notes in Computer Science*, Vol. 4143 (Springer-Verlag, Berlin, Heidelberg), pp. 297–311.

Bravenboer, M., Tanter, É. and Visser, E. (2006b). Declarative, formal, and extensible syntax definition for AspectJ, in *OOPSLA '06: Object-Oriented Programming Systems, Languages, and Applications* (ACM Press, New York, NY, USA), ISBN 1-59593-348-4, pp. 209–228.

Burbeck, S. (1992). Applications Programming in Smalltalk-80: How to use Model-View- Controller (MVC), URL http://st-www.cs.illinois.edu/users/smarch/st-docs/mvc.html.

Christensen, A. S., Møller, A. and Schwartzbach, M. I. (2003). Precise analysis of string expressions, in *SAS'03: International Conference on Static Analysis* (Springer-Verlag, Berlin, Heidelberg), ISBN 3-540-40325-6, pp. 1–18.

Clark, J. (1999). W3C recommendation. XSL Transformations (XSLT) version 1.0, http://www.w3.org/TR/xslt (accessed on December 18, 2011).

Cleophas, L. G. W. A. (2008). *Tree Algorithms: Two Taxonomies and a Toolkit*, Ph.D. thesis, Technische Universiteit Eindhoven, URL http://library.tue.nl/catalog/LinkToVubis.csp?DataBib=6:633481.

Cleophas, L. G. W. A. (2009). Private communication.

Comon, H., Dauchet, M., Gilleron, R., Löding, C., Jacquemard, F., Lugiez, D., Tison, S. and Tommasi, M. (2008). Tree Automata Techniques and Applications, http://www.grappa.univ-lille3.fr/tata (accessed on December 18, 2011), release November, 18th 2008.

Conallen, J. (1999). Modeling Web application architectures with UML, *Communications of the ACM* **42**, 10, pp. 63–70.

Crockford, D. (2008). RFC 4627 - The application/json Media Type for JavaScript Object Notation (JSON), IETF RFC, URL http://tools.ietf.org/html/rfc4627.

Donzeau-Gouge, V., Kahn, G., Lang, B. and Mélèse, B. (1984). Document structure and modularity in Mentor, *ACM SIGPLAN Notices* **19**, 5, pp. 141–148.

Earley, J. (1970). An efficient context-free parsing algorithm, *Communications of the ACM* **13**, pp.

94–102.

Engelfriet, J. (1974). Tree Automata and Tree Grammars, Manual written lecture notes.

Engelfriet, J., Rozenberg, G. and Slutzki, G. (1980). Tree transducers, L systems, and two–way machines, *Journal of Computer and System Sciences* **20**, 2, pp. 150–202.

Ernst, M. D., Badros, G. J. and Notkin, D. (2002). An Empirical Analysis of C Preprocessor Use, *IEEE Transactions on Software Engineering* **28**, 12, pp. 1146–1170.

Favre, J. M. (2004). Towards a Basic Theory to Model Model Driven Engineering, in *WIME '04: Workshop on Software Model Engineering*.

Floridi, L. and Sanders, J. W. (2004). Levellism and the Method of Abstraction, Tech. Rep. 22.11.04, Oxford University.

Futamura, Y. (1999). Partial Evaluation of Computation Process—An Approach to a Compiler–Compiler, *Higher-Order and Symbolic Computation* **12**, 4, pp. 381–391.

Gamma, E., Helm, R., Johnson, R. and Vlissides, J. (1995). *Design patterns: elements of reusable object-oriented software* (Addison-Wesley Longman Publishing Co., Boston, MA, USA), ISBN 0-201-63361-2.

Goodman, D. and Eich, B. (2000). *JavaScript Bible*, 4th edn. (Wiley & Sons, New York, NY, USA), ISBN 0764533428.

Halstead, M. H. (1977). *Elements of Software Science (Operating and programming systems series)* (Elsevier Science Publishers, Amsterdam, The Netherlands), ISBN 0444002057.

Hartmanis, J. (1967). Context-free languages and Turing machine computations, in *Symposia in Applied Mathematics, Mathematical Aspects of Computer Science*, Vol. 19 (Amer Mathematical Society), pp. 42–51.

Hayes, I. (ed.) (1987). *Specification case studies* (Prentice Hall International (UK) Ltd., Hertfordshire, UK), ISBN 0-13-826579-8.

Heering, J., Hendriks, P. R. H., Klint, P. and Rekers, J. (1989). The Syntax Definition Formalism SDF — reference manual, *ACM SIGPLAN Notices* **24**, pp. 43–75.

Heidenreich, F., Johannes, J., Seifert, M., Wende, C. and Böhme, M. (2009). Generating safe template languages, in *GPCE '09: Generative Programming and Component Engineering* (ACM Press, New York, NY, USA), ISBN 978-1-60558-494-2, pp. 99–108.

Herrington, J. (2003). *Code Generation in Action* (Manning Publications Co., Greenwich, CT, USA), ISBN 1930110979.

Hopcroft, J. E., Motwani, R. and Ullman, J. D. (2001). *Introduction to Automata Theory, Languages, and Computation (3rd Edition)* (Addison-Wesley Longman Publishing Co., Boston, MA, USA), ISBN 0201441241.

Hotz, G. (1980). Normal-form transformations of context-free grammars, *Acta Cybernetica* **4**, pp. 65–84.

Huang, S. S., Zook, D. and Smaragdakis, Y. (2005). Statically safe program generation with SafeGen, in *GPCE '05: Generative Programming and Component Engineering*, *Lecture Notes in Computer Science*, Vol. 3676 (Springer-Verlag, Berlin, Heidelberg), pp. 309–326.

Hunter, J. (2000). The problems with JSP, http://www.servlets.com/soapbox/problems-jsp.html (accessed on December 18, 2011).

Hunter, J. and Crawford, W. (2001). *Java Servlet Programming* (O'Reilly & Associates, Inc., Sebastopol, CA, USA), ISBN 0596000405.

Johnson, S. C. (1975). Yacc: Yet Another Compiler-Compiler, Tech. Rep. 32, Bell Laboratories, Murray Hill, NJ, USA.

Johnstone, A., Scott, E., and van den Brand, M. G. J. (2011). LDT: a language definition technique, in *LDTA*, p. 9.

Kang, E. and Aagaard, M. D. (2007). Improving the Usability of HOL Through Controlled Automation Tactics, in *TPHOLs '07: Theorem Proving in Higher Order Logics*, Vol. 4732 (Springer-Verlag, Berlin, Heidelberg), pp. 157–172.

Klint, P., Lämmel, R. and Verhoef, C. (2005). Toward an engineering discipline for grammarware, *ACM Transactions on Software Engineering and Methodology* **14**, 3, pp. 331–380.

Knuth, D. E. (1965). On the Translation of Languages from Left to Rigth, *Information and Control* **8**, 6, pp. 607–639.

Kohlbecker, E., Friedman, D. P., Felleisen, M. and Duba, B. (1986). Hygienic macro expansion, in *LFP '86: LISP and Functional Programming* (ACM Press, New York, NY, USA), ISBN 0-89791-200-4, pp. 151–161.

Kong, S., Choi, W. and Yi, K. (2009). Abstract parsing for two-staged languages with concatenation, in *GPCE '09: Generative Programming and Component Engineering* (ACM Press, New York, NY, USA), ISBN 978-1-60558-494-2, pp. 109–116.

Koorn, J. W. C. (1994). *Generating uniform user-interfaces for interactive programming environments*, Ph.D. thesis, Universiteit van Amsterdam.

Krall, A. (1998). Efficient JavaVM Just-in-Time Compilation, in *PACT '98: Parallel Architectures and Compilation Techniques* (IEEE Computer Society Press, Washington, DC, USA), ISBN 0-8186-8591-3, pp. 205–213.

Krasner, G. E. and Pope, S. T. (1988). A description of the model-view-controller user interface paradigm in the Smalltalk-80 system, *Journal of Object Oriented Programming* **1**, 3, pp. 26–49.

Leijen, D. and Meijer, E. (1999). Domain specific embedded compilers, *ACM SIGPLAN Notices* **35**, pp. 109–122.

Moonen, L. (2001). Generating Robust Parsers using Island Grammars, in *WCRE '01: Working Conference on Reverse Engineering* (IEEE Computer Society Press, Washington, DC, USA), ISBN 0-7695-1303-4, pp. 13–23.

Moreau, P. E., Ringeissen, C. and Vittek, M. (2003). A pattern matching compiler for multiple target languages, in *CC '03: Compiler Construction, Lecture Notes in Computer Science*, Vol. 2622 (Springer-Verlag, Berlin, Heidelberg), pp. 61–76.

Murata, M., Lee, D., Mani, M. and Kawaguchi, K. (2005). Taxonomy of XML schema languages using formal language theory, *ACM Transactions on Internet Technology* **5**, 4, pp. 660–704.

Nijholt, A. (1991). The CYK approach to serial and parallel parsing, *Language Research* **27**, 2, pp. 229–254.

van Emde Boas, G. (2004). Template Programming for Model-Driven Code Generation, in *19th Annual ACM SIGPLAN Conference on Object-Oriented Programming, Systems, Languages, and Applications, Vancouver, CA*.

de Jong, H. A. and Olivier, P. A. (2004). Generation of abstract programming interfaces from syntax definitions, *Journal of Logic and Algebraic Programming* **59**, 1-2, pp. 35–61.

Parr, T. J. (2004). Enforcing Strict Model-View Separation in Template Engines, in *WWW '04: International Conference on World Wide Web* (ACM Press, New York, NY, USA), pp. 224–233.

Parr, T. J. and Quong, R. W. (1995). ANTLR: a predicated-LL(k) parser generator, *Software: Practice & Experience* **25**, 7, pp. 789–810.

Pemberton, S., Austin, D., Axelsson, J., Çelik, T., Dominiak, D., Elenbaas, H., Epperson, B., Ishikawa, M., Matsui, S., McCarron, S., Navarro, A., Peruvemba, S., Relyea, R., Schnitzenbaumer, S. and Stark, P. (2002). XHTML 1.0 The Extensible Hypertext Markup Language, W3C Recommendation, URL http://www.w3.org/TR/xhtml1.

Ramsey, N. (1998). Unparsing expressions with prefix and postfix operators, *Software: Practice & Experience* **28**, 12, pp. 1327–1356.

Rieback, M. R., Crispo, B. and Tanenbaum, A. S. (2006). Is Your Cat Infected with a Computer Virus? in *PERCOM '06: International Conference on Pervasive Computing and Communications* (IEEE Computer Society Press, Washington, DC, USA), ISBN 0-7695-2518-0, pp. 169–179.

Roth, M. and Pelegrí-Llopart, E. (2003). JavaServer Pages Specification Version 2.0, Sun Microsystems, Inc.

Schmidt, D. C. (2006). Guest Editor's Introduction: Model-Driven Engineering, *Computer* **39**, 2, pp. 25–31.

Scott, E. and Johnstone, A. (2010). Gll parsing, *Electronic Notes in Theoretical Computer Science* **253**, pp. 177–189.

Sheard, T. (2001). Accomplishments and Research Challenges in Meta-programming, in *SAIG 2001: International Workshop on Semantics, Applications, and Implementation of Program Generation, Lecture Notes in Computer Science*, Vol. 2196 (Springer-Verlag, London, UK), ISBN 3-540-42558-6, pp. 2–44.

Sheard, T. and Peyton Jones, S. (2002). Template metaprogramming for Haskell, in *ACM SIGPLAN Haskell Workshop 02* (ACM Press, New York, NY, USA), pp. 1–16.

Spinellis, D. (2001). Notable design patterns for domain-specific languages, *Journal of Systems and Software* **56**, 1, pp. 91–99.

Sturm, T., von Voss, J. and Boger, M. (2002). Generating Code from UML with Velocity Templates, in *UML '02: International Conference on The Unified Modeling Language* (Springer-Verlag, London, UK), ISBN 3-540-44254-5, pp. 150–161.

Taha, W. and Sheard, T. (2000). MetaML and multi-stage programming with explicit annotations, *Theoretical Computer Science* **248**, 1-2, pp. 211–242.

Tratt, L. (2008). Domain specific language implementation via compile-time meta-programming, *ACM Transactions on Programming Languages and Systems* **30**, 6, pp. 1–40.

Vandevoorde, D. and Josuttis, N. M. (2003). *C++ Templates: The Complete Guide* (Addison-Wesley Longman Publishing Co., Boston, MA, USA).

Veldhuizen, T. L. (1999). C++ Templates as Partial Evaluation, in *PEPM '99: ACM SIGPLAN Workshop on Partial Evaluation and Semantics-Based Program Manipulation* (ACM Press, New York, NY, USA), pp. 13–18.

Vinju, J. J. (2005). *Analysis and Transformation of Source Code by Parsing and Rewriting*, Ph.D. thesis, Universiteit van Amsterdam.

Vinju, J. J. (2006). Type-Driven Automatic Quotation of Concrete Object Code in Meta Programs, in *RISE '05: Rapid Integration of Software Engineering Techniques, Lecture Notes in Computer Science*, Vol. 3943 (Springer-Verlag, Berlin, Heidelberg), pp. 97–112.

Virágh, J. (1981). Deterministic ascending tree automata I, *Acta Cybernetica* **5**, pp. 33–42.

Visser, E. (1997). Scannerless Generalized-LR Parsing, Tech. Rep. P9707, Programming Research Group, University of Amsterdam, http://www.science.uva.nl/pub/programming-research/reports/1997/P9707.ps.Z (accessed on December 18, 2011).

Visser, E. (2001). Stratego: A language for Program Transformation based on Rewriting Strategies. System Description of Stratego 0.5, in *RTA '01: Rewriting Techniques and Applications, Lecture Notes in Computer Science*, Vol. 2051 (Springer-Verlag, Berlin, Heidelberg), pp. 357–361.

Visser, E. (2002). Meta-Programming with Concrete Object Syntax, in *GPCE '02: Generative Programming and Component Engineering, Lecture Notes in Computer Science*, Vol. 2487 (Springer-Verlag, Berlin, Heidelberg), pp. 299–315.

Visser, E. (2008). WebDSL: A Case Study in Domain-Specific Language Engineering, in *GTTSE '07: Generative and Transformational Techniques in Software Engineering, Lecture Notes in Computer Science*, Vol. 5235 (Springer-Verlag, Berlin, Heidelberg), pp. 291–373.

Völter, M. (2003). A collection of patterns for program generation, in *EuroPLoP '03: European Conference on Pattern Languages of Programs*.

Völter, M. and Gärtner, A. (2001). Jenerator – Generative Programming for Java, in *OOPSLA '01: Workshop on Generative Programming*.

Wachsmuth, G. (2009). A Formal Way from Text to Code Templates, in *FASE '09: Fundamental Approaches to Software Engineering* (Springer-Verlag, Berlin, Heidelberg), ISBN 978-3-642-00592-3, pp. 109–123.

Wassermann, G. and Su, Z. (2008). Static detection of cross-site scripting vulnerabilities, in *ICSE '08: International Conference on Software Engineering* (ACM Press, New York, NY, USA), ISBN 978-1-60558-079-1, pp. 171–180.

Watt, D. A. (2004). *Programming Language Design Concepts* (John Wiley & Sons), ISBN 0470853204.

Wile, D. S. (1997). Abstract syntax from concrete syntax, in *ICSE '97: International Conference on Software engineering* (ACM Press, New York, NY, USA), ISBN 0-89791-914-9, pp. 472–480.

Index

FSC
www.fsc.org
MIX
Papier | Fördert gute Waldnutzung
FSC® C083411

Kolibri 360 GmbH
Ferdinand-Jühlke-Straße 7
99095 Erfurt, Deutschland
produktsicherheit@kolibri360.de